# REGIONAL FLASHBACKS

THE REGIONAL FLASHBACKS SERIES IS PUBLISHED BY THE
EUROPEAN ETHNOLOGICAL RESEARCH CENTRE
CELTIC & SCOTTISH STUDIES
UNIVERSITY OF EDINBURGH
50 GEORGE SQUARE
EDINBURGH EH8 9LH

REGIONAL FLASHBACKS

# Lochmaben:
*Community Memories*

EDITED BY
Isabelle C. Gow
and
Sheila Findlay

in association with
THE EUROPEAN ETHNOLOGICAL RESEARCH CENTRE
AND NMS ENTERPRISES LIMITED – PUBLISHING
NATIONAL MUSEUMS SCOTLAND

GENERAL EDITOR
*Mark A. Mulhern*

Published in Great Britain in 2023 by
European Ethnological Research Centre
Celtic & Scottish Studies
University Of Edinburgh
50 George Square
Edinburgh EH8 9LH

and

NMS Enterprises Limited – Publishing
NMS Enterprises Limited
National Museums Scotland
Chambers Street
Edinburgh EH1 1JF

ISBN 978-1-910682-50-0

**British Library Cataloguing in
Publication Data**

A catalogue record of this book is
available from the British Library.

Cover design by Mark Blackadder.
Front cover: Mill Loch photograph by
   kind permission of David Mair;
Back cover: Lochmaben School from
   the Dalton road showing classrooms,
   drill hall, office and bell tower photograph by kind permission of Lochmaben and District Community
   Initiative.

Internal text design by
   NMS Enterprises Ltd – Publishing.
Printed and bound in Great Britain by
   Bell & Bain Ltd, Glasgow.

This product is made of material from
well-managed forests and controlled
sources.

For other titles in the Flashback and
Regional Flashback series see page 196.

For a full listing of related NMS titles
please visit:
**www.nms.ac.uk/books**

# Contents

# Acknowledgements

Firstly we would like to thank the people of Lochmaben, especially those who volunteered to interview and be interviewed. We owe them a great debt for this permanent and comprehensive contribution to our local oral and written history.

Thanks are also due to Tom Russell and David Mair who, as members of the Lochmaben and District Community Initiative, kick-started, developed and encouraged the 'Lochmaben Voices' project on which this book is based. David also helped to identify place names and their locations and supplied many of the images.

With thanks to Lynne J. M. Longmore for information about the Waterlow Curling Cup bonspiel and McCall curling cup.

Grateful thanks are also due to Mark Mulhern for the involvement and support of the EERC.

# Editorial Note

This book is the product of collaboration between the people of Lochmaben; the Lochmaben and District Community Initiative (LDCI) and the European Ethnological Research Centre (EERC).

In 2011 some within LDCI were keen to capture something of the memories folk of the town had. They decided that the best way to do this was to hold recorded conversations with a few people from the town. This lead to the creation of 17 recordings which were stored and transcribed. This phase of work was completed by 2014.

In 2012 the EERC began its work in Dumfries and Galloway as part of its Regional Ethnology of Scotland Project (RESP). As this project got underway, the work of the LDCI became known to the EERC. After meeting with David Mair and Tom Russell it was decided that the EERC and the LDCI would collaborate so that the recordings that the LCDI had made to date would form part of the RESP collection. At that time Isabelle Gow – who had made many of the initial recordings – became involved as a volunteer fieldworker on the RESP. Isabelle went on to conduct a further seven interviews of folk from the town with a view to possibly producing a book about life and society in the town.

Once Isabelle had conducted the second phase of interviews, she and the EERC decided to work together to produce the book which you are now reading. In forming the interviews of the LDCI into a book, Isabelle worked with Sheila Findlay as joint editor.

This book is therefore the culmination of the work of many. Both a communal and individual endeavour this is a representation of the generous insights of:

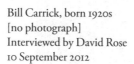

Bill Carrick, born 1920s
[no photograph]
Interviewed by David Rose
10 September 2012

Tom Allan, born 1930s
Interviewed by David Mair
10 September 2012

Beth Corrie, born 1990s
Interviewed by Isabelle Gow
3 March 2016

Bill Gibson, born 1930s
Interviewed by Isabelle Gow
25 January 2016

Isabelle Gow, born 1950s
Interviewed by Paul Gow
2 May 2012

Alan Hannah
Interviewed by Isabelle Gow
20 February 2012

Anne Hills, born 1950s
Interviewed by Isabelle Gow
28 August 2013

Betty Hutt, born 1930s
Interviewed by Tom Russell
10 May 2012

Allison Laurie, born 1970s
Interviewed by Isabelle Gow
5 February 2016

George McCall, born 1920s
Interviewed by David Mair
5 December 2011

Andre McCrae, born 2000s
Interviewed by Isabelle Gow
23 February 2016

Hal McGhie, born 1930s
Interviewed by Tom Russell
16 October 2012

Lynne McNeish, born 1950s
Interviewed by Isabelle Gow
23 February 2016

James McWhirter, born 1940s
Interviewed by Isabelle Gow
18 February 2014

Maitland Pollock, born 1950s
Interviewed by Isabelle Gow
27 March 2016

Paul Roxburgh, born 1930s
Interviewed by Tom Russell
10 September 2012

Hazel Sloan, born 1930s
Interviewed by Isabelle Gow
17 March 2016

Roy Thorburn, born 1930s
Interviewed by Tom Russell
21 March 2013

Three Ladies
[no photograph]
Interviewed by John Reid
10 September 2012

Ian Tweedie, born 1930s
[no photograph]
Interviewed by David Mair
27 February 2014

Wilma Twidale, born 1930s
Interviewed by Isabelle Gow
10 September 2012

Isabel Wells, born 1940s
Interviewed by Isabelle Gow
18 February 2014

Jack Wilson
Interviewed by Isabelle Gow
27 August 2011

# List of Illustrations

# Introduction

The Royal Burgh of Lochmaben, Dumfries and Galloway, is situated near the River Annan on the banks of three lochs: Mill Loch, Castle Loch and Kirk Loch. It lies eight miles east of Dumfries and four miles west of Lockerbie, between the A74(M) motorway and the A701 trunk road – the main routes from north to south. The area has historic connections to the family of Robert the Bruce, whose father built a keep on the site of the present golf course. This connection is further evident in the town motto '*Ex Nobis Liberator Rex*' ('From Us The Liberator King'). These connections are evident today in the names Castle Loch and Bruce Street, and the Bruce Arms and Kings Arms public houses. The majestic statue of Bruce in the town centre and the stained glass windows of Bruce and Wallace in the Town Hall are Victorian reminders of that period of history. Positioned on the main route into Scotland from Carlisle, the town has played a role in Anglo-Scottish history.

Today Lochmaben is friendly and welcoming – a close knit community with plenty of activities. It is also a town which, unfortunately, over the years and, most recently, has lost several of its basic amenities. Some things do thrive however, and the recent community buyout of Castle Loch has been a real success. The paths are well maintained by a good number of volunteers; a ranger encourages the whole town to participate in events and a huge number of visitors to the loch has brought more attention to the castle, the grounds of which have been excavated.

'Lochmaben Voices', a project set up by Lochmaben and District Community Initiative after one of its members, David Mair, saw the value of a similar scheme on a visit to Derbyshire, provided the material for this book. The aim of the 'Lochmaben Voices' project was to collect the memories of the town's residents – of different ages and backgrounds – with the intention of creating a resource which would give an insight into life in the town in the recent past. Financial support to fund the project was received from Dumfries and Galloway Council, with volunteers giving their time and skills to undertake the work. This work comprised recording the interviews, transferring the sound files to CD and transcribing them. The interviewers were Tom Russell, Paul Gow, Isabelle Gow, David Rose, John Reid and David Mair. The interviews were transcribed by volunteers, including

Angela Rae and Doreen Beveridge. The work began in 2011 and by 2016, 24 of the town's residents had been interviewed. Three friends who preferred to remain anonymous were recorded together and are referred to in this book as 'Three Ladies'. One contributor, Bill Gibson, wished not to be recorded but was happy to be interviewed and his story used, although he later did record a small contribution. The project resources are available to peruse at Lochmaben Library and on the Regional Ethnology of Scotland Project website:[www.regionalethnologyscot land.llc.ed.ac.uk].

Alison Burgess, at the time, Local Studies Coordinator at the Ewart Library, Dumfries, became aware of this work and brought it to the attention of Mark Mulhern of the European Ethnological Research Centre. After discussion it was agreed that the recordings would be shared with the EERC's Regional Ethnology of Scotland Project. The aim of the RESP is to explore the lives and society of the people of Dumfries and Galloway, past and present. The RESP aims to gather this information through extensive fieldwork carried out by the people of Dumfries and Galloway themselves. Training and equipment have been made available via the RESP and, so far, the volunteers have gathered over 400 recordings across Dumfries and Galloway which are available to listen to on the project website (see above).

The eldest of the Lochmaben interviewees was born in the 1920s and the youngest in 2000s, most of them having lived in the town from birth. Some spent time away while serving in the armed forces and others moved away for work purposes, before later choosing to return to the town. This collection of interviews enables us to observe the changes that the town and its residents have experienced over almost 100 years.

In preparing the material for this book, a survey of the recorded material was made in order to identify the key themes and topics that occurred within the interviews. These fell into three broad categories: Lochmaben, both as a physical place and a community; personal recollections of living in the town; and military connections to the town during the Second World War. Within these three sections there are a total of seven chapters in which the recorded material is set out and contextualised.

Chapter one shows how the town and the community have changed over the years. The importance of the natural landscape is recalled in memories of the lochs which have supplied the town with water, both prior to the installation of a public water supply and in times of drought. Several interviewees commented on the summer weather being better than that nowadays while winters were remembered as being more severe. In summer, boating and swimming were popular pastimes but, sadly, there were also tragedies associated with these activities. Curling on Castle Loch was a popular winter sport and recollections of this pastime and the prestigious Waterlow Cup (sometimes referred to as the Waterloo Cup) curling bonspiel can be found in chapter six. Anglers have also been attracted to the lochs and there are several mentions here of the vendace, a native freshwater fish. There are recollections of Victory Park, on the banks of Castle Loch, being a popular recreational space in the town for both local people and visitors. Memories of the lochs being used for military training during the Second World War also appear in this section. The built landscape of the town has expanded over time and the Town Council's contribution to this, with the replacement of older, substandard housing, and of new build developments in the town are recalled. The older inter- viewees remembered winters before central heating was commonplace, when iced windowpanes were the norm during colder weather.

Several interviewees spoke about the town's railway station, which closed to passengers in 1953 and to goods traffic in 1963. In its time, the line offered a useful travel link for the townspeople enabling them to travel to Lockerbie and to bring visitors to the town. The goods yard was a busy hub where commodities arrived and were collected by, or delivered to, the townspeople. Coal supplies for the area arrived here and were collected by coal merchants who weighed and bagged it straight from the wagons. When times were hard, some local people caught rabbits and took them to the station, to be sent further afield and sold on by game merchants. The cash generated from this activity made an important contribution to family income.

The community coming together to have fun at the annual Gala Day, an event which has taken place for over 70 years, is recounted here along with details of the celebrations for the coronation in 1953. Every town and village have their worthies – those people whose character or personality ensure that they remain in the communal memory. Lochmaben is no different and there are fond memories here of some of its well-kent characters. The chapter closes with comments from inter- viewees who have considered the reasons why people might move to Lochmaben and reflect on the contribution that they could make to the community.

In chapter two we move on to memories of Lochmaben Hospital. This facility opened in 1908 as the Infectious Diseases Hospital for Dumfriesshire, specialising in the treatment of illnesses such as scarlet fever and diphtheria, which at that time were major killers. In 1926 this facility expanded to become the County Sanatorium, as an important treatment facility for the prevalent illness of tubercu- losis. This illness was highly contagious and required prolonged treatment which necessitated patients being isolated from their families and the wider community. The sanatorium has been one aspect of Lochmaben life that has remained strong in the collective memory of the town. There are memories here from former nursing staff who worked at the hospital and from two patients who were treated there – one for tuberculosis, the other for diphtheria.

Also remembered is Christopher Clayson, a very popular and well-respected man, who was appointed Medical Superintendent at the hospital in 1943. The interview extracts included here tell how treatment for tuberculosis changed over time from large doses of rest and fresh air to new drugs, which were much more

successful in curing patients. Although the sanatorium was very much a self-suffi-
cient entity with staff accommodation, meal preparation and laundry all provided
onsite, it was also very much part of the local community, providing employment
and social interaction with the residents. In more recent times the original facility
has been demolished and has been replaced by a new building which is used mainly
for geriatric care. A housing development has also been built in the grounds.

In the third chapter the older interviewees recall Lochmaben being a busy
town with many shops and businesses, a bank, a post office and a café, all serving
the needs of the people living in the town and in the surrounding area. At one time
as many as 38 shops sold their wares in Lochmaben, some from dedicated premises
and some from front rooms in houses across the town. There were butchers, with
their stock of carcasses hanging up in the shop, bakers, grocers and greengrocers.
Ladies selling confectionery from their front rooms were popular with children
who would stop on their way to and from school to buy sweets. Some of the
grocers and bakers took their goods to outlying areas in travelling shops; before
the implementation of strict food hygiene regulations which made this imprac-
tical. There are memories too of wartime food rationing and co-operative society
membership. Clothing and footwear were sold in the town and there are recollections, for example, of cloggers who made footwear for work purposes. Local
tailors and drapers reduced the need to travel further afield for clothing, at a time
when travelling to obtain provisions was much less common than nowadays. In
more recent times the number of shops in the town has reduced, as is the case in
so many other places. Supermarket chains and stores in nearby larger towns, such
as Dumfries and Carlisle, along with increased car ownership, have markedly
changed shopping habits. There were also, at one time, at least five licensed
premises in the town, three of which, The Crown Hotel, The Commercial Inn
(now the Bruce Bar) and the Kings Arms were at the time of writing still in
business. The memories of the public houses shared here illustrate how licensing
hours and attitudes to women frequenting this type of establishment have
changed over time.

Other recollections demonstrate the changing working pattern of life around
Lochmaben. At one time, blacksmiths in the town mended tools and shod
working horses. There are memories of children, who came to watch them at work
in the smiddy, getting too close to the forge for safety and being chased away.
Nowadays, horses are mainly kept for recreation and local farriers travel to them to
attend to their needs, rather than the horses being brought to them.

There are memories of Corncockle Quarry, which operated at nearby Templand and was an important source of employment for local people. Stone from this
quarry was taken by rail and used to build tenements in Glasgow and Edinburgh
and public buildings such as Edinburgh's Scottish National Portrait Gallery. The
quarry closed for a while but has since re-opened, operated by Dunhouse Quarry
and stone is now transported by road. Also remembered is McGeorge's, a knitwear

manufacturer which employed local people at its branch in the town where, during the Second World War, it made gloves for the armed forces. Local doctors who worked from private premises, prior to the formation of the National Health Service, are also recalled here.

This chapter concludes with substantial extracts taken from the interviews with two local businessmen, Roy Thorburn and Hal McGhie, who both joined their fathers in family businesses and were each instrumental in expanding them.

Roy Thorburn served his apprenticeship with a local joiner and undertaker before joining his father's business, H. K. Thorburn and Son. With Roy's vision and ambition the company expanded to become the first in Scotland to specialise in manufacturing and erecting timber-framed houses. It has also served the community as a funeral undertaker.

Several interviewees could remember farmers in the district bringing their milk into the town on a cart to sell in McGhie's dairy, which started its business in the town. On leaving school, Hal McGhie began working for his father and, in the extracts from his interview, he described how the family business expanded over the years. When Alan Hannah worked for McGhie's he delivered milk to the six hospitals in Carlisle. He also reflects on other business ventures he has been involved with and the positions that he has held in the business community over his working life.

Chapter four takes us from the physical town and the community to the personal experiences of the residents who were interviewed. The interview extracts presented here recall the experience of being a child in Lochmaben. All but one of the interviewees attended Lochmaben Primary School and, for the older interviewees, their experience was quite different from that of youngsters today. Discipline was strict, with the tawse being the ultimate punishment for transgressions, demonstrating how such procedures in the education system have changed over time. Some subjects taught were gender specific, with boys taken out of class to play football and to tend the school garden, and girls left behind to learn domestic skills such as sewing and knitting. This divide was sometimes obvious in the playground too in the games that were played: marbles and football for the boys and beds [also known as peevers or hopscotch] for the girls. Classroom layout, members of staff, the curriculum and the school garden are all recalled, along with sporting activities and playground skirmishes. The move from primary to secondary education was not an easy transition for some Lochmaben pupils, as it involved moving to school in Dumfries or Lockerbie, being separated from friends and having to make new ones.

Play is an important and enjoyable part of childhood and when not in the classroom there were various activities for children to choose from. There are recollections here of ball games, marbles, skipping and hopscotch played with friends, either in the playground or, nearer home, in the street. Solitary activities, like guddling for fish, trapping rabbits and bird nesting were also enjoyed. Away from the watchful eyes of adults, the great outdoors was a playground offering a freedom that children nowadays rarely experience. There was little regard to the present culture of risk assessment or health and safety measures and increased traffic flow now limits the opportunity to play out in the street. Youth organisations in the town attracted some of the interviewees to their activities and one recalled the formation of its first Boy Scout troop. The youngest of the interviewees, Andre McCrae, spoke about moving to the town from Manchester when he was eight years old and noted the differences between his childhood there and what Lochmaben had to offer him. There are also memories here, from the immediate post-war years, of a nationwide campaign to gather wild rosehips which were sent off to produce rosehip syrup, a widely used vitamin C supplement. This activity was evidently enjoyed by some informants who happily recalled some of the scrapes that this led them into. The chapter ends with some individual memories such as seeing the first cars and television in the town.

Working life is the topic of chapter five. The interview extracts show that, when the older interviewees left school, employment appeared to be readily available in the local area and that it was relatively easy to move from one employer to another. On leaving school, it was a priority to find employment. For boys, serving time in an apprenticeship to learn a trade was encouraged by parents. George McCall recalled his father sending him to Dumfries with the instruction not to come home until he had found a job. This had a happy ending for him, as he met up with a group of plasterers who took him on. By the end of his working life, George had progressed to teaching the skill to young apprentices at a local college. In this chapter we are made aware that some jobs which were once commonplace, are less so now. Chimney sweeps and milkmen may be making a comeback at the present time, but petrol pump attendants and coal merchants are now, largely, a thing of the past. Interview extracts from women highlight the expectation that they would give up their employment when they married, despite being trained and qualified in their roles. Also included are memories of the soup kitchens in Lochmaben and Dumfries and 'parish money' being distributed by the district registrar, when times were hard and unemployment was common.

Chapter six gives a glimpse into ways that the interviewees spent their leisure time, both as children and adults. The town has had a long association with sporting events which have attracted contestants from a wide area and there are extracts here recalling some of these.

The Waterlow Cup curling bonspiel was played on Castle Loch with rinks from all over the county invited to compete. The competition was initiated in 1869 by Sir Sydney Waterlow, member of parliament for the county. It was open to all clubs in Dumfriesshire and Sir Sydney donated a silver trophy for the winners. Castle Loch was frequently the venue in the past, due to its large expanse which made it suitable for hosting the number of competitors and spectators attending. There was a special halt on the Dumfries to Lockerbie railway line, close to the loch, enabling competitors travelling to the event, with their stones and equipment, to gain easy access to the venue. Lochmaben Castle Curling Club still takes part in this annual competition but nowadays there are fewer clubs competing and it is held at the ice rink in Lockerbie. A curling trophy which was donated by local building company McCall Wells is also mentioned here.

Another major event, which attracted competitors to the town, was the National Quoiting Championships. This also used a designated halt on the railway line for competitors travelling to the event. The competition began early in the morning and was played late into the evening. The Lowland Games, held annually, also attracted competitors from further afield and offered a range of sporting activities such as athletics, greyhound racing and equestrian events as well as cultural activities such as bagpiping and highland dancing competitions.

Football has been popular in the town over the years and several interviewees recalled enjoying the sport, both as players and spectators. There is a thriving golf club in the town and the development of this over the years, driven by the hard work and enthusiasm of its members, is proudly remembered here. The original nine-hole course was designed by the five-time Open champion and noted golf course designer, James Baird.

Castle Loch is the home of the Annandale Sailing Club of which interviewee, Paul Roxburgh, is a founder member. The abundant lochs and streams in the area have been used for the more solitary pastime of angling, memories of which are also included here. There are recollections too of playing snooker, of bowling and of equestrian activities.

In its time, the town's cinema, a converted church building, was a popular attraction for some of the interviewees who, as children, enjoyed the latest film releases there. At that time the genre of Western movies was very popular, with heroes such as Roy Rogers and Hopalong Cassidy appealing to audiences. The popularity of these characters often influenced their time at play and memories of this are recalled here. A travelling circus, which paraded its animals through the streets, is remembered too. Regular dances were held in the town hall with dance bands from the local area providing the music. Personal hobbies were also remembered, including recollections from Hal McGhie, about horse racing, an interest passed on to him by his father, one of the local farriers.

The final chapter tells of the military activity that took place in the town and surrounding area during the Second World War, along with post-war experiences of those interviewees who joined military service soon afterwards. For the duration of the War, there was a high level of military activity in the local area. The War Ministry requisitioned 40 acres of land at Halleaths Estate, to be used as a training camp for over 2000 personnel. The camp was constructed by Royal Engineers who were billeted with families in the town. Once operational, troops were housed in Nissen huts in the grounds and officers were accommodated in Halleaths House. Facilities at the camp included a parade ground, minefield, shooting gallery, rifle and machine gun ranges, as well as a NAAFI [Navy, Army and Air Force Institutes] canteen. Jardine Hall was also requisitioned and used as a military hospital for wounded personnel. Prisoners of war were encamped at nearby Hallmuir and at Parkgate, near Dumfries, and were sent out to work on local farms after the War ended. The Army had a visible presence in the town when troops practised manoeuvres in the streets and derelict buildings. They also built jetties and bridges on the town's lochs. There were social interactions with the townsfolk on open days when the public were given access to Halleaths and on occasions when military bands performed in the town. The memories in this section are of some of these activities observed by those interviewees who were children at the time; there was excitement to be had by playing with discarded ammunition and other debris left over from training operations in the streets. Blackout conditions, lying in bed listening to German bombers flying overhead at night, being given sweets by passing troops and receiving toys made by prisoners of war – many of whom worked on farms around the town – are all remembered here and remind us of the reality of living through war.

After the War some interviewees were given their own taste of military life, when they were conscripted into the armed forces as a result of the 1948 National Service Act. This legislation extended the conscription of the Second World War and continued until the last conscripts were called up in 1960. Unless registered as conscientious objectors, employed in exempt occupations such as coal mining and farming, or in the Merchant Navy, able-bodied young men aged between 17 and 21 were called up. This peacetime conscription initially lasted for 18 months, however was extended to two years in 1950 during the Korean War. Memories of this interruption to their normal working lives are recalled here by several interviewees and another one spoke about serving in the regular Army post-war.

It was the aim of the 'Lochmaben Voices' project to record the memories of townspeople to create a resource for the future, giving an insight into life in the town in the recent past. Oral history is a valuable tool for informing us of the lived experience in a particular place at a particular time and the collection of excerpts used here does just that, giving us an insight into almost 100 years of life in the town. It also allows us, through recording small, personal and specific details of life, to observe that which may otherwise go unnoticed or unrecorded. When we compare the material collected here with that of similar projects, we are given the opportunity to witness change and continuity across location and time. While each place is unique, change is often influenced by external factors, common to many, as well as a result of more local influences. 'Lochmaben Voices' is a valuable resource recording both the external and the local influences which have shaped the town and the lives of those who lived there.

# Change Over Time

The extracts in this chapter tell us about Lochmaben the physical town and community life within the town. The natural landscape and how that has been used over time by the townspeople are recalled. There are memories of the lochs supplying water to the town and of them being used for recreation along with the popular Victory Park. There are recollections of changes to the built landscape over the years as the Town Council replaced substandard dwellings with modern housing and new build developments. The railway line and station, once a vital communications link carrying goods to and from the town – as well as providing a useful passenger service – are remembered. Community life and the coming together of the inhabitants for special events are also remembered along with local worthies who were part of the community.

## Town Lochs

The importance of the lochs to the people of the town: Mill Loch, Castle Loch and Kirk Loch is evident in the following extracts. In times of drought, they were used to augment the town's public water supply. They have provided popular locations for recreational activities such as fishing, swimming and boating. Springs – one of which was reputed to have restorative properties – are also recalled. Curling on Castle Loch has been a popular pastime and more about this is found in chapter six. Victory Park, situated on the northern side of Castle Loch, has long been a favoured recreational space in the town, attracting locals and visitors alike.

During the Second World War, the lochs were used for training purposes by troops stationed at nearby Halleaths Camp and some evidence of that still exists. When he was a schoolboy Paul Roxburgh discovered an ancient wooden canoe on the shore of Castle Loch, indicating that this area has been populated for over 2000 years.

## Paul Roxburgh

*We've come through Dumfries Academy time, that certainly was the time that you made your big discovery on the Castle Loch, would you like to tell us about that?*

Aye, well, Ah used to like walking. Ah walked aw round the lochs an the hills in Lochmaben, very, very often on my own. An on this occasion, Ah was walkin round the Castle Loch. It had been a very, very dry spell. Ah would be twelve year old then, an near the Vendace Burn, near that bay there, there was quite a large piece of wood protrudin out o the mud, an Ah could see that it was handmade. So, the next night, Ah brought a couple o ma friends doon, wi shovels an [we] dug it oot. An it was a perfectly formed canoe. Ye could even see the marks on it where it had been hollowed out. And Ah was quite excited by this an told ma history teacher, a Mr Russell. The next day he informed a Mr Truckle from the museum, Alfie Truckle, an two or three days later a flatbed council lorry arrived out wi some workmen on it, an it wis manhandled onto the back of the council lorry. But it was waterlogged, mind, but in perfect condition, and taken into Dumfries Museum. No doubt today it would have been better handled and they would have had [some] means of preserving it. They would have, probably, have kept it in water for some time. There'll be treatments today that could preserve it perfectly, but when Ah see the auld bit o twisted wood that it is nowadays, it's unrecognisable. That was dating back to the time that there were crannogs in that area, roughly about, over 2000 years ago.

*I think that was also a route across to the castle?*

Aye, that's right, from the Castle Hill area. Ah kept goin back roond there for many, many months afterwards but Ah never found anything else. An within a year it was all overgrown, ye wouldnae have been able to dig it.

The importance of the lochs for the town's water supply and a spring with supposed curative powers are recalled by George McCall:

## George McCall

There were also a well there, [Castle Loch] an it was good water. In fact, the well, Ah think it was Tom [Russell] that got it shifted because it was making a mess o the bowling green, but that water, it was very important to Lochmaben. In fact, during the summer when water wis scarce a bit, at the water works, when the levels went down, that was used quite a lot for water. Even in the middle o summer it was very, very cold. But Ah remember o ma uncle, John Wells, you know, you'll hae heard o McCall Wells the builders? Well, he was an uncle o ma father's, actually, but Ah always called him Uncle John and when he was on his deathbed, Ah had tae go an get water for him …

*Oh right, frae that spring?*

… because he reckoned it was the best water, he reckoned there were a cure in it, you know. But whether it was imagination or not Ah don't know. Lochmaben got their water supplies fae wells. One o them wis up Ravenshill, that wis a main one, that was where people went for their water, and there was also one down at the Kirk Loch Brae, a water well.

*And people went for their water, did you say, they carried it every day, did they?*

Oh aye, that wis before the water works. Ah can't just tell ye, the water works were there before my day, Ah think. The water works wis at Bankhead, it wis Lochmaben, worked by the workers, Lochmaben workers. There wis aboot three workers at that time, and it was a good water supply. In fact, it's still there yet. If ever ye want tae go a walk up that way, ye can go right up to it. There's no a road up to it, well there is a road, but Ah think ye've got tae walk up the field but it's aw there to be seen.

*So, it was much later that the water was piped into the houses then, was it?*

It was piped intae the houses, aye.

… Aye, the water, the wee fountain that they had, they had a fountain, an a cup an a chain, where ye could go and have a drink. Dr Longmore, he always took pains, an he still does, to test the water an it's still drinkable. But Ah was kinna saddened to see it being done away wi but they always blamed that [on] the bowling green moving when it got flooded and it was causing the bools to go off. So, they took it out into the, further intae the loch and sealed it up. But it was a grand wee water drinking area, especially in the summertime, because it was always that chill, that cold.

The spring is also remembered by Roy Thorburn.

### Roy Thorburn

*Near where the boating hut was there was another interesting relic that you don't see now, at the edge o the bowling green, right at the corner.*

Aye, yes, aye, we had a spring there and summer and winter most of the locals, an even the visitors in years to come, used it. An it was always ice cold but, unfortunately, it disappeared from the scene so whether it had been drained into the loch – obviously it was – but it's a bit unfortunate that it wasn't retained.

*Aye, it was covered to allow access to the car park.*

Victory Park, on the shore of Castle Loch, has long been a popular public space for townsfolk and visitors alike. The next three extracts recall some of the activities that took place there.

### George McCall

*And Victory Park, at that time, would be used quite a lot, was it?*

Victory Park was used quite a lot for people goin in. A lot o people went down there and sat on the seats and read. There was a tree planting – for the Coronation and the Jubilees and that sort o thing. You'll see there's signs on the trees, Ah think, to say why the trees were planted.

*And did many people come to Lochmaben just to sit in the park? As visitors, aye?*

Yes, they did, they used to come for picnicking as well, aye. Ah always dreamt that some time we would have a wee platform in the summer an we could hae had entertainment down there, outside entertainment, because we had good summers in wur young days. They're a wee bit changed now.

*Did they come into Lochmaben on the train or on a bus?*

The train, yes, the train, yes.

… The Castle Loch was quite popular. We had a sort of bit fenced off for a swimming pool. It had a sandy bottom an it had a diving board. It had two huts for tae change, changing huts, an it had a veranda. The veranda, the foundations o the veranda, are still there but they've got that into a flower bed now and a summer seat. The tennis court was very popular, Ah don't think tennis is so popular as it was.

### Roy Thorburn

*You also have quite a number of memories of life in Lochmaben, for instance, what went on at the Victory Park.*

Aye, the Victory Park, there was a bandstand in the middle of the park in these days and the Army bands used to come on a Saturday and Sunday. On a Sunday in particular, they'd play all day, obviously they'd quite a lot of musicians. There was quite big crowds used to go down there in the summertime tae hear them an watch them, an they were very, very entertaining. We also had a wee swimming pool down there, a man-made pool, which was just a fenced-off area on the water. We used to go and swim in the summertime, which ye got good summers at that particular time.

*Ah believe there was a beach.*

There was, there was a beach but probably only about two lorryfuls of sand or something like that, which they put in to make it look like a beach.

### Paul Roxburgh

There used to be a paddling pool in the Castle Loch at the bottom of Victory Park. …

Aye, it had a beautiful sandy beach, there's no sand along there now, an it was fenced off, quite a defined area that you could, well, paddle in or attempt to swim.

Angling was, and still is, a popular pastime on the lochs and one species of fish, the vendace, once native to Mill Loch and Castle Loch, is no longer found there. In this extract Paul Roxburgh considers why that might be:

**Paul Roxburgh**

There was vendace in two Lochs, in the Castle Loch and the Mill Loch, Ah think the last vendace to be found were found in the Mill Loch. Ah remember a chap, Professor Maitland, comin and doing surveys. He came to do surveys quite often but eventually it was decided that there were no vendace left. Of course, the vendace were never caught by fishers because they only fed on vegetable matter. Any vendace that were caught were either accidently [sic] hooked or deliberately netted. They used to have a day, Ah don't know whether it was once a year, where they netted the Castle Loch for vendace. But quite a few people in Lochmaben used to have a jar with a preserved vendace in their hoose, there used to be one in the Town Hall.

*That's right and Ah think they're in Annan and Dumfries Museums and SNH[1] have a supposedly long-term aim to reintroduce vendace.*

Ah don't know whether they … Ah think they had second thoughts and decided that the water, well, Ah think they would decide: 'Why did they die off in the lochs in Lochmaben?' An the water probably wasnae suitable for them, so why reintroduce them because they would probably just die off again?

*Aye, well, Ah think they … certainly had to wait for the pH value, or something, being right and they wouldn't even think about it until that is stabilised, Ah think that was partly due to a lot of effluent coming off the land.*

An that'll not stop, Tom, no, this was another thing that possibly caused the decline in fishing. The effluent, modern farming and the effluents that come off the fields into the rivers and lochs, was causing the decline in the fishing.

While serving in the Army in Malaya [although referred to as such throughout, is now Malaysia], Ian Tweedie received a letter from his mother in which she mentioned that a vendace had been caught.

**Ian Tweedie**

Ah used tae fish as well, on the loch.

*All the lochs? Or was it the … which?*

Well, mostly the one at the head of the town, you know, the Castle, no the Castle—

*The Mill Loch?*

The Mill Loch, aye, that one. Regular.

*What did you get there? Did you get pike and things?*

Pike, uh huh, Ah'll tell ye a thing, there was a man, you've heard the thing aboot the vendace?

*Yes, aye.*

Yes, well it was when Ah was in Malaya, an my mother sent me a letter, he had actually got a vendace in the loch at Lochmaben.

13

*He caught a vendace?*

Aye, he did.

*So that must have been one of the last ones that was caught?*

Aye, definitely, because ma mother wrote tae me.

Boating and swimming were popular pastimes recalled by some interviewees. There were rowing boats for hire on Castle Loch and George McCall remembered the boats being made locally and the hut where the equipment was stored. Paul Roxburgh was employed in the evenings to hire out the boats and was reimbursed by being allowed the free hire of a boat, which he used to fish from.

### George McCall

There was the golf course, where we spent a lot of time there, an of course, the Castle Loch, which was good for fishing. We had free fishing at that time. They had boatin, the people that stayed across the road fae us, her father, he actually built boats. That was his business, making, building these boats, and it was very, very popular, the boatin.

*So, how many boats would be on Castle Loch at any one time do you think?*

Oh, Ah would say there could hae been a dozen. Aye. The pier, they had a concrete pier right out and a rail, an they had a hut for keeping aw the oars in, an everything.

*Sorry, the concrete pier, would that be where the car park is now?*

Where the car park is now, yes.

### Paul Roxburgh

When Ah was a young lad, well, slightly later on, Ah used to look after the boats in Lochmaben, at night an at the weekends, sometimes, an for hiring the boats out. There would be about six or seven boats for hire, and we moored them out on the Loch. They were brought in, in the winter. But if Ah hired the boats oot Ah wis allowed the use o a boat maself, an Ah used to go around fishing for pike in all the wee bays. And there was a super boathouse as well, which was burned down in the early 1950s, Ah think it was, Ah don't know whether it was accidental or—

*Well, rumour has it [that it] was a local youth.*

Aye, Ah know who it was supposed to be (laughs) but it's an old Lochmaben, it wis a member of an old Lochmaben family, in fact his grandfather was Provost.

*Where exactly was this boathouse?*

It was beside the loch, of course, jist beside the bowling green on the right-hand side.

*Presumably the boats were hired out an there was no life jackets issued?*

Oh, no, nothing sophisticated like that, Tom.

*Was there ever an accident?*

No, never.

*And what age would you be when you were hiring the boats out?*

Oh, Ah would be probably be about twelve or 13. …. The soldiers fae Halleaths built an extension onto the jetty there as well which was eventually taken away of course, the whole jetty was taken away.

## Roy Thorburn

*And other things went on at the Castle Loch near there … next to the bowling green, there was a hut.*

Well, yes, an they had boats, small boats, probably about seven or eight, maybe more, to hire.

*Rowing boats?*

Rowing boats, aye. They were quite popular with the local ladies and the soldiers from the camp.

The Brummel and Grummel lochs are now drained: the site of the Brummel is now partly forested and there is a football pitch on the site of the Grummel. In the following extracts Hal McGhie remembered the Brummel and Paul Roxburgh recalled the Grummel.

## Hal McGhie

*There's one activity you told me about that Ah was interested in and that was—*

Punting?

*Rafting, yes.*

Not rafting, but punting, aye, we made a makeshift raft of some sorts on a loch near Halleaths. Ah think you said you've got a name for the loch.

*It's known on the maps as Brummel Loch and you're the first person that I have spoken to, in Lochmaben, who has experience of it being water.*

Water, yes. It wouldn't be very big, and it was obviously pretty secluded amongst the trees, so Ah suppose one o the reasons we would go there [was] because nobody would see us there. Because Lochmaben lochs were considered very dangerous, obviously because nobody could swim in these days, and if ma father caught any of us near the lochs he would not be very happy, to say the least of it. Ah think all the parents were the same, because there were occasionally people drowned in the lochs.

*… I only know Brummel Loch as being on one of the older maps and it was bigger than the current Mill Loch which is surprising. And my experience of it was in 1970, going in with my family to explore and sinking rapidly and coming out very quickly.*

Yes (laughter).

*So, you've actually, interestingly, rafted on it.*

There must have been more water in the late 1930s and early 1940s.

## Paul Roxburgh

*There wasn't any trace of the Grummel Loch at that time was there?*

Ah well, of course the Council dump was there an that was another attractive place tae me because Ah used to get worms an maggots for the fishing in the Council dump. And they had great difficulty keeping the water at bay because that would be the Grummel Loch an it used tae flood. Ah was intrigued because Ah thought it was infested wi water rats but thinking back they werenae water rats at all, they were voles. But [REDACTED], jist used tae dump aw their waste meat down there, that's where we got the maggots from. You know, when you think ae what people got away wi then, an of course the old horse and cart yaist tae come doon that wee road an dump their load in the water.

*Do you think it was a bit of a health hazard?*

Oh, by nowadays' standard it was very much a health hazard.

While the lochs supplied water to the town and were used for leisure and relaxation, they were also the scenes of several tragedies. Paul Roxburgh, Roy Thorburn, James McWhirter and Isabel Wells all recalled some of their childhood contemporaries drowning in the lochs while swimming or boating.

## Paul Roxburgh

Aye, the lochs in Lochmaben have always had a great attraction but they've had their dramatic side as well. There's been quite a few locals drowned in the lochs at Lochmaben. The first one Ah remember was a chap called [REDACTED] who stayed in Bruce Street, and James Wright, the nephew of the Misses Wrights, … had built a canoe and [REDACTED] was paddling the canoe along the bottom of the gardens and went upside down and couldnae right himself and that was the end o [REDACTED]. An a chap who went tae school wi me, cawd [REDACTED] who stayed in Queen Street, in Lochmaben, was drowned in the Mill Loch, jist off where the houses are built now. There's seemingly a very deep shelf that goes off there, an [REDACTED] had been swimmin in there. An another friend o mine at Lochmaben School, a lad called [REDACTED], who stayed in the wooden houses at Halleaths, was bathin in the Annan there and got into difficulties in the big pool an he was drowned. He was drowned there.

## Roy Thorburn

*You mentioned a sad aspect of Lochmaben's situation, in that a few youngsters lost their lives in the lochs and river.*

It was in these days, the summers were much better than what they are now … there was two Ah can recollect on Mill Loch and one on the Castle Loch, Ah can't remember their names. [REDACTED] was one o them, an he was only, he would be the same age as maself, an he got tangled up with wire. It was very dangerous, everybody seemed to go [there] and nobody seemed to see the dangers in these days. [REDACTED] was another lad, that was one who was drowned as well.

*Paul Roxburgh mentioned [REDACTED] in the Kirk Loch.*

That's right [REDACTED] was drowned in the Kirk Loch. He had a small canoe. He drowned there but, yes, that's right, [REDACTED], he was the other one Ah was trying to remember, in the Mill Loch.

## Isabel Wells and James McWhirter

JMcW: Aye that's right, we used to dae oor swimming roond at the Point, they used tae caw it, the Mill Loch.

IW: Aye.

*Swimming?*

JMcW: Aye we used to swim in the Mill Loch.

IW: Oh aye, in the Mill Loch.

JMcW: There used to be hundreds and hundreds of people there.

IW: It was so deep.

*Really?*

JMcW: Ah'm no joking, aye.

IW: Frae the Point jist straight across tae where the boat went doon.

JMcW: Because that's where we used tae swim.

*You would have thought that would have been really dangerous. Ah mean folk drowned in that loch.*

JMcW: [REDACTED]

IW: Aye.

*But you were allowed to go swimming in the loch.*

JMcW: Aye, oh, hundreds o us.

IW: Aye, loads.

JMcW: We used to swim from there across tae the paddling pool an then there was a bit at the paddling pool where ye could dive off.

*Goodness, Ah didn't know that.*

IW: Well, they used to dae water skiing up there an aw.

JMcW: Aye, they did, aye.

IW: Later on.

*I remember when the paddling pool was built and it was used, it wasnae used for very long.*

JMcW: No, it wasnae.

IW: No, it wisnae.

During the Second World War, troops stationed at Halleaths used the Mill Loch and the Kirk Loch while training.

### Roy Thorburn

*They also used the lochs for another activity, the Mill Loch and the Kirk Loch.*

Oh yes, during the War, the Mill Loch was, they had a pontoon bridge across there from approximately the swimming pool and Vendace Drive, an Ah remember [on] one occasion they lost a tank there. The water's very, very deep in that particular place and they also had a jetty at the Kirk Loch which is still visible to this day.

The built landscape of Lochmaben has changed over the years. The town has expanded in area although the population has not increased greatly over time. New housing was built by the Town Council in the 1930s and 1950s and older, substandard housing demolished and replaced by new developments. Land at the site of the former sanatorium has also been used for house building. Most of the interviewees were resident in the town all their lives and, in this section, some of them recalled the housing conditions of their childhood. There was no central heating, fireplaces in bedrooms were rarely lit and frost on the windowpanes on a winter's morning was common. Houses were small with several children sharing a bedroom. Some interviewees also recalled the older dwellings which were demolished.

George McCall lived in Queen Street, when he was a boy, and recalls the council starting to build new housing developments. He also remembered older parts of the town such as Marjoriebanks, known locally as Bogle Hole.

### George McCall

Queen Street was completely different, there wis a lot of houses that's been knocked down. Where Ah stayed ... there could have been four or five families just opposite, but there's only two houses there now where there could be four or five. Times were really hard, because when Ah was a kid Ah remember going round Queen Street, and yin o the chaps ... he had been workin and been forced to gaun away an work aboot Whithorn, an he came back and he brought a wife back wi him. An aw that they had was a camp bed and a chair, no linoleum, nothing. An then he stayed across the road.

*And did he move into a tied house? Would it be a tied house?*

No, he moved intae Croft Terrace. They were startin tae get better in these day, times wis getting better an they [the Council] started [building]. Halliday Terrace was the first, that took over all the overpopulated area o Marjoriebanks. Marjoriebanks, the name wis changed through Burns, Ah believe he termed it in one of his poems, Marjorie o the Many Lochs, an Ah think that's why it's called Marjoriebanks.

… The Bogle Hole, God it was rough, it really wis rough. In fact, my vision o Bogle Hole wis [the residents] empty[ing] the fires, the ashes oot the fire, they jist threw them out the window and they were ash paths. An Ah remember o goin intae one house and aw ye could see wis bunk beds and it mair or less filled a room; there were that many people stayed [there]. The corridor, or the lobby as we call them, they went right out on to the pavement, same level and everything else. Ah don't know how they didn't flood. But it was rough quarters, in fact, it wis that bad that they said you couldn't walk through it at night.

*And was it single people that was staying there or married?*

Families, families, well Ah don't know whether [it was]. But when they built Halliday Terrace a lot of these people shifted.

*And it was the Council that built Halliday Terrace?*

The Council built it, Halliday Terrace. Another thing wis they wouldnae have tiled roofs, the old Council, everything had tae be slated. There wis, still there yet, what we call a [Paddy can]. It wis for tramps and they could stay there the night. Ah don't think there was anybody had any control of it, it was just an open door where they could walk in and sleep.

*Is this a house? Was it a house or a shed?*

Aye, it is still there yet, yes, aye.

*Where is it about?*

It's right at the end, in fact Ah think it's got a sign on it. [Used from 1851 to mid-twentieth century, this was the Poorhouse.]

*Oh, going down Marjoriebanks and over the hill, on the left, aye?*

Aye.

Ann Hills explained how building work at Annandale Crescent started before the Second World War and continued after it, giving rise to the house numbers being changed and the different house styles found in the street. She also recalled having a fireplace in her childhood bedroom.

**Anne Hills**

*Anne, could you tell me a little bit about growing up in Lochmaben in the 1950s and 1960s?*

I lived in Annandale Crescent, it was, when I was a child, number 52 Annandale Crescent. We lived in the same house all the time, but it had, Ah think, two numbers before I went in. Ah think it started off as number 22, or something, in the scheme because they kept building different bits onto the scheme. So, although Annandale Crescent, the original Annandale Crescent, has 82 houses now, when I was a child there weren't 82. Ah can't remember how many there were because they built a bottom section when I was there, as a child.

*So, were a lot of the people who lived in Annandale Crescent born and bred [in] Lochmaben?*

Ah think so. I was under the belief, until a couple of years ago, that it all started in the 1950s, when ma mum and dad moved in. They moved into our house in 1952, Ah think. I was a baby and the plaster was still wet. They must have moved in December, January, because Ah was born 7th January. So, that was when I thought all of Annandale Crescent was built, but I've heard recently that the front part, when you go in from Queen Street, those houses up there and the first lot as you turn right, they were built in, Ah think, the 1930s.

… An if you actually look at the houses, those older ones are a different style to the one I lived in, which is now number 52.

… So, I thought everybody moved in at the same time, but some came earlier.

*That was maybe called something different then.*

No, it was Annandale Crescent. That's all that was built because Ah think the War came along and stopped the plan, because the plan was to build it all. And then the War came an it stopped it, an then after the War everybody moved in.

*So, what kinna size were these houses … at that time?*

Well, they're still the same today, they're three bedrooms, it's a lovely house. A good-sized house. There was single houses, not double frontage, an there was a living room, a kitchen with a pantry at the back o that, bathroom downstairs, hallway, stairs up for the half-landing and three bedrooms upstairs.

*An a garden?*

An a garden. Ours was an end house so we had a longer garden. Also, there were fireplaces in the bedrooms, because I remember ma mum and dad's bedroom, at the front, had a fireplace and my bedroom, at the back, had a fireplace. …

An when it was ma birthday Ah was allowed to have the fire on an my friends to play in the bedroom, so that was special. They were cold houses, really cold.

*No central heating?*

No central heating, ice on the windows, the ice patterns on the windows.

Wilma Twidale explained how her and her husband came to be allocated a council house in Annandale Crescent on moving back to Lochmaben when his Army service ended. Later, they exchanged houses with another council tenant to enable them to move to a larger one.

**Wilma Twidale**

We left [Elgin] in 1952, Jim was demobbed from the Army [in] 1952, and we come back tae Lochmaben. We got allocated a house because we'd put oor names in as soon as we got married. So, we got allocated a house, jist after he was demobbed really, and we got into it in about November, in Annandale Crescent, and so we lived there and Jamie was born when we were there. And we lived there for quite a while and then a couple round the corner wanted tae exchange their house, they had a bigger house than us, so we exchanged with them. And we lived in that house, near Queen Street, right at this end, for four years.

Bill Carrick's boyhood home no longer exists.

**Bill Carrick**

*Whereabouts did you actually live, Bill, when you were in the village? When you were a boy?*

When Ah was a boy? The Buffer's Castle.

*Buffer's Castle?*

Buffer's Castle.

*Buffer's Castle. Where is that?*

That's knocked doon now.

*Whereabouts was it?*

Ye ken where [UNCLEAR] heads into Annandale Crescent.

*Yes.*

Jist ten, twenty yairds up fae there. There's a big hoose.

*And you had the whole house?*

Aye.

Isabel Wells and James McWhirter both lived in Croft Terrace and recalled some of the other residents and the cast iron ranges that were used for cooking and baking.

**Isabel Wells and James McWhirter**

*Right, what can you tell me, Isabel, about in the 1950s? Croft Terrace, for instance, where you lived? And Jimmy, you might be able to add something about that as well.*

IW: … where the car park is now, there used to be—

JMcW: A builder's yard.

IW: Aye, Carruthers & Green, builder's yard, aye. Wee Mrs Johnstone staiyed at the corner where the car park wis.

JMcW: That's right, aye.

*That wee house with the wee window?*

IW: Jimmy can remember mair folk in Croft Terrace as Ah can. Oor block was like the last block added on, wasn't it?

JMcW: When they built them six hooses, Mr Clough, Bob Clough, Alec Clough's dad.

JMcW: … He was in there an then somebody called—

IW: Mrs Warbeck, Jim Warbeck.

JMcW: Aye, Jimmy Warbeck.

IW: Then it wis—

JMcW: Harold Brooks.

IW: Then it wis Duke Paiterson.

JMcW: That's the name Ah was looking for.

IW: Duke Paiterson.

JMcW: Duke Paiterson, aye.

IW: [UNCLEAR] an then maself, that was that, six.

IW: But the rest o them had been there for a number of years before.

*So, when was Croft Terrace built then, just after the War or—?*

IW: There's a sign there or there used to be.

JMcW: Aye, 1935, or something?

IW: Something like that, Ah think.

*Before the War? Before the War started.*

IW: Aye, well, but those last six, Ah was five when we went intae that hoose.

JMcW: Ah can mind o the hooses being built like, we were 14. Ah wis 14 then when 14 Croft Terrace, sorry, it was 14 Croft Terrace, aw they did was change the numbers. …

IW: Aye, that's right, aye.

JMcW: We became 20 Croft Terrace.

IW: So, if Ah was five when oo went in there, 46 an five's 51, so that block must have been built in what 1950, 1951, cos Ah think it would be the April when we moved intae that block.

*So, they'd be good solid houses.*

JMcW: Oh, aye.

IW: Oh aye, they're grand hooses, aye

*Ye'd have coal fires.*

JMcW: That's right, aye.

IW: Aye, that's right. There wis nae central heating.

*No, oh, no.*

JMcW: A big range, ye had a big kind o cast iron range.

*Aye, for cooking on as well.*

IW: Oh aye, you had thaim, we never had that in oor hooses, but you had them cos Ah mind ma Aunt Dorothy having yin.

JMcW: That's right, Ah can mind ma mother [polishing] it with lead or something, black lead.

IW: Black lead, that's right.

JMcW: Everything was done in there like pan scones and everything.

When talking about the changes in Lochmaben, Allison Laurie recalled her feelings about the residential development at Vendace Drive when she first visited it.

## Allison Laurie

*Anything else you want to add, maybe generally about Lochmaben? What kinna changes do you see?*

It's got a lot bigger, more houses, especially round the Vendace Drive, round there.

… When Ah first went round there after they built it, Ah could have been anywhere, it didn't feel like it was Lochmaben. But you soon get used to it and your friends move in there and it becomes part of the town, like everywhere else did when it was first built.

The railway was an important means of transport to and from the town. The line serving Lochmaben was opened in 1863 by the Caledonian Railway company, its route being between Dumfries and Lockerbie. The line closed to passenger trains in 1953 and goods trains in 1963. In its heyday the station was the delivery point for goods such as domestic coal, newspapers and parcels and the dispatch point for livestock and other produce to markets in Lockerbie, Dumfries and further afield. The station was equipped with a loading platform, hand crane and cattle pens and a Station Master and a porter were employed there.

The following extracts describe a time when the station was a hive of activity with parcels arriving and then being delivered to their recipients by a porter with a barrow. Coal merchants would arrive to empty the wagons of coal, bag it and put it onto their lorries. In times of hardship, to supplement earnings, rabbits were caught by locals and sent away to be sold to game dealers. During the severe snow falls of the 1947 winter, when road transport was impossible, McGhie's dairy used the railway to distribute its milk further afield. One interviewee recalled having to jump out of the window of the train he was travelling on, as the door had jammed closed. The railway track was sometimes also used as a short cut when walking in the countryside.

Tom Allan recalled working on the railway line, carrying out line maintenance.

## Tom Allan

So, Ah seen this job advertised on the railway. There was one at Lockerbie an one at Castlemilk, so Ah applied and Ah got the job. Ah went for an interview at Lockerbie Station an the man went away to the end o the platform an he waved a red flag and he shouted: 'What colour's that?'
Ah says: 'Red.'
He said: 'You'll do, ye're in.'
So, Ah had tae gaun tae Motherwell for a medical an come back. An, as Ah say, I cycled fae Lochmaben tae Castlemilk sidings, which would be aboot

23

seven miles, night and morning. Then Ah got a chance of a job on [the] Lochmaben length. Ah'd a wee bit swither whether tae take it or not but Ah thought *Aw well*, so worked on there for a while, at Lochmaben. Ah enjoyed it, it was grand. Aye, walking the length fae Lochmaben to Mareheid [Muirhead] at Lockerbie and back up the other side to the Blind Lochs at the top … back doon the other side again, wi yer hammer across your shoulder an yer key in your bag, knocking the blocks in as ye went along.

*Maintaining the line, is that maintaining the line?*

Maintenance, aye. Well, these blocks got rumbled oot, you ken. Then they werenae screwed doon, they were knocked in again.

*An you said you had weeding to do as well, eh?*

Well, ye'd tae start at one end and weed as much as ye possibly could. Of course, ye had tae maintain the level o the tracks, the site boards and what. An generally keep it tidy, keep the weeds at bay. Scything was … ye'd twae swathe tae cut either side, fae Lockerbie tae, as Ah said, to the Blind Lochs and back doon the other side. Ye're eether standing, yin leg up in the air or the other way.

*You needed one shorter than the other?*

Aye, like a mountain goat.

*How many trains would come through there every day?*

Oh, there wis two or three, there wis a couple of trains at night, there wis the fish train an the milk train would come through at night. Then you'd get a couple of goods through the day bringing coal in and shunt it into Lochmaben, because there wis three coalmen. Eventually there wis only two workin in the goods yard in Lochmaben.

*And would the stuff, the coal, say, if the coal was offloaded fae the train and then the coal merchants would come and pick it up there, did they?*

They eether bagged it there on site.

*They bagged it.*

Of course, they had tae get it done quick because there was the murage tae pay if ye waited, kept it too long. An, of course, there wis potatoes an things goin away as well. All these sorts o things went away in wagons.

*So yes, the railway was used quite a lot then?*

Aye, then it was, an as Ah say there was a holiday coach sat through the goods shed, right up to the area towards the back o the station.

*And that was where the Barras is now, is it, up where the Barras is?*

Aye, where the houses are now where the station yard wis.

*That's the station yard, aye.*

It wis quite a big yard.

*Was it?*

Aye.

*And there'd be the wagons wi coal on?*

There were three spurs. One went through the goods shed and then there wis another three efter that, spurs, that wagons could be shunted in. An there was a crane, there wis a crane as well.

*An was there a wee shunting pug or something?*

No, jist the one that brought the stuff …

*Just used to shunt it.*

… used to knock it on the track.

*And the local men, the local coalmen, say, would go in and just offload the stuff fae the wagons?*

That's right.

*Is that how they did it?*

An bag it up. They'd just reverse the wagon in, open the door and then just bag it up and so on.

*So, it's wagons they were using too, it wasnae horse and cart?*

No, it was wagons.

*It wis wagons.*

It wis, oh there were Austins and Fordsons.

*So, it would be quite a busy place at that time …*

Aye, it wis quite busy.

*… the goods yard and the station, aye.*

Aye. But as Ah say, lorries became, contractors became more common an, of course, the railway lost aw these contracts because the lorries could go as far as Glasgow an aw these places then.

*That's been the problem, hasn't it, as you say, it was more convenient …*

Aye.

*… to load it up onto a lorry then?*

Well, to put it on a lorry, you took it to the destination. When they take on the railway, to take it fae the distributor to the railway, fae the railway to the next station, to the station worker and transport it again, you know.

*So, you were handling it two or three times rather than once.*

Aye, aye, that's right.

The busy railway goods yard and a particular train which regularly brought people into the town in the evening, are recalled by George McCall.

### George McCall

The train was very popular. The station was up at the Barras of course. The station yard was very industrial, that's where the, the houses across from the Railway Inn, that was all a work area for the railway. The parcel services wis aw done by the railway and they had people come down wi barras delivering the parcels.

*So, you remember the railway well then?*

Ah remember the railway well. There used to be the, Ah cannae remember what they called the train, but it used tae come in aboot seven o'clock, and a lot o people used tae [go to] the Railway Inn for a drink, tae drink. And they used tae load it up with different stuffs. Rabbits wis very pop—, rabbit food wis very popular in oor young day. Of course, Ah mean things were hard, times were hard, an Ah remember them, they used to come down absolutely loaded with rabbits on their bikes for to put on the train … tae go on to the game people, to sort them out.

Local livestock were transported to market by rail, as remembered by Bill Carrick.

## Bill Carrick

[They] used to bring the sheep up an intae Lockerbie tae the slaughterhouse.

*Did they walk them or put them in carts then?*

They were in trucks and they used tae … they dropped them off at the main street like, jist doon tae the slaughterhouse.

*That's right. They didn't go on the railway?*

Ah suppose maybe some o them did because the amount o sheep that they were handlin, they couldnae aw come by road anyway, ye ken.

*So, some would come on rail?*

Some would come on rail.

*Did you ever go on the railway from Lochmaben to Dumfries or anywhere?*

Aye, Ah used tae travel fae Lochmaben tae Dumfries, well fae [Sheildhill?] tae Amisfield?

*To Amisfield?*

Lochmaben to Amisfield, Ah used tae traivel.

*Did it stop at Shieldhill?*

Aye.

*You'd walk from there probably, did you? It wouldn't stop in Amisfield, did it stop in Amisfield?*

Aye, it stopped yin night an Ah couldnae get the bluidy door tae open. Ah threw ma case oot an scrambled oot through the window and then down (laughs). [This stop may have been Locharbriggs.]

*You had to jump out through the window? Oh dear.*

When you think of the things you done.

*That's right.*

They'd say ye were mad nowadays.

… A lot of stuff came bi train because we used to go up at night tae the train, when it came in, tae get the papers and aw that, ye ken. Oh, there were some massive engines in these days.

*It was only a single line, wasn't it? Was it a single line, a single track?*

Aye, aye. A single track.

*Single track.*

Aye, aye and there wis double track at the stations like.

*Aye, to let trains pass.*

Paul Roxburgh used the railway line as a shortcut when out walking.

## Paul Roxburgh

*Now, you mentioned walking Castle Loch an Ah think over to Beacon Hill and Graham's Monument. Were there any other favourite walks you had?*

Ah used to enjoy going up the Blind Loch[s], but it was quite dangerous up there, well, Ah don't know whether you would describe it as dangerous, but there were, you know, the floating logs went up and down as you walked across them. It all added the excitement but Ah quite often got into trouble for no coming back home, missin ma dinner.

*Now, at that time there would have been trains goin past that area, do you have any recollection of that?*

Aye, oh aye, very much, aye. Ah used tae walk up the railway quite often and often got chased off by railway workers, not supposed tae be there.

*Was that the easiest way out to the Blind Loch[s] then, along the railway?*

It was the most direct line.

*Did you travel much by train?*

Aye, we used to go to Lockerbie, to the pictures, on a Saturday afternoon.

*You don't remember how much it cost you, do you?*

No, I don't really, no.

*Was that the Rex Cinema that you went to?*

Aye.

*Did you go to Dumfries by train?*

Ah never went tae Dumfries by train, no. But I remember walkin across the viaduct because there were some awfy good mushroom fields on the Holmes, on the River Annan, at the far side of the viaduct.

James McWhirter also used the railway line as a shortcut and Isabel Wells recalled the goods yard.

## Isabel Wells and James McWhirter

*Do you remember the trains stopping in Lochmaben, an the station?*

JMcW: Ah can mind o the station an Ah can mind o Alec Grierson being the ...

IW: Station maister.

JMcW: ... station maister, can mind o that. An Ah can mind o the station quite well cos we used to play, we never actually played in the railway, but if

27

we were walking up to the three lochs, the two Blinds and [Upper] we were always up by the railway.

IW: But they kinnae, the coal yaird was up there tae, ye ken.

JMcW: Well, where my daughter stays, where Martin Burns stays now it was the Victoria Cottage, that's where Mair's stayed.

IW: Yes, that's right.

JMcW: An everything came in tae that yard, aw the—

IW: Aye, there was big gate in through there.

JMcW: Everything was shunted in there fae the railway, aw the coals and that.

IW: The coal came in that way, that's right.

*It would probably be quite busy then.*

IW: Aye, it was.

The 'Big Sna' of 1947 brought severe winter weather and heavy snowfall from mid-January to mid-March, road transport was difficult, so McGhie's dairies used the railway to get milk supplies as far as Dumfries. At one time the railway network was important to the dairy trade in the area as it enabled milk supplies to be delivered quickly into the centre of big cities such as Manchester and Edinburgh.

### Hal McGhie

Yes, we've only once been unable to get into Dumfries because of the weather and that was when Ah was still at school in 1947, where the Dumfries road was blocked. Ah remember when we did get in on the double decker bus the drifts were as high as the double decker bus. But what we did was, we loaded the milk onto the trains at the station at Lochmaben, took it into Dumfries, then Heyton's lorry delivered it with Heyton's lorries. That was an interesting experience, delivering milk by train.

*And, of course, milk went the other direction up to Edinburgh, in the Edinburgh and Dumfriesshire Dairy.*

Well, a lot of the Dumfriesshire milk, it went to Manchester, Edinburgh, everywhere, in the 1930s. Ah mean, before the Milk Marketing Board became around, in 1934, they were undercutting one another but milk went, the railways were very successful for the distribution of milk because it was, you could get fresh milk straight into the towns. It went from here, in cans, to Edinburgh dairies. It went to, as far as Manchester, as Ah understand it, but that's long before my day.

*Did you travel much by train to Dumfries?*

No, no, we would occasionally get it to Lockerbie, because Ah think at one time it was cheaper to go by train to Lockerbie than it was by bus. But it was purely finances that … would make ye go by the train.

*You didn't personally travel by train to Dumfries much?*

Ah can never remember travelling by train to Dumfries.

*It always appears to me it must have been quite a scenic journey.*

Ah suppose so. We had a good, we've always had a good bus service, Lochmaben to Dumfries. And it was very much more convenient than the train, this end of the town.

*It's a big regret that they didn't grasp the nettle and use the old railways for cycle tracks and walkways.*

Yes, Ah could never believe why they, all the railways were just disbanded. They were huge methods, shortcut methods, of communicating with one another, whether it was cycle tracks or walking tracks. They're now trying to spend millions on cycle tracks which I approve of very much. Because the only reason why Ah don't cycle much here now is because Ah'm afraid to go on the roads because it's so dangerous. But to go on a cycle track when we go on holiday, we hire bikes and when we go to Portugal, we actually have bikes and we cycle a lot but there, cycling's very safe.

The following extract taken from an interview of the three ladies who wished to remain anonymous has information about the route that the train took and memories of one of the station porters.

**Three Ladies**

*You were talking about the railway, how different Lochmaben was then, when there was the station and the regular trains. Was it by, was it passenger trains or other trains?*

And goods used to go through. It wis used a lot.

It was, it went fae Lockerbie right through tae Dumfries, didn't it, stopping at aw the stations, like Shieldhill, that would be the first one. Was there one at Amisfield? Was there a station there, no?

Ah don't know.

Or did it gaun fae Shieldhill to Locharbriggs? There wis a station in Locharbriggs.

An then on tae Dumfries, Ah don't know about Amisfield.

*Are there any memories of the station, what it was like in Lochmaben, what it looked like or did you have much to do with it when you were younger?*

Was Bella Arthur was the porter?

Bella? That would be when Bob Brown, Bob Laurie worked there once, did he?

Bella Arthur

…

And then, what's the … Grierson?

…

What did you caw the Grierson man that yaist tae be the porter up there an he aye delivered the parcels in a barra?

29

Jenny Grierson's man?

…

That's right, Jenny wis his wife. He brought her on. Do ye no remember
when he was a porter?
They used tae push the barra down the street.
Aye, deliver the parcels, fae the station.
Alec Grierson. For he used tae stay in that house, across fae the railway, the
railway house, the wee cottage at the other side.

…

Aye, it was Alec Grierson, I remember him wi the black jacket and the
trousers and the waistcoat, pushing the barrow, deliverin the parcels. He
had a sort of limp.

Prior to local government restructuring in 1975, the affairs of the town were
managed by the Lochmaben Town Council. The administrative body for the area
is now Dumfries and Galloway Council. The town has a Community Council
made up of elected residents who care about their community. Community
Councils have a role to play in campaigning for and influencing consideration of
local issues by Dumfries and Galloway Council as well as organising community
events. There is an active Church of Scotland congregation in the town and in the
following extract George McCall speaks of his time as a community councillor and
his family's connection with the Church of Scotland over the years.

### George McCall

*Aye, so you've had a busy time, George, a busy life in Lochmaben?*
I've enjoyed doing [things] for Lochmaben, you know.
*Because you were in the Community Council as well, weren't you?*
I was in the Community Council; Ah was voted on at that time. They done
an election an Ah was voted on. It wis a lot of good work. But it started and
sort of fell … Dr Wilson was the chairman and Bennet Miller, Professor
Bennet Miller, he was the chairman for a while. You wouldn't know Bennet
Miller, he stayed up the Mill Road.
… He was quite a character as well, like. Ah think he was [a] university-
trained professor. He was a Professor o Marine Law, that was his actual job.
He kinna looked after the rights of way in Lochmaben, he was very good at
that. And then there were Dr Wilson after that, an Ah took over. Ah took
over for a year because nobody wanted the job an Ah done it for three years,
but three years was plenty, Ah was quite happy, although ma dad … Mark,
ma brother, he was aboot 30-odd years as a councillor, like.
*Was he?*
Aye, an ma dad, he was a Baillie, of course, and my grandfather was the
Dean o Guild.

*Aye, a long association with the burgh.*
> A long association wi the burgh, aye.

George also recalled the amalgamation of two of the town's churches and two of their ministers.

*And changes, you've seen a lot of changes?*
> Ah've seen a lot o changes, where the flats wis. Ah mean Ah worked on them as well, down Queen Street, St Margaret's, flats.

*Yes.*
> It was the church.

*And you remember it as a church, do you?*
> Ah remember it was a church, actually, we were members o the Parish Church. Ma dad was the beadle an Ah think he fell out wi the minister an we went tae the Free Church, an they turned it intae flats at the finish-up, like. They joined the two together. We had a good minister here at one time, they cawd him McCall, he came frae aboot Hamilton. Actually, he filled the church and a lot o people that had children, they cawd their children after him. McCall Wells, they were a big contractor at one time, they used to employ about 112 people. McCall Wells ... the chap that, who had the business, he was called for McCall the minister. Mr Gibb, Dad was the beadle, but Mr Gibb, he was Lochmaben born, well, he came tae Lochmaben from his early days and brought his family up in Lochmaben. One o them was the Director of Health for Aberdeen, one of his sons, and one o them was a judge in Kirkcudbright, Forbes Gibb. Ah don't know what the other one done. But he was a good minister as well, a good preacher, and we had some good preachers at the Free Church as well.

Another interviewee with family connections to the Parish Church is Wilma Twidale who explained how the local congregations have merged over time.

**Wilma Twidale**
> Ah was gonna to tell you about the church because we have always, the family [has] always been very involved with the church. Ma father was brought up in the Barras Kirk and that united with Victoria Church, which the two became St Margaret's in 1921, Ah think. So, he'd grown up in it, and then after they united, when he was 19, he became the Assistant Clerk.

*Harkness, is that the name?*
> An he did that right through and then when St Margaret's united with St Magdalene's, as it was, it became jist the Parish Kirk, he was still the Clerk. He did it for about 50 years, so we have got a connection with all those ...

*A long, long connection, yes.*

… in Lochmaben, with all three, we've got connections with. An we still do quite a lot in the church.

*Oh, yes.*

Because we're elders and we sing in the choir.

Lochmaben has, for over 70 years, held an annual children's Gala Day in the summer months, attracting locals and visitors alike. An event like this would not be possible without goodwill, help and co-operation from residents, local organisations and businesses. Roy Thorburn explained how his business, as well as local farmers, were involved in the Gala Day.

## Roy Thorburn

*And the second event that your name is intimately associated with is 'It's a Knockout', which happened in the 1970s. Now, everyone talks about the swimming pool game. Could you maybe explain to people what you did in that game?*

Well, we had to form a pool o some description at the games, it was always a water game. We tried to have something new every year and we used to get straw bales from the local farmers, and they were very good, we used to get them for nothing. But Ah had tae have the boys off maybe two days or three days prior to the event to set them up. It was jist, it wasn't always my own idea, it was like yourself had different ideas which, Ah constructed it, but people had different ideas in what we should do. But we had some quite clever games and we had a lad there, Gough, who was only aboot 16 at the time, an he used tae try them out for us. Ah think in the present day the Health and Safety wouldn't even let us into the field, never mind make the competitive games, but we had some marvellous times wi these and everybody seemed to appreciate it.

*Yes, … an there certainly were crowds of over 1000 that used to come from outside Lochmaben.*

Yes, yes, far and near and in the entrance into the football park it used to be lined and lined there, it was amazing the amount of people there. Ah don't know how many would be there but there would be well over a thousand people some nights.

*And Ah don't think we ever charged for it, it was just a can at the gate.*

That's right.

*And Ah think the other thing Ah remember is that there were over 100 youngsters went on the first hour and over 100 adults usually the next two hours.*

Aw the competitors over that time, an Ah mean it was all done in one evening, which was quite an achievement, when ye look at it now, for the committee to have it aw set up the way it was. Ah mean Ah only took part in it, Ah only put one game up, it was usually something reasonably special and how the committee … it certainly was a marvellous time.

*Ah, you're being modest about it because Ah remember an aerial ropeway down into the pool and so on and the main object was to get people wet, Ah think.*

Well, that's right, there was no chance of getting out without getting wet. It doesn't matter how athletic they were, they had to fall into that pool.

*A lot of the team leaders had a great time, like Willie Edgar and Colin Davidson, Keith Creighton, Lindsay Maxwell, Davie Hewitson, Sandy Grant and John Wilson.*

We were quite fortunate at that time, there were all these people. An Davie Hewitson was another one, he got a big entrance into it. We were quite fortunate at that particular time, everybody seemed to blend together, and there was no problems at all.

*One Ah do remember was Keith Creighton's cow which you had to milk, that caused a bit of amusement.*

Aye, Keith was quite a character.

*As you rightly say, Ah don't remember gettin a bill for anything connected to the 'Knock Out'.*

Ah might jist send it yet, though. Ye might get it yet (laughter).

Betty Hutt took part in the Gala, as part of a team representing the sanatorium. Along with other family members she also participated in the Gala parade.

## Betty Hutt

*So, are there any other recollections of the hospital that you want to say anything about?*

Well, we used to take part in the Gala. We used to put a team into the Gala in the knockout and we called ourselves 'The Skeletons'. And for effect we got some bones from the butcher. They were our spare parts. But we didnae go to win, there's no way we would have won anyway, but we went there tae have good fun and to let people have a good laugh.

*Well, I always thought that you were there because you were determined to get the booby prize.*

Well, we did get the booby prize every year, Ah think (laughter). Ah think we were cheatin an everything, but it was good fun.

*It was good fun an Ah mean, we got over 1000 people coming to that event.*

We did.

*It was great fun, great memories.*

It was.

*And Ah think ye remember one or two o the games?*

Oh, yes.

*If Ah mention Roy Thorburn?*

He had a paddling pool, and we were always in there and we used to take a thermometer down to test the water. It was always freezing but it didnae matter.

*Well, it's the first time Ah've heard it described as a paddling pool.*

Well, it wasn't really a paddling pool.

*I would have said it was more of a swimming pool.*

It was a swimming pool (laughter). Whenever you went in ye had tae swim. But no, it was good fun.

*Yea, that's right. Anything else? You mentioned the Gala and, of course, you and Tom were stalwarts of another part of the Gala, the parade.*

Yes, we enjoyed goin into the parade. Sometimes ma father and Tom went in but, latterly, Tom an I went in thigither and now ma daughter. Maybe reluctantly, but she comes in wi me.

*So that's three, four generations you can say have been in the Gala?*

Yes, because ma father, he used to go intae the Gala. He was on the Gala committee, he always took part in the Gala.

*Ah believe you didn't know until the eleventh hour that you were going into it?*

Well, Ah could come off night duty …

*On the Friday?*

… the night before we werenae goin in, the Saturday morning Ah came in an we were goin in. He'd been up to the Russell's to get the placards written an that was us.

*It was good fun that. I say, a couple I can think were following in your footsteps were the Davidsons.*

Yes, they were, an they always used tae say: 'We'll beat you next year.' (laughter). But they never managed.

One of the younger interviewees, Beth Corrie, has been a participant in the Gala all her life.

**Beth Corrie**

*What about the Gala, that's always been a big thing in Lochmaben?*

Yea, I've always been a part of the Gala. So, for 16 years Ah've done that but Ah missed it last year because of the school trip. And we always did something as a, like the families were all really close so we did it together and we always dressed up and did the lorry. It's just nice to see everyone walk past and all these people and you got to talk with them, it's nice and it's still happening and … it's good.

A significant community event remembered by the older interviewees was the town's celebrations for the coronation of Queen Elizabeth II. The coronation took place on 2 June 1953 and, to mark the occasion, the centre of Lochmaben was decorated and a bonfire held in the evening. At that time Tom Allan was employed by local building company McCall Wells and was involved in building a decorated archway over the town centre. The events of the day are also recalled by Isabel Wells and James McWhirter.

## Tom Allan

*And you also had something to do with the celebrations for the Coronation?*

Aye, Ah was set tae work cutting this conduit intae lengths and then grooving oot the ends so they fitted in, ye know, and they were welded up. And it covered fae one side o the Town Hall, right to the statue and right across the street. They were [UNCLEAR] over to where the dentist is now, from there, right across back tae the centre and back across. Double decker buses could pass underneath it and we decorated [it] on the corners. It was great.

*I believe there's a photo of that too, somebody's got a photo, aye.*

Aye, somebody's got a photo, Ah hadn't seen it for what, 60 years, isn't it, really? Mrs Milligan brought it up and let me see it. It was taken at the dark but ye can see it fine. It was a, aye, it was a marvellous thing for Lochmaben at that point.

… And the celebrations were great as well, up on top o the golf course, the big bonfire and everything. Aye. Mr Bell that led Lochmaben Pipe Band, was piping there, Jock Bell. There were two men holding him up an he was still piping (laughs).

*Oh right. Well that's dedication, as they say.*

## Isabel Wells and James McWhirter

IW: We aw got Coronation mugs didn't we?

JMcW: Aye, we did aye. Ah don't know if there was anything on, no like what they have now, these street tea parties an that. Ah don't know if it went as far as that.

IW: No. Ah think aw the kids came up tae the Cross. Ah think they were aw roond there an Ah can remember Billy's dad pitting up this big fancy crown, frae the library tae the toon hall, right ower that area.

*So, it would be all lit up, would it, at night?*

IW: Oh, Ah cannae remember that.

JMcW: Wisnae allowed out.

Hogmanay was an annual event to celebrate and the Three Ladies recalled participating as young women.

## Three Ladies

Well, they were great, they really were, then. You went first footing, didn't ye? But there wis no lights. They didnae put the lights on through the night then. So we had tae [UNCLEAR].

Lanterns.

The lanterns, aye.

*When would that be, that you would start?*

Well, aboot 1960 maybe?

Aye. Was that when you were married?

When was Ah married?

No, was that when you started going in the celebrations, [UNCLEAR] younger than that .... Go oot first footing.

It was after Ah was married anyway.

Aboot 1960 would it be?

Aye, it wouldn'ae be far away, 1959, 1960.

*And can you remember much about New Year when you were much younger?*

Aye, Ah remember the housefuls ma mother used tae have. I mean, Ah've seen no gettin tae bed till seven o'clock in the morning, you know, worse than they will be now (laughs). And she'd the carpets clear and she'd tae turn it over, ken, at New Year time.

... And Janet Moore, she ... stayed across the road. Her mother and father were Irish and the mother used to run back and forwards. Well, she'd been wakened this time and she brought her over and ma mother wis standin an Janet's pousslin at her: 'Mrs Beattie, can Ah say my wee poem?'

Ma mother said: 'If you can get anybody tae listen, dear, you say yer poem.' (Laughter).

In every community there have been residents who, for various reasons, stick in the minds of its inhabitants. Perhaps these people had a particular talent, were eccentric, or are remembered for their kindly nature or outgoing personalities. In the next extracts the interviewees have recalled some of the characters they remember from their early years.

First, Paul Roxburgh spoke of two elderly ladies from his childhood, as well as a blind fiddler who used to play in The Crown Hotel, a Lochmaben hostelry, for free drinks.

## Paul Roxburgh

Lochmaben had its share o characters as well, when Ah was young. There wis an elderly lady called 'Mag the Bully'. I don't know why she was called 'Mag the Bully', but she was quite a character. And another one cawd 'Aye, aye', Ah think she was cawd 'Aye, aye' because she finished nearly every sentence with 'Aye aye' (laughter). Another one called 'Blund Jimmy', he was a fiddler. He was definitely blind because [he] had tae wait at the corner at Bruce Street for someone tae take him across the road to the Crown. He yaist tae play his fiddle in the Crown to get a couple o free pints.

Another lady Paul recalled gave children apples from her employer's garden.

> On the road to school ... at the Old Bank House, lived a man called David Rome, who had the local threshing mill and visited aw the farms and he kept it in the courtyard at Old Bank House. And he had a housekeeper, cawd Miss Lorraine, who used to look after him. She was very generous wi the apples, kept aw the children going wi apples. They would have been stolen anyway (laughter).

Anne Hills recalled Tom Cockburn, a local worthy. She also recalled an elderly lady who children used to tease and a neighbour who grew tobacco in his garden.

## Anne Hills

*The only other thing Ah was gonna ask you, [can you remember] any memorable folk?*
> Well, one that sticks in my memory, of course, is Tom Cockburn. I mean Tom, always with his bicycle.

*His bike, yep.*
> Singing in church when he could give it laldy, [I] always remember Tom. ... So, as a child, ... I tell you who Ah remember. There was a lady lived on the corner of Castle Street. She was an elderly lady and she kept cats and everybody used to call her a witch. An Ah often think, not that I did it of course, but a lot o the kids, we used to go round the church hall, we used to batter on her door an we must have given her a terrible fright. She was an old, old lady in an old, old, dark house, oh dear, next to Ashton House on the corner, there.
> ... There was one of the chaps in Annandale Crescent, he grew tobacco. Now, that was memorable for us kids, he grew it in his garden, next to Shirley Arnold's. An he had, like us, he had a big, long side garden and he used to grow tobacco. He used to watch these tobacco leaves an then he would pick them all. An then he would put them into his shed and obviously he did whatever you did with tobacco.

*Really?*
> Yes, he grew tobacco. That was memorable.

Tom Cockburn was also remembered by Hal McGhie.

## Hal McGhie

*You also mentioned that one of the Lochmaben's local worthies played the violin.*
> Aye, Tom Cockburn, he made noises. Ah think his playing would be reasonable, although Ah don't think he would be very skilful ... he came and entertained us, Tom. He was a, as ye would know, he was a real worthy o Lochmaben.

*That's right, Ah mean, I still can vividly remember … we don't have the same worthies now, Ah don't think.*

No, Ah don't think we're allowed the scope to be a worthy now.

*No, yet he wasn't abused by the local population at all.*

Oh, no, he was all part of it, Ah mean, he would take over directing the traffic. Ah remember him once directing it when there was a huge tournament, a huge curling tournament in the Kirk Loch there, and of course after Tom had directed it, it was pretty chaos (laughter). Nobody could get out, it was a gridlock.

*And he did a great job for Jim Henderson at the shop too, didn't he?*

Yes, yes. Aye, he worked in Dumfries, in the grocer's shop in Castle Street, before he went to work for Jim Henderson. And he had a, well in my days, he had a bicycle. And we had a bicycle repair shop at Townhead, and Ah used to repair his bicycle. He would bring it in tae 'get tuned', as he said.

*Ah remember picking him up on the dairy straight, between Lockerbie and Lochmaben, he'd broken down. Ah took his bike and Ah took it up to, I can't remember who I took it up to, to get it repaired.*

There'd be nobody in Lochmaben, was there, then?

*No, Ah don't think so, Ah don't know.*

He went tae Kirkpatrick's in Dumfries, Ah think, after that.

… Ah can remember one occasion in the dairy when, Tom Cockburn used tae come into the dairy and go into the fridge and help himself. And somebody shut the door and said that he couldn't, said that it was locked, we couldn't unlock it. And, of course, Tom fainted so we got him out and he got a big, Ah think he got a brandy or something, and he was ok. But he was quite a character …

*Oh yes, he was.*

… but very likeable.

Roy Thorburn recalled a patient at the sanatorium who stayed on to work there after he was cured and who wrote poetry.

## Roy Thorburn

*You also mentioned one or two characters you remember, Sammy McLurchan for one.*

Yes, Sammy he was a great guy. He was a, he actually was a patient at the sanatorium, well over 50 years ago. An, after he was cured, he worked as a boiler man. An that's what he finished [as], as a boiler man at the sanatorium. An he was like McGonagall the poet. He used to make up rhymes which Ah've already, Ah think Ah've told ye aboot.

*Well, Ah wonder if you could repeat them for me?*

Ah possibly could. One was:

> There's beauty in the Highlands and in the Lowlands too,
> There's beauty in old England where the skies are always blue
> There's beauty in old Blackpool where the flags are always wavin'
> Ah think you'll all agree with me there's nowt to beat Lochmaben.

That was his first one an I used tae sit an listen tae him when he had had a few halfs. He repeated them so often Ah remembered it. His next one was:

> When Scotland's Lords and Ladies for their King would build a hoose
> He was a royal monarch by the name of Robert Bruce
> But where to build this castle they all began to guess
> Some said build in Glasgow and some said Inverness
> They took their troubles tae the King, His Majesty was shavin'
> Says he 'Take my advice and build it in Lochmaben
> For if you choose Lochmaben you'll have chosen well
> There are brave men in Lochmaben that would follow me through Hell.

*Well, Ah've never heard these before, that was very good, thanks.*
Well, funny, he used to repeat them an Ah used tae say tae him: 'Say that again.'

In more recent times one popular person in the town, David (Davie) Shankland, has left behind fond memories of his wit and kind nature and there are many examples of these to be found in interviews throughout this publication. His career as a clinical nurse, leading him to become a nurse tutor in the region, is remembered by some of his former colleagues. He is also remembered as a keen angler and footballer, and for his enthusiasm and involvement in the local Gala Day.

The population of Lochmaben is a mix of long-established local families and people who have moved there from elsewhere. Incomers have generally been well received and their contribution to community life welcomed. The next extracts consider why people might move to the town and how they can be welcomed and integrate into the community. Isabel Wells and James McWhirter commented on people moving in and explained how, at one time, it was not possible to be allocated a council house unless you were a native of the town and how that has changed.

### Isabel Wells and James McWhirter
*So, how do you feel, how has Lochmaben changed?*
JMcW: Well, you dinnae like to call people interlopers but (laughter) …
*Too many of them now.*
JMcW: … but nowadays there a big change cos when you were … if you were born in Lochmaben you got a house in Lochmaben, right? If you were born outside Lochmaben you couldnae get a house in Lochmaben.

*Really?*
> JMcW: But nowadays they come fae Glasgow.

*Oh yes.*
> JMcW: They come from all ower the road.
> IW: Everywhere, everywhere.
> JMcW: That's how things are changing as quick.

Hal McGhie considered that the mix of old families and new has worked well, especially when the newcomers have been willing to become involved in the affairs of the town.

## Hal McGhie

*There still is, I think, a community spirit here.*
> Yes.

*Which is lacking in other communities, Ah think.*
> [It's] thanks to people like you, Tom, that that's the case. Because a lot of people have come from outside Lochmaben but have become more and more part of the community and put a lot into the community.

*Aye, well that's very kind of you to say that, but I would say in reply that it's been the marriage, if ye like, of the locals and the incomers that have made the success.*
> Well, we welcome the incomers.

*Yes, and we couldn't have done things without—*
> Our immigration policy is quite good?

*Pardon?*
> Our immigration policy (laughter). We welcome … especially, immigrants who will put something into the community, as most of them do.

Andre McCrae, one of the younger interviewees, moved to Lochmaben from Manchester when he was seven years old. In the following extract Andre compared Lochmaben and its environs to the area of Manchester he moved from.

## Andre McCrae

*Andre, can you tell me a little bit about yourself, where were you born and where were you brought up?*
> Well, I was born in Manchester, England, and I was brought up there for about seven years until I moved here, just before my eighth birthday.

*So, how did you feel coming to Scotland? Had you been to Scotland before?*
> No, I had actually never been to Scotland. I'd never actually been anywhere outside the city because we lived in the central part of the city and when I saw the fields and stuff, I was just amazed at it, you know.

*All the green space.*
> Yea, and I had a lot more freedom than what I did back in England.

… I could go pretty much anywhere because it was a lot safer than the city. We lived in flats in the city and we could only play in the car park because we weren't allowed out of the [flats?] because no one could get in because of the gate.

*Oh, I see.*

But here, we'd—

*Go and play football.*

Yea, and even snow was a good thing to see here because in the city it—

*It disappears.*

Yea, it would snow, but all the vehicles and stuff, also the smell as well. Like even when we go back down to Manchester, just every now and again, you can tell the difference, just with the amount of vehicles. It's the same going up to Glasgow but, you know, it's a lot more—

*Fresher atmosphere.*

Yea, fresh air, yea. And a lot nicer as well.

*So, do you find there's plenty to do in Lochmaben, that's one of the problems sometimes with young folk?*

A lot of people try and say that there's not a lot for them to do. But they're not actually thinking about it because we do have woods, but it's in the main woods. The bigger one that we had, it was cut down and I wasn't sure if it was due to the tree disease that was happening a wee while ago because they were cutting a lot down in Dumfries and Galloway. So, it had been cut down so it wasn't as fun as it used to be but when it was up you could do so much there, you know, build dens.

… Even just, you know, like play soldiers or something.

… Yea, there's actually more than what you would expect and you can go on walks around the lochs. You can go fishing, it's something that I quite, personally, like to do. I get out as often as I can and there's quite a bit of fish so you don't really get bored when you're doing it.

Hazel Sloan explained why people might be attracted to Lochmaben, especially to retire.

## Hazel Sloan

*Lots of people have come to Lochmaben to live here.*

Oh, a lot of people come to retire to Lochmaben because it's near the motorway for going north or for going south.

*What facilities are there for people in Lochmaben?*

Well, actually, there's quite a lot, depending on your age group. There's quite a lot of care for pre-school and they have quite a lot of various activities. And for senior citizens there's a friendship club.

*That's right.*

There's a luncheon club and we also have a very good bowling club where all ages can participate.

*Anything else?*

And there's a local golf course, there's a lot of very good walks we have. We're surrounded by three lochs and there's one particular one that has a very good walk, which is about three point something miles, that a lot of people come and use.

*So, it's a nice place to retire to.*

Definitely, definitely

In his younger days Maitland Pollock was a professional footballer. During his footballing career he lived in Nottingham, Luton and Portsmouth. In his interview he reflected on how these other communities compared to Lochmaben and whether it is a good idea to return to one's roots, as he has done.

## Maitland Pollock

Nottingham's a lovely place, it has its areas, like every other place. Luton is exactly the same, I stayed in a village just outside Luton called Thorpehill, between Luton and Bedford. And then Ah moved to Portsmouth and every time you move it's got a culture change.

*That's right.*

Obviously, a dialect change as well. Nottingham's very 'Midlandy', if you can call it that. Luton is more akin to a London … and Portsmouth is as well, [a] very sort of London accent. Places like that you hardly know your neighbours because everybody goes about their own business. You don't see, people go out to work, they don't see their neighbours, maybe at the weekend, but they don't often fraternise with their neighbours. And Ah found that as you go further south, Ah found that [to be] more of a case.

*Really?*

Here it's a community, it's a small community.

*Yes, most folk know each other.*

That's right. You know, people, where Ah stayed in the village of Thorpehill, either worked in Bedford or they worked in Luton or London.

*So, like a dormitory town.*

More or less. Ah suppose the conurbation of London's spreading all the time so it takes in Watford and places like that.

*And then after Portsmouth, you came back to Lochmaben?*

I came back to Lochmaben, ma father died in 1978, and Ah had the opportunity to come back. And Ah thought, well, it would be nearer Mum, it was more a sort of personal decision rather than a career decision, at that time. And things didn't quite work out, football-wise, here, when Ah came back to Queen of the South. And Ah actually retired playing when Ah was 27.

*You played for Queen of the South?*

I played for Queen of the South, yea. Things, you expect people to be the same, your friends, you expect the place to be the same but they're not, you change, people change. And there's some people that I knew then I'm still close to now but, on the whole, people move away to find their own life and the way I look at it is that you really shouldn't go back and stay.

*Aye.*

You and I have both done it.

*Yea.*

We've been away, we've come back, things are different, you're different, people are different, you know. Times change.

2

# Lochmaben Hospital

In this chapter former staff and patients recall the time they spent at Lochmaben Hospital, also know as the County Sanatorium. Medical advances during the lifetime of the interviewees resulted in new treatments which used drugs replacing the regime of fresh air and bed rest, previously thought to be the most effective treatment. This significant change is remembered here by former nursing staff and patients. Betty Hutt and Lynne McNeish, who started their nursing careers at the hospital some 20 years apart, provides some insight into life at the hospital for both staff and patients. Bill Gibson, who received treatment there for tuberculosis, and Hal McGhie for diphtheria, shared their experiences of being patients at the hospital. Christopher Clayson, who was appointed to the post of Medical Superintendent at the sanatorium in 1943 is fondly remembered, along with Davie Shankland.

The feeling that the hospital was a community within the wider Lochmaben community is apparent in the interviews. Meals were cooked and laundry done on site and patients enjoyed recreational activities such as billiards, film screenings and concerts. The hospital was very much part of the community, providing employment, and allowed the patients to interact socially with the community. There was accommodation in the grounds for nursing and domestic staff and a house for the gardener. In more recent years the facility has changed and is now mainly used for treating elderly patients. A housing development has also been built in the grounds.

This first extract is from Betty Hutt whose nursing career began at the hospital in 1953.

**Betty Hutt**

Ah worked in an office, but Ah wanted to be a nurse, so Ah started at Lochmaben as an auxiliary nurse when Ah was 17. At that time, there was a fever ward and there wis five TB [tuberculosis] wards: two male wards, two female wards an a children's ward.

*And you mentioned something about your wage?*

Oh, ma wage, it was £5 a month but, Ah mean, we got fed and we had our

44

uniform and our digs. But, at that time everything was rationed. So, you had a wee dish, an that's when, every Monday morning, you took your dish and you got your sugar weighed out.

*And you would stay in the Nurses' Home?*

Yes.

*I remember there was a two-storey building on the right-hand side as you went into the hospital [grounds]?*

That's right, that was it.

*So that was in 1952, and then in 1953?*

Ah started ma general training at Dumfries Infirmary[1] and we were in the preliminary training school for three months out at Gribton. That's out by Holywood. And after that we went into the infirmary. And if we were satisfactory after six weeks on the ward, they gave us a nurse's cap. A proper cap. An Ah was there for three years.

*And at that time Davie Shankland was crossing your path, I believe.*

David Shankland and I, and another three young girls, started our training thegither. That was in January 1953. Davie was very patient with us.

*Aye, but he enjoyed it, I would think.*

Oh, maybe. We gave him a rough time sometimes (laughs).

*So, in 1956, you were now a fully qualified Registered General Nurse, having completed your training at Nithbank, what was Nithbank Hospital, later Dumfries G. R. Infirmary? … And you went to work in Lochmaben. Can you tell us something about your two years at Lochmaben?*

Yes. At that time, Lochmaben was mostly tuberculosis. There was no fevers at the hospital and one of the wards was used for TB patients, female patients, and they were called 'the spinsters.' And there wis two male wards, three wards and a children's ward. But the new treatment had been discovered for tuberculosis, an it wis good. It got good results and they even brought patients from Greenock and Glasgow to fill the beds because, with the new treatment, patients didnae need tae be kept in as long. The patients who had been in maybe five or six years, it gave them hope, but that was about it.

*Now, you mentioned about the new treatment. Ah think people would be interested to hear what life in Lochmaben Hospital was like when you were there in 1952, before the new treatment came. Can you give people an idea of what the traditional treatment for TB was like?*

Yes. All they had was fresh air, good food and rest. And as they progressed, they'd be assessed every six weeks an x-rayed. And it all depended how they were getting on as to how many hours they were allowed out of bed. But everybody had to have a rest hour between eleven and twelve and four and five. It didnae matter if they had been allowed to stay up twelve hours, they still had tae have their rest hour. And some of the patients slept out on the verandahs. And they had red mackintoshes at the end of their bed to stop the rain wettin the bed.

*So, it was rain, hail or shine, they were out on the verandas?*

Oh, they were out, even snow. An there were no windows or doors closed when it was TB. That was the only treatment they had. But as they progressed, they all had wee jobs to do, maybe cleaning brasses or that sort of thing.

*Ah mean, Ah remember, when Ah came to Lochmaben, that all the wards had these verandas but at that time they weren't used for the purpose that you've just described.*

No, at that time, Ward 1, they used to take surgical patients in Ward 1; Ward 2 was a chest ward; Ward 3 was a children's orthopaedic ward and Ward 4 was an orthopaedic ward. An Ward 5 was really geriatric.

*Is that not where Norma Foggo did some work?*

We did have an occupational therapist, an she stayed where Michael Dickie stays now. An the basement in the Nurses' Home, that was where the occupational therapy place was. And, ye know, they used tae make trays and baskets and that sort of thing. But everything, when it was tuberculosis, everything had to be autoclaved, or sterilised, before they left the hospital, anything they made.

*… and then in 1958 you took a break from nursing until 1971 … you came back to Lochmaben in 1971 and stayed there until you retired in 1997.*

Yes.

*Now you mentioned some things about the operation of the hospital, like what the night sister did and how patients went into the dining hall and so on. Would you like to say something about that?*

Yes, this is when it was tuberculosis. But even when Ah went back in 1971, the night sister locked the Nurses' Home at night and there was also a maids' home, adjoining the Nurses' Home. They were locked in at night too. An when it was TB, the male patients who were able to go to the dining room, had to go in the right-hand-side door and the female patients had to go in at the left-hand-side door. They ate thegither, mind, but they werenae allowed to go in the same door.

*Now, you also mentioned some characters, Davie Dall and Mr Watson. Would you like to say something about them?*

Yes. Davie Dall, he was the patients' pal. That's what he wrote on his Christmas cards. Davie sent every patient a Christmas card. An he had been a patient himself. And he actually stayed in the basement in Ward 1 and he was really a type of message boy. Ah would think he would maybe get £2 or £3 for doing it, but Ah'm not sure. And there was a Mr Watson, who was a telephonist there, an he was blind, and we thought it was great because he could read without putting the lights on in the winter. You know, he never got cold hands because he could read his Braille.

*You also mentioned that the hospital really was a community in its own right.*

Oh, it was when it was tuberculosis. They had everything but dances. They were allowed whist drives, the patients that were on shorter bed rest, they were allowed whist drives, concerts, films, but no dances.

*But you also mentioned the facilities that were there.*

The recreation hall, an they also had a billiard hall. An a wee shop, an the shop was staffed by patients that were allowed to stay up for maybe ten hours.

*And there was a dining hall?*

A dining hall. The staff dining hall was upstairs and they had a laundry too, they did all their own laundry.

*An, of course, most important of all, there was a very good kitchen, wasn't there?*

Oh, it was excellent, yes … Kay Morton was in charge …. That would be … when Ah came back in 1971.

*And you also said that, at this time in 1971, numbers [of patients] had gone down. Can you tell us why the numbers went down?*

Well, they transferred all the orthopaedic patients to the new infirmary. They transferred any TB patients that we had in the wards to the infirmary as well. An then we really went to all geriatric.

*So, that was a major change?*

It was.

*And, at this time, Irene McMichael, Ah think, came to the hospital.*

Yes. Shortly after that she came.

*And that began a long connection with the hospital. And you mentioned that with the advent of her being in charge there was quite a reputation built up for entertainment?*

Yes. Every year the staff, Ah don't know if they volunteered or not, but they took part, shall we say, in a concert. And that was mainly for the patients, but visitors were invited as well. But we did it for the patients, an it was good fun but sometimes things didnae turn out the way they were supposed to. An they also had fashion shows an again, the staff, we were the models. So, we had many a good laugh about that. An the patients could try the clothes on and, if they liked them, they could buy them. So, it was giving them choice, which is very important. We also had, not the Olympic Games, but we did have games for them. Throwing big dices and that sort of thing, and they all enjoyed that.

*One other thing I remember from my time here was that they had wonderful Burns' suppers.*

Yes, we had. An they continued well after the hospital closed. When the new hospital was built, we used to have them in the hall in Lochmaben, you know.

*In the Leisure Centre?*

Yes, it was. But it was a lot of hard work, we were all getting older, so we retired when it was still good.

*And one person we haven't mentioned is someone who is really connected to the hospital in a big way, and that was Christopher Clayson and you, Ah think, served under Christopher Clayson.*

Yes, Ah did.

*Would you like to say something about him?*

Yes, Ah thought he was a wonderful man who did a lot for tuberculosis. And he had also been a patient himself, not in Lochmaben. He had tuberculosis himself an Ah thought he was a great man.

*But you mentioned that he was quite strict.*

Oh, he was strict (laughs). Oh, definitely, he was strict, but he looked after his staff. When it was the tuberculosis hospital, we were weighed every month and x-rayed maybe every three months.

*He was quite a pioneering entity, wasn't he?*

Oh, he was, yes, he was.

*Aye, he was a wonderful man.*

Lynne McNeish, whose training at Lochmaben started in 1971, also shared her memories.

## Lynne McNeish

*So, what sort of duties did you learn when you were at training?*

Training? Well, … at Lochmaben at that time, there was orthopaedic surgery, cold surgery, there was medical—

*Sorry cold …?*

Cold surgery.

*What's that?*

That's just like orthopaedic surgery, you know, like a hip replacement, a cartilage in your knee, or whatever, but it was all done at Lochmaben, at that time. We even had children in Pavilion 4 at that time, so that was there. The theatre was done in the main hall at the hospital so the ambulance used to come and ferry them back fae Pavilion 4 to the main reception area. And there was geriatrics and there was medical, quite a variety o medical. Also TB.

*Still TB at that time.*

Still TB at that time.

*And we're talking about 19 …?*

1971 to 1974 Ah was at Lochmaben.

*So, there was still TB then?*

Not so many, but there was still odd cases of TB.

*So, what did you do, … did you administer injections or, what sort of things?*

Yes, uh huh. It was just like doing any of your training. Any of these procedures that had to be done, like giving injections or giving out the medication. We used to do a lot of bronchoscopies at that time, which was taking biopsies of the lung, so you would be part and parcel of watching that procedure. Very much, again, because of the TB, you were checking sputum.

*Oh, yeah?*

All the time, you know, I mean you were doing that on a regular basis. So it was, at that point it was like, you know, very much a full training.

*So, you were training at Lochmaben, … what happened when you qualified?*

Oh well, when Ah qualified, I got a post in Pavilion 4 and Ah worked in there, Ah think, roughly about six months … that was the orthopaedics. And so, Ah was involved in that, which was a very good learning curve, you know, because of the all the orthopaedics and the preparation you had to give for patients. And so, it was very interesting.

… Ah left the hospital in 1974 so, I mean, there's big changes in the hospital now. I mean it's, well even the new build, all the pavilions were done away with.

*Yes.*

So, there's a big, big change.

*Aye there's not much left up there [now].*

No. In fact, Ah don't know if there's anything at all. I mean when, it was like a wee place on its own, the hospital, with having the bowling green, the canteen, it was such a community. But, of course, these patients were in for such a long time.

*Yes, somebody else said that about the TB as well, they werenae allowed tae leave.*

That's right. So, it was a wee community in itself, yes.

The next two extracts give an insight into the patient experience at the hospital. Bill Gibson was admitted to the hospital with tuberculosis, in 1949, and benefitted from the new drug treatments that were emerging. Hal McGhie contracted diphtheria as a teenager, although he had been vaccinated for this, and was treated at the hospital. Diphtheria is a highly infectious and potentially fatal illness which, due to a successful vaccination programme beginning in the 1940s, is now rare in this country.

## Bill Gibson

*Bill, you were in Lochmaben Sanatorium. Can you tell me a wee bit about that?*

Well, I was 19 when I was in the Lochmaben Sanatorium, that was 1949, and Ah was in there for six months, came out in the January 1950. But when Ah was in there, Ah mean, Ah lay in ma bed for the first four months, never out o bed. And ye'd only visitors three times a week, a Sunday and a Saturday, and a Wednesday, and that was the only visitors. Ma sister wasnae allowed to visit me. She was too young to be allowed into the hospital.

*So, you were a bit isolated?*

Aye, I was really.

*So, where exactly in the hospital were you?*

Ah was in Pavilion 1, that's the first bit as you went up. Aye, that's where Ah spent ma time.

*… where was your bed, did you have to go out onto the veranda?*

Well, at times, if the weather was good in the summertime, ye were put out on the veranda. And there used to be … quite a fuffle if it came a windy shower … Ah mean if the rain blew into the veranda, and they had to get all these beds back in quick haste. Aye.

*Can you remember … was it all female nurses or …?*

It was all male nurses.

*All male nurses?*

Yes, jist the sister was the female – Sister Durie. … Davie Shankland was one of ma nurses.

*Oh right, ok. And what treatment did you get other than going out to the veranda?*

Treatment. Ah wis actually on what they called PAS [Para-aminosalicylic acid], it was streptomycin, that was a new cure, and that certainly was a big difference really. Ah was only in six months. Some of them up there, they were there for years. And a lot of them never came out … . I mean I was frightened when Ah went in there first, there was somebody dying about every night … it was terrible.

*That's scary.*

And being sae young, well, Ah can see them lying, jist breathing their last. It was really scary.

*And some younger than you, as well?*

No much, oh well, there was a kids' ward. … Aye, they had TB too, I mean it was rife in these days.

*So, what did you do? Can you just lie there, I mean?*

Jist mair or less. Ah hadnae many interests masel. Some o the nurses, some o the patients, had different things that they did, right enough. And another thing, a Sunday morning, some o the fit patients was allowed to make a fry-up, so we all had a fry-up on a Sunday morning (laughter). Ma mother used tae bring tattie scones and eggs.

*Oh, my goodness. And what was the food like generally when you were there?*

It was quite good, aye. There was nothing wrong wi the food.

*And it would be made at the hospital?*

Aye, it was made at the hospital. Once ye got a wee bit better ye went to the kitchen for your meals, later on.

*And outside, in the grounds, you were able to walk about there?*

Well, eventually, Ah mean eventually Ah managed to walk home.

*Goodness. And that's how many miles, that's maybe what …?*

Two and a half miles, Ah was struggling to start wi but, and Ah got ma brothers to run me back.

*Very good. So, when you came out of the hospital did you just go straight back to work?*

No, Ah had six months convalescent, aye.

*I see, just at home, yeah.*

Just at home. It was quite an experience. It was frightening, as Ah say, however, I survived. I'm 85 now, so it certainly didnae do any harm (laughter).

## Hal McGhie

*Now, your schooling at Dumfries Academy was disrupted by ... illness wasn't it?*

Yes, along with a lot of other people. A lot of people in Lochmaben had caught diphtheria. Ah caught diphtheria in ma third year at Dumfries Academy. Ah remember going in and we were sitting exams, it would be in early December, Ah think, and [I] became very ill and Ah'd been pretty healthy most of ma life. And, at lunchtime, Ah got the bus back home and went in and the doctor arrived. And Ah'd already had a sister, at least one sister, in hospital. Ah was diagnosed with diphtheria and taken up to the hospital in Lochmaben, where the sister just two years younger than me died. Ah don't, Ah can't remember anybody else dying of it. But it was obviously, although we'd all been vaccinated, it was an unusual strain that came and it was pretty severe. I was in for ten weeks and three days in the hospital ... and they took ma tonsils out, because it was your throat, it blocked your throat, Ah gather, tac try and get a clear swab. And eventually Ah got out. Ah missed a whole term at Dumfries Academy, which kinna set me back a bit, but Ah was told not to repeat the year, just to go on and work away.

*You were mentioning about [having] your tonsils taken out, that was quite a common event in the past. ... You don't hear about that now, at all.*

No, Ah don't know ... presumably antibiotics would sort it out. But they just took them out.

*Lochmaben was a big hospital in those days, 90 patients.*

Yea, a lot for TB. There was a lot of TB patients in the hospital. And then there was the scarlet fever and diphtheria, it was an infectious diseases hospital. Christopher Clayson was in charge.

*Was he in charge when you were there?*

Yes. Ah didn't see him but Ah'm told he was in charge. Ah must have seen him at some time, but Ah can't remember seeing him.

*Aye, he was a fine man.*

Yes, Ah'm nearly a neighbour to Christopher, so Ah used to go and see him. He liked his malt whisky. Ah used to take him a bottle of 18-year-old Macallan and [we'd] have a little sip together, occasionally.

In the following extract Paul Roxburgh recalled Davie Shankland, who trained as a nurse and worked at the sanatorium. Later, Davie's career took a different path when he became a nurse tutor and taught many student nurses in Dumfries and Galloway.

## Paul Roxburgh

The sanatorium was a hospital in Lochmaben which was originally established to fight tuberculosis. They found the cure for tuberculosis and it's been used for many things since but Ah remember one of the cures for tuberculosis was the fresh-air treatment. The patients were wheeled out every day, summer and winter, rain, hail or shine an Davie was of the opinion then, and still is, that it was a complete and absolute waste of time.

*That's partly why they had the verandas.*

Aye, that's right.

*Along the front of the wards, they were still there when I came tae Lochmaben, an of course the famous Christopher Clayson was in charge of the sanatorium and he did a lot of pioneering work. And Davie, of course, was he the Chief Nursing Officer, there?*

Aye, he was Dr Clayson's right-hand man. And then Davie went away tae teacher training college, well he actually went tae university in Edinburgh, to qualify as a teacher, nursing teacher.

*Uh huh, an he trained a lot of nurses in Dumfries.*

Oh, aye.

*And have you any memories of his humour?*

Oh, yes, aye, he had a joke for every occasion. The one that springs tae mind is, there was always a lot of antagonism between Lochmaben and Lockerbie, you know, in sports and many, many aspects. An one o Davie's jokes was: If there was a pile of furniture outside a house in Lochmaben, it would be flitting, if it was a pile put out in Lockerbie it was a warrant sale.

*That wouldn't go down too well in Lockerbie!*

In this final extract Tom Allan recalled moving to a tied cottage in the hospital grounds when he was a child when his father took the position of head gardener at the sanatorium. The cottage was of a quite distinctive style but is no longer there.

## Tom Allan

*Ah believe you came to Lochmaben when you were a boy.*

That's correct, yes. Ah was nine year old when Ah came tae Lochmaben on the back of a flitting fae Boreland. An the first thing Ah did was jump off the back o the wagon an banged ma head on a metal lamp post, which was a big introduction. Ah lived at the sanatorium. Ma dad wis gardener, head gardener, there, and we lived in the Inkbottle, which was a wooden house as you go in the gate tae the hospital.

*That's all gone now.*
    It's all gone. The gates are away.
*And how did it get the name Inkbottle?*
    Because it jist, the four chimneys were in the middle o the roof, an it wis just like somebody wis dipping in ink, for ink, ye know, like a pen in it.

# 3

# Town Life

The memories in this chapter, from the older interviewees, recall a time before widespread car ownership, when people relied on shops and businesses in their locality to supply their essential needs. Mobile shops also served the outlying rural area. These extracts are recollections of some of the many shops and businesses, along with their owners, that traded in the town in the past.

## Iain Johnston

My grandmother and grandfather, Jack, had run the shop for many years, several generations since before the 1860s. I think there were about 40 shops: a butcher, two chemists, a greengrocer, three hairdressers, a cobbler, as well as a glove factory and a cycle shop. And there were three tailor's shops.

## George McCall

*There were a lot o shops in the place.*

There were 38, Ah've counted.

*Thirty-eight, goodness.*

In the High Street alone, there was Teenie Dalziel, she wis a sort o sweetie, confectioner's shop. That's where the kids, aw the school kids, went and got their sweeties for school. Mrs Hart, or Miss Hart, she had a sort of chocolate, sort of grocery shop, very old woman. Across the road was the bakery, Thomson's the bakers. There was Miss Duff's fruit and veg, the Post Office was still there, [and] A. Y. Johnson's was the drapers. Oh, the chemist, Roland Bisset's, McMichael's, the grocers. Next door was Johnny Bell's, the chemist, and along [from there] was Maxwell and Hare's, draper. And then across the road was the butcher's. So, it shows you how many [there were].

*Absolutely.*

Aye, and in Queen Street, there were shoemakers, Graham's, the shoemaker, and confectionery; Somerville's, the bakers; Murray's sweetie shop; again, Tweedie's grocers; Davidson's grocers; Tweedie's, shoemakers, shoe repairers.

*Of course, at that time nobody went away anywhere to shop, did they?*

It was all local.

*It was all local, aye.*

Aye, on Bruce Street, Roxburgh was the bakers and egg merchants. Further up there was Halliday's grocers and tea merchants.

… King's was the cycle shop wi fishing tackle and toys for kids.

*And these shops just gradually closed did they, just gradually?*

They closed aye, the big stores took over, the big stores. There were two cycle shops in Lochmaben. McGhie had a cycle shop as well. Two blacksmith's shops, McGhie had a blacksmith's shop. Ah don't know whether … he kept it open as a museum, but Ah don't know whether it still exists or no yet. It was at the Townhead.

Tom Allan recalled wartime rationing and some of the shop keepers in the town.

## Tom Allan

*Is there anything you would like to say about how Lochmaben has changed in all the time you've known it?*

From when Ah was a boy, when Ah arrived here, the shops in Lochmaben wis, as Ah went tae school, there was Roxburgh's. John Dickson was the chappie that was behind the counter, a very thorough man, John. Paul Roxburgh would tell ye. He used to say, 'Plain, pan, cut or new?' when ye went for a loaf. An Ah remember Ecky McLean saying him an his brother had a penny to spend gaun tae school and one didnae want to spend his halfpenny at that shop so they thought they wid get it changed, they said: 'Mr Dickson, could Ah have two halfpennies for a penny, please?'

'Run along, sonny, this is not a bank.'

*'This is not a bank!'*

That was John Dickson.

*And what kinna shop was that, then?*

It was general groceries, ye know. Of course, coupons and rationing was still on the go then, you know.

*Aye, it would be.*

Aye, ye didnae get much cheese or butter or anything then.

*And most people would shop in Lochmaben, they didnae go anywhere?*

Aye, aye, everybody shopped in Lochmaben. They did a big trade in eggs, Roxburgh, at one point, you know. They'd go out in the country and bring the eggs in and exchange, like a barter system, Ah presume, wi their customers.

*Because they had a mobile shop, hadn't they?*

They had a mobile, Paul drove the van. Uncle Dinky drove the van in the beginning.

*Dinky?*

Aye, aye, McWilliam, Dinky McWilliam, which would be Mrs Roxburgh's brother. Then there were three cloggers and woodmakers in Lochmaben. There was Scott.

*Tweedie, was Tweedie one of them?*

Tweedie, Johnny Tweedie. An then there was Easton, Easton the clogger. It wis jist at the end of Welldale Place, opposite the coal yard office, ye ken.

*So, was everybody wearing clogs then?*

Ah wore clogs. Ah wore clogs when Ah wis on the railway even, aye. Clogs were a common thing then, guid clogs.

*And was there a shop where you could buy medicine or was there a chemist or what?*

Well, Mr Bissett wis in where the chemist is now, it wis Bissett. An there was Johnny Bell, which is next tae, Johnny Bell the chemist an his daughter wis next tae the Indian shop, you know, behind the Town Hall? That was two shops then.

*That's where the Kennedy's is, is it?*

No, that was Maxwell and Hare, which was a tailor. So, across the road was A. Y. Johnson, where the hairdresser's, Loc o Hair, is now. That was A. Y. Johnson.

*And what did he do?*

They were tailors.

*Tailors as well.*

And drapers.

*So, there was a whole row of shops round there then?*

Oh aye, a busy place, aye. Wee Johnny Bell, the chemist, someday he'd come oot the door an his trooser zip was open, or his buttons were open, and somebody said: 'Johnny, your shop door's open.'

'Is that right,' he says, 'Bessie's in.' This was his daughter; she was behind the counter.

*Aye. Good.*

Then there was Chippie Joe, ye ken, Joe Crolla, was next tae the ice cream shop, Tony, who was his brother.

*So, where the chip shop is now, that's always been a chip shop, has it?*

Aye, Joe had the chip shop plus he had, up [Blacklocks] Vennel, he had a games room wi a billiard hall an he had accommodation for fishermen and what have ye. Aye, he was a worthy, Joe.

*And that's the brother of Lou?*

An uncle, an uncle of Lou.

*Lou's uncle? Right.*

Aye, Joe. Now Joe, there's a man that could tell you a few tales, Lou (laughs).

*You mentioned tearooms, was there a tearoom still in Lochmaben?*

No then.

*Not then?*

No.

*So, it was Crolla's—*

Crolla's ice cream shop.

*But if somebody wanted a cup o tea or something, … [was] there nowhere like that?*

That was the only bit, mair or less, ye could go.

Bill Carrick recalls being sent to the fishmonger who also sold fruit and vegetables.

## Bill Carrick

*And you also told me about the time when you used to go for two leeks. Tell me about going for two leeks, when you could buy two leeks or wherever it was, for your mother's soup pot or something, do you want to tell me that?*

Maybe Ah did.

*You were sent somewhere and they used to call you 'two leeks', when you went for them, a penny for two leeks or something like that?*

Oh aye. Delvers, he was a fishmonger an fruit shop.

*Where was that?*

You know where the vennel is up at Annandale Crescent, that was the hoose there, there wis a wee shop then.

*Ah, right.*

Kipper Haddie, they cawd him.

*Kipper Haddie?*

Aye.

*He would get his fish off the train, did he, from Glasgow or somewhere like that?*

Possibly would.

The Three Ladies discussed the shops and businesses that they could remember, from earlier years.

## Three Ladies

*The shops in the town, which ones can you remember?*

Where do we start, at the top of the town?

Well, there was Dubbs [Duff's], where Costcutter is now.

Yes, they had two shops.

*And what kind o shop was that?*

Fruit shop, both fruit shops.

Grocers, an then were wis Pollock's, where the flats are up there now.

Pollock's, it wis a grocery. And Miss Tweedie's sweetie shop.

Miss Tweedie, aye.

Across the road was McGhie's.

McGhie's, a tailor's shop.

The father came further down here, to the one next door to you.

Miss Murray's.

Miss Murray. The clogger next door. Across the road was the bakers and Davidson, the grocer's.

Aye, Jimmy Davidson.

Further down was the butcher's. Across was Maxwell and Hare, the draper's.

Then we're going off to Costcutters. It was McMichael's along with Miss Bell.

Aye, the chemist.

No, they were Hare's the drapers before the Co-operative come in.

Ah remember Hare's.

Maxwell and Hare.

And then there was Charlie Johnstone as well.

Ferris.

An then there wis the McMichael's shop, grocer's shop. Across the road from Johnstone's, draper's, that sold everything.

And Mr Little.

Aye, Mr Little.

Next door tae them.

That's where Alex served his time.

Did he?

Post Office, the bank.

Aye, Bissett the chemist.

Dowlin's [Dowling's], that's where the café is now, you know the bakery?

Yes.

They used to have all the fancy goods, didn't they?

Ay, there wis a lot of shops then.

Frae Bruce Street to the ironmongers.

King's.

King's up next to The Crown. Roxburgh's further down Bruce Street, Ritchie's, the baker's, on the corner.

Webber's.

…

McMichael's was a great baker across there.

Aye you worked there.

They baked all the bread up there.

Up the back.

Aw their vans.

*Were there many mobile shops?*

The vans went out aboot every day, McMichael's. They went out every day away round the country.

Willie Kennedy used tae come, he went out wi Bill Dirom.

*What did they sell?*

The baker's, McMichael's, was most all jist bakery.

Aye, Robert Kennedy was the baker.

They would sell big bottles o lemonade, for McMichael used tae make that.

They used tae buy the lemonade from him. He sold it as well.

Aye, then he'd the hairdresser further down here.

That's right, 'Much off?' (Laughter). That's right, 'Much off?', and before him there was Mrs Gray, an she sold sweeties an things like that.

And did he not play the fiddle?

Aye, Gray, the tin whistle as well.

The tin whistle (laughs).

Aye, for the daughter yaist tae come and play the piano.

That's right.

Aye, Margaret, aye.

She played in the orchestra.

Is she still living?

I don't know, she left the district. I don't know if she's still living.

In the following extract Wilma Twidale, interviewed with her husband James Twidale, recalled how her father became a baker and came to start his own business in the town.

## Wilma and James Twidale

WT: Ma dad worked at Somerville's, the baker's, which was in Queen Street. Ah need tae tell ye aboot ma dad. Ma brother Edgar was born an then brother Johnny, then there was a big space and Nancy came along, but ma dad worked at Somerville, the baker's. Now, ma dad was the youngest of his family, and there was nine of them, an he was only 13 when his father died. So, he was meant for the bank, that was kinna to be his career, but he had tae leave school because his mother had nobody else, and he was apprenticed at the bakers. So, that was how he got there. So, when I was, well, Ah was quite young, ma dad took a shop, we had a shop in Bruce Street, a baker's shop, and he didn't drive, ma dad, so he did his deliveries with, Ah don't know if you'll remember the ice cream things with bikes? Well, it was a square box like that, with the bike an, it opened up an it had shelves in it, an that was how he did his deliveries. And so, we were there, he was there for a while, an then he got the shop in High Street, which is the café now, The Village Fayre. And that was our shop, and we were there for a wee while, but the people he rented it off were goin to do wonders to the house, an never did, an the house was really, got too small for us. An Ah think, too, the War was jist coming, again, I don't know but Ah'm looking back thinking, things were becoming quite difficult and so he closed the shop and went to work in Lockerbie, for

Currie's, which was a bakery. Well Mr Currie had been a rep for a flour firm and he'd opened up this shop an he came an asked him if he would work for him, so he went there as the foreman and we moved up to Mossvale, which was just being built, an that was in 1938. So, we were there, well I got married from there, so we were there a long time really....

*... now you were gonna tell me about the shops in Lochmaben.*

WT: Yeah, well, Ah counted, an I counted 25.

*And that was in 1942, about then.*

WT: About 1942, yes.

JT: It was these wee houses with a room as a shop.

*Oh, ah yes.*

WT: There weren't so many of them, there was one, there was a wee shop at Marjoriebanks, a sweetie shop, it's Rosemount Cottage or something, that's the house, it's still there, now she had a sweetie shop. Now Ah've come down from there, where would the next one be? It would be this one across here, which was Duff's.

JT: An Miss Tweedie's.

WT: No, that wasn't there in 1942, then there was Tweedie, the tailor, an Tweedie, the shoemaker, at the top of the hill. And go down Princes Street, Mrs Brown, who was Mrs Dixon's mother, not Sheila Dixon, this was Sheila's granny, she had a sweetie shop in her house. And further down Princes Street, there was, oh Ah forgot McGhie's, up at the Townhead, there was McGhie's cycle shop and hardware. He sold paraffin and he did batteries for radios, for the wireless an everything, an he sold bikes, an he had a blacksmith's place. An then down Princes Street there was, there was nae shops up the top of Princes Street after Mrs Brown but when ye got further down, there's an empty shop now next to the Crown Hotel, that was Mrs King's, another hardware shop. An then Sandra's Bazaar was a grocer's and then on the Dumfries Road there was Roxburgh, the grocer. And then we come to the High Street, no, wait a minute we come to Castle Street first, and there was Crolla's café, an there was the chip shop next door. Then you go to the corner where the hairdresser's an that is now, that was Johnstone's the draper's, then the Post Office, then the chemist, and then ye crossed over and there was another shop which was a sweetie shop, oh Teenie Dalziel's, Miss Dalziel.

*I remember someone telling me about that one.*

WT: It was a wooden bit built on the end of the house, all the children went there, all the school children. An ye come further up an there was another sweetie shop, at Russell's, an then ye come up tae the fruit shop, that was Duff's as well, an did they have, no Ah think it was jist one big fruit shop then, there was a house next door, that's right. An then behind the Town Hall there was Maxwell and Hare, the tailor, Johnnie Bell, the chemist, an another grocer, there wis three shops there. Ye come up Queen Street and there was Mrs Graham's, coming up the street, it was on the left-hand side, Mrs Graham's shop and that was a sweetie shop but her husband repaired the shoes, and further up there was Miss Murray's shop, another sweetie shop.

*That's about four or five sweetie shops!*

WT: Aye, and on the other side of the road there was Jimmy Davidson's, the grocers, an, no, Ah've missed somebody.

*What about, do you remember Scott Paul had the big shoe shop, what was that before that was there?*

WT: It was a shoe shop, that was Scott's Shoe shop then, it was called Scott's, but oh—

*That's a lot of shops.*

WT: Aye, there wis a lot o shops, but Ah missed one an Ah jist remembered it after Ah had spoken tae ye but it's gone out ma head again.

*What was where the bank is?*

WT: Oh, that was the bank.

*It was, and where the café is, the Village Fayre?*

WT: That was the one, it was a baker's.

*Well yes, the baker's, yes, an you had the baker's for a wee while.*

WT: That's the one Ah had forgotten, that was the baker's, it has been various things, we had it as a shop an, after it was closed down, people bought it and they used it as a room, they didn't use it as a shop, it was part of the house, then some more people came and took it on. Remember that guy … [REDACTED]?

*[REDACTED] … Ah remember that name, yeah.*

WT: Well, he had it as a gift shop and then there was people came after him, Bridges, an they had it as a gift shop, an they moved tae down tae, what do you call the place in Derbyshire? The spa place? Oh, Ah've forgotten, it's a well-known place.

*Chatsworth Ah always think of in Derbyshire.*

WT: No.

*Buxton, Buxton?*

WT: Buxton. An they moved there but they called their shop Bridge's of Lochmaben.

*Oh really, in Buxton?*

WT: In Buxton.

*Oh, that's interesting.*

WT: But they probably aren't there now.

*No, no, no. Gosh. And there wasn't anything further down, after the chemist's really? Towards the school, there was nothing, no?*

WT: No, no.

*But a lot of sweetie shops.*

    WT: Although Ah think there had been.

*Yes, maybe at one point, yes.*

    WT: Ah've got an old almanac somewhere and it's got them all. A lot.

*I've got a copy of an almanac. Yes. Round about 1900.*

    WT: An of course, it was self-sufficient because we had plumbers, we had joiners.

*Blacksmiths.*

    We had blacksmiths.

What about butchers, was there a—?

    WT: Oh aye, there was the butcher's, Ah'd forgotten aboot the butcher's. It was Brown's the butcher.

*Were they always there? Opposite, near the Town Hall? You know the butcher's shop there?*

    WT: Yes. But Ah believe before that there was a butcher's. You know the shop on the corner, the big shop on the corner which is the hairdresser's [Loc Of Hair] now in the [UNCLEAR]. Well just beyond that, in my day, it was a garage and electrical, Ah forget what.

*Oh, yea.*

    WT: That had been a butcher's shop, Wright's the butcher, Ah gather.

*Yes. That's right. Ah remember, did Paisleys not have their wee electrician's shop there at one point as well?*

    WT: Yes. Maybe.

*Yes, they did. Paisleys, Paisleys?*

    WT: Oh, did he have it? Ah didn't know that.

*Was it Paisleys? Ah thought maybe they did, Ah couldn't remember.*

    WT: Now, his son used to do shoe repairs, in his own house. It was like a shop.

*Yes. And the dressmaker's as well?*

    WT: They were in Castle Street. Aye well, Ah mean, I don't remember a dressmaker but there were dressmaker's in Lochmaben.

*Again, when women had bought the dress and then, well they bought the material and made their own dresses, didn't they, and trimmed it themselves?*

    WT: That's right.

*Gosh.*

    WT: And there had been a fish shop at one point. Ah kind of think that was where the butcher's ended up, Brown's. And there was also—

*Somebody said there was a slaughterhouse there as well, would it be behind the butcher's?*

    WT: Behind the butcher's. Oh, they had their own slaughterhouse when Browns had it. That's right, they did.

*That's right. Ah remember them.*

WT: An there was a jeweller's, but I don't remember the jeweller's. It was in Queen Street.

*An Ah remember where the coal merchants were, was there not a baker's shop there for a wee while, before it became the coal merchant's?*

WT: Aye, well, Ah've mentioned that one.

*Ah, we've talked about that one.*

WT: That was Somerville's, where ma father worked, an then it became McMichael's.

*Yes, and then they had the vans as well.*

WT: That's right.

Paul Roxburgh worked for his family's grocery business and could remember farmers coming into the town to sell milk. He also recalled the travelling shops which served the outlying area and the reasons for this stopping.

## Paul Roxburgh

Ah was always struck about how many thriving businesses there were in Lochmaben. Ah remember there being six grocers, three sweetie shops, two bakers, three shoemakers an a clogger who also sold McMichael's lemonade, which was a big attraction, two chemists, three tailors, a chip shop, a café and five pubs or hotels, several builders and joiners, Green's buses, Simon Smail who had the Crown Hotel also had a bus, a successful milk retailer, an two farmers who came around wi a wee pony and trap sellin milk from the back o it from a big container, door to door, so there were other big business in Lochmaben, as well, that started off.

*Had the tile factory started by then?*

No, no, there was just Gibson's, the slater in Bruce Street, an he started the tile factory off....

*You were general manager of Roxburgh Stores?*

Aye, aye.

*And at that time, you hadn't a horse-drawn mobile?*

No, it was a wee van, aye, a wee Ford van. A very temperamental old van, Ah would say.

*An were you still covering the whole of Annandale then?*

Aye, well, up tae Johnstonebridge, up to Wamphray Ah would say, and down as far as Dalton.

... Being a grocer too Ah'm, it's really quite sad, the amount o travelling shops there used to be, Ah mean coming out of Lochmaben, there would be at least four grocers, travelling grocer's shops, and God knows how many vans set off fae McMichael, the baker's, an Brown's had three vans.

*That just shows you that the communications from the country weren't the same as they are now and of course there were a lot more people.*

The supermarkets.

*A lot more people were living in the country at that time probably too.*

Aye, Ah know from ma own experience, because we eventually found it wasnae economical to run the travelling shop. An, really, the business wasnae worth running withoot the travelling shop because 75 per cent of the trade was done in the travelling shop. But you just couldnae compete against the supermarkets. You know, you wid get a customer comin oot 'Ah'll have half a dozen loafs', because they're too bulky tae bring back fae Dumfries, an ye couldnae run a business on that basis. Even the cost o the fuel alone was prohibitive. An you've also got the hygiene question, you know, ye'd butter an bacon an a lot o perishable goods like that, that would never be allowed to be sold at that temperature today.

The shops found in the town, later, in the 1950s and 1960s are recalled here by Anne Hills.

## Anne Hills

*Ah suppose you remember quite a lot o the shops in Lochmaben?*

Yea, Ah do remember them all.

*Other people who have been recorded and remembering all the shops maybe in the 1930s and '40s but what about the '50s and '60s?*

Well, starting at the top o the town at the Mill Loch it was Duff's, Duff's shop, then it was Mary Tweedie's sweetie shop up at the Townhead, and then, coming down, it was Jim McCall's, [*that*] was the draper.

*The drapers.*

And next door was Yolanda's, the hairdresser, Yolanda Crolla, the hairdresser.

… Then the other side o the street was the baker's and then Jimmy Davidson's. The thing Ah always remember aboot Jimmy Davidson's was he had a cheese wire and he used to cut his cheese wi the cheese wire. Then it was down to the butchers.

*Ah remember that, sawdust on the floor.*

That's right and the carcasses hangin behind you.

*Ah know.*

An ye could get Smith's crisps wi the blue bag in them.

*Yes, that's right, ye could.*

That was the only place ye could get crisps. …

Then there was the Co-op, with your number, trying to remember yer number. Mother kept [receipts?] in a jar. An then it was along to, now, what was the grocer's there, before Jimmy Henderson, who was in there?

*Was that McMichael's the grocer's? Ah can't remember, it could have been Roxburgh's?*

No, Roxburgh's, that was further down the other street, Bruce Street. An then there was another bakers along past the police station, on the corner where Sandra's Bazaar is now, that was the bakers, and there was Roxburgh's and there was, was it not McMichael's was the drapers on the McMichael's corner? That was a drapers, Bernard Mann, who had the electrician's, the Post Office, can't remember who was in the Post Office and Jepson's of course.

*I remember Jepson's, yes.*

And the sweetie shop, Dowling's, used to go into Dowling's, and then the chemists. Ah think that would be them all.

*There was a bakers down there as well.*

Oh, no that was Dowling's.

*Was that? Because Ah think Wilma said they'd had a bakers down there at one point.*

That's maybe earlier, maybe. The one that was the Village Fayre?

*Yes.*

That was Dowling's sweetie shop, and, Ah mean they maybe did sell groceries as well because they also had a gift shop. They sold toys and gifts and they had a separate room where that was. It was a two-roomed shop that, but we just went for sweeties.

*Yes probably, probably.*

Yes, that's how we've all got bad teeth.

*Oh, exactly.*

School dentist coming filling our teeth.

*Yes, Ah remember that as well.*

The van, the grey van used to come (*laughter*).

Several interviewees mentioned the Crolla family's café and fish and chip shop. In this next extract Hal McGhie recalled the fish and chip shop during the wartime years.

**Hal McGhie**

Crolla's, I don't know whether Lou Crolla can remember, but Crolla's Café was heaving. It was a very successful business at that time.

*Was that when they had a fish and chip shop as well? That was next door.*

Well, his uncle had a fish and chip shop, Joe. But the café seemed to be the more successful, Ah don't know, although Ah remember queueing at Joe's, too, to get a poke o chips. We could never afford a fish (laughter). Lou's grandmother used to make peas, used to dae whatever it is wi peas, they used to stew, they'd buy hard peas and you could get a pie and peas in there, which was always one of our favourite sort of dishes during the War.

*Aye, rather than fish and chips, aye.*

Well, they were cheaper (laughter).

Local public houses are remembered next, including one which also traded as a petrol station. Changes to licensing hours and attitudes to women drinking in pubs are evident in these extracts.

## Tom Allan

*And what about pubs, how many pubs were there then?*

Well, there was The Crown, which was a busy place; The Commercial, which is The Bruce now, it was called The Commercial then; The Kings Arms and the Railway Inn, of course. Balcastle was still a house then.

*Oh, it was a house then. So, it was a house and then a hotel and then a house again.*

Aye. A hotel, then there was a petrol station in it as well at one point.

*A petrol station?*

Aye, what happened was, the petrol station was in Castle Street in the beginning, you could get petrol at the garage in Castle Street. Then when Ah came back from the Army, the petrol station was built in Bruce Street, which was Esso. So, the contract was, wi Esso, was that they wouldnae build another station, another Esso station, in the area. So, what they did was they had another subsidiary firm and they put it in Balcastle. So, Willie Noble said: 'Right, we'll sort that.' So, he built a petrol station beside the yacht club, well, the yacht club wasnae there then.

*Bill Carrick, his place, aye?*

Bill Carrick, aye. So, there was a Shell station there, so it cut the yin in the middle oot.

*Aye. It's never recovered really, has it?*

No. So, it's a shame really that the Shell station went. There's nae petrol stations left now. Ye could come fae as far away as Castle Douglas and come doon that road, and through this way, and ye'll no get a petrol station.

*That's right. Aye, you're right.*

An there yaist tae be yin, every ten miles ye'd hae got yin. Different days altogether now.

## Paul Roxburgh

The pubs used to close at nine o'clock at night sharp and of course there were always many heavy drinkers in Lochmaben, and it was, one of yer entertainments was to see the pub coming oot at nine o'clock, particularly on a Saturday night, because a lot o them were well and truly inebriated. It was possible, if you were in the know, to be taken to the Sergeant's Mess at Halleaths Camp and ye could get a bit o extra time drinkin there.

Anne Hills recalled her aunt's marriage ceremony being held at The Balcastle, originally a private residence. She also mentioned visiting the Bruce Arms, as a child, when her grandfather was the landlord.

## Anne Hills

*Movin on a wee bit, what are your memories of Balcastle?*

Not a lot, well Ah say not a lot, one in particular. My Aunt Nan got married in Balcastle, in the conservatory. It was because it was the time that the church was being renovated so she couldn't, she and ma Uncle Derek couldn't, get married in the church, so they were married in the Balcastle conservatory. An Ah do remember it was a wet day and the water dripping down on everybody. An then, after that, Ah didn't go to the Balcastle at all, as a youngster. You know it wasn't, it was kinda frowned upon an—

*Ah remember a disco there once. When would that be, '68 maybe, something like that?*

But Ah would be married before Ah would be goin to the Balcastle because under-age drinking was—

*Well, in Lochmaben.*

Well, that's the other thing, yes, no under-age drinking was done in Lochmaben (laughter). And after that Ah was in Lockerbie.

*Any of the other pubs in Lochmaben?*

Ma grandfather used to have the Bruce Arms.

*The Bruce.*

Ah've got memories of the Bruce Arms, a lot, Ah used to go in there as a child, on a Saturday, and bottle up and do things, an Ah do remember the Bruce Arms had these fantastic old, old mirrors, the very old, original Johnny Walker mirrors and McEwan mirrors. Ah don't know if they still have them, now, but Ah do remember them.

*Ah remember going to the Railway Inn. Rhoda Smail, you remember the name? Ah remember her having a party there at the Railway Inn.*

Yes, because she lived there, didn't she?

*And Ah remember that well.*

You see, ladies didn't drink in those days and ladies didn't go to bars so I never was in the Railway Inn. Ah've only once been in the Railway Inn and that was at a funeral, in [unclear] time. Ah think Ah've once been in the Crown, Ah've never been back in the Kings Arms, the Bruce Arms, since ma grandfather was there. Kings Arms, Ah've been to funeral teas and some weddings but Ah've never had a drink in the Kings Arms.

*No, Ah think Ah'd be the same.*

An Ah think the Balcastle, latterly, they used to do, sort o dinner dances and discos, maybe, then. That was it.

The blacksmiths who served the town, sharpening tools and making cartwheels with the local joiners, are remembered next. In the past, working horses from farms would be walked to the forge, and hunters taken in horseboxes, to be reshod. However, nowadays horses are owned for recreation and the farrier travels to them with his mobile forge. One blacksmith is remembered as a good runner who had competed at Powderhall Stadium, in Edinburgh, where the Powderhall New Year's Sprint used to be held.

## Tom Allan

*An was there a blacksmith? Was Tweedie something to do with the blacksmith's?*
>No. Irvine was the blacksmith, Bob Irvine was, and his dad. Ah used tae gaun doon there, when Ah wis on the railway, and get picks sharpened, ye ken. The old man was still on the go well in his nineties.

*Aye, and were there still horses coming in tae be shod?*
>Aye well, there were more of the hunter type, an by that time they were starting to go oot and dae them then, traders bring them. Ah've seen horse-boxes stopped on the Queen Street and horses gaun up the vennel tae the blacksmith's shop aye.

## Bill Carrick

*Where did the blacksmith come from, for the horses?*
>Amisfield.

*Did you take the horses down to them?*
>Took the horses to Amisfield, aye.

*That would be to Stoorey, what was he called, the lad down … no, Look-up, the blacksmith was called Look-up, wasn't he?*
>It wis Bob Warden that was the blacksmith.

*Uh huh. They used to have a lad there called Look-up … . They used to put hoops around cartwheels and all sorts down there, didn't they?*
>Aye, beside the burn an—

*Uh huh, that's right. There was a circle where they could put the—*
>Hoop in.

*Heat it and stick it—*
>An then in the water

*Stick it in the water, old Bob used to work for the joiner's that made the wheels.*
>Aye, aye.

*Made the wheels. So you would walk the horses down there, would you, to get shoed.*
>Aye.

*Or ride them down, would you ride them?*
>No, Ah used tae walk.

*Just walk them.*
>Sitting on the back of a Clydesdale's no very comfortable.

*Is it not? A bit too wide, Bill? It's a bit wide, eh?*
>Oh aye. It's like sitting on a ledge.

## Three Ladies

*Ah think you mentioned there was a blacksmith's and a couple of stories about him?*

There wis actually two blacksmiths. There was Bob Irvine. Would he be after Kit?

Aye, Bob was after, up that vennel, up there.

You would hear Alex saying his hands were covered, like, Alex's hands were covered wi warts and he went roond, an somebody told him he had tae put his hand in the water, you know where they cooled the—

*The horseshoes, Ah remember that?*

Aye, that. An he says it did, it worked. Aye, Ah remember him saying that.

Aye, Bob used to have that cottage up there wi the hens in it, Bob Irvine. Who's in it now? A biggish chap.

Ah don't know, Ah don't know, Nell.

Ah think his sister stays in that big house, once ye go through to [?] at the right-hand side. He bought that wee house at Lochmaben, big, hefty chap. Don't know his name but Ah remember Bob gaun up tae feed the hens.

Ah can remember, he was a good runner, too.

Aye, he was.

He used to run at Pow … was it Powderhall?

Aye, he used tae be at all the sports.

Aye, he was a good runner.

Ah can picture him wi the leather apron, a big man. Better playing wi him as against him (laughter).

Children who went along to see the blacksmith at work weren't particularly welcome, as recalled in the next two extracts.

## Anne Hills

Oh, Ah tell you another thing that was memorable, the blacksmith's yard. He used to keep us, what was his name again? Ah've forgotten, it'll come back to me. He didn't encourage children round about but, if ye stood quietly away back, you could see the big horses being shoed.

## Isabel Wells and James McWhirter

IW: Well, Ah remember, ma dad was a blacksmith, well that wasnae the blinkin easiest job in the world. An after we moved doon to Croft Terrace ma dad used send me on a Saturday morning, across the road, ma grandfather stayed across the road.

JMcW: That's right.

IW: And he had sent is for the pay, well Ah think it would be £3 or something that's aw he got, it wisnae very much, no it wisnae.

*But a blacksmith was really needed, Ah mean, a lot o horses.*

69

IW: Aye.

JMcW: [Ye] used tae get chased by Bob quite a lot, when ye went intae his yaird: 'Don't dare to disturb my horses!' (Laughter).

IW: He used to get intae a row fae Agnes Broon and them, because the weans would come in an he would be like that wi the hot shoe an he would burn their jackets and things cos they were stannin too near. They used tae gang an complain tae him but he said: 'The boys were too near.'

*They wouldnae be allowed to do that now.*

Hal McGhie's father and grandfather were blacksmiths and farriers.

## Hal McGhie

*Now, you've mentioned that your grandfather and father had interests in livestock, could you maybe tell us a little about both of them?*

Well, both … were blacksmiths and farriers. Ma grandfather – ma father was actually born in the Gorbals in Glasgow – ma grandfather was up there as a blacksmith, working for Glasgow Corporation. Ah think they came back in 1905 to Townhead, Lochmaben, which I understand belonged to the Tweedies, next door at Townhead, and they leased it from them. There was a shop and the smiddy and some outbuildings. My grandfather, and why Ah remember, ma grandfather was obviously getting older, he died in May 1950, but he bred greyhounds, he had a good greyhound bitch and thought he would breed them. We would break them in as you were, walk them, four at a time, we eventually, once ye trained them, and then he sold them on to various tracks. Ah remember one lot going to Belle Vue[1] and some going to, Ah think it was White City, in Glasgow. He seemed to, it was quite a good hobby, Ah think he got his pocket money from that.

*You mentioned your father, grandfather, were farriers, now I think that would be a word that not many of the current generation know about. What was a farrier?*

Well, there are more farriers now than there were, just about, in the 1930s. There were blacksmiths and farriers, and it was all heavy horses. It was working horses, a thing that was dying but now it's hobby horses, but you see horses and ponies all over the place. And we have farriers now, rather than blacksmiths and farriers, who just purely shoe horses or look after horses' feet.

*Aye there's some mobile farriers, aren't there?*

Yes.

*They go round in their vans.*

They can now hot shoe a horse from a gas-operated forge. So, things keep changing.

The Three Ladies spoke about Corncockle Quarry, near Templand, which had a dedicated train line to take the stone out.

## Three Ladies

*… You knew quite a bit about Corncockle Quarry because you were born, brought up in Templand.*

Oh, Ah was still at Templand when you used tae hear the hooter gaun at night and they'd aw come down an cycle tae Lochmaben and it's opened up again.

*You were saying that, yes.*

How do they manage in without the train? It's the lorries that take [the stone] away now. They used to have a railway and it used to go up round the back of Spedlins and Jardine Hall. An Ah think the way she was talking, it used tae drop off at Nethercleugh. They lifted aw the railway up. But Mrs McKinnon was up there for years, wisn't she?

She was in a big house up there.

*Is there anything else about the quarry?*

Ah don't know why they closed it down but it's jist no long opened up again. Maybe the stone's of some value or something, Ah don't know.

It'll be the sand lorries come down here, sandstone. It's that big, it's like Rob Walker's lorry, big, you know, sandstone, I've seen them wi trailers on as well.

Well, that's it, they'll be getting the sandstone out again.

Ah would think so.

…

*If you could think when that was, when the men were cycling back to Lochmaben. Can you remember roughly when that would be?*

Well, we were still at Templand then. Did we move to Lochmaben when Ah wis aboot eleven?

Ah cannae remember now.

You were born in, when, 1927, 28?

28.


Another concern which operated in the town, employing local worker during the Second World War, was McGeorge's, a knitwear factory producing gloves for the military.

## George McCall

*OK, right, good. And you said you remember the glove factory in Lochmaben?*

The glove factory that was on Princes Street, they made gloves during the War for the forces.

*Oh right.*

An in the forces' colours for the RAF, the Navy an the Air Force. An they also made socks. It was McGeorge's, but they had a big factory in Dumfries, they called it the Nithdale Factory, it wis up by the infirmary. It's the flats now, an it closed down during the War Ah think. Ah was asking ma wife – that's the only job she ever had, she worked in the factory – an Ah was asking her how many were employed. She said she couldnae remember but it did employ a few. Ah think it would be Wilma's grandmother was in charge, she was the manageress o the factory, it employed a few.

*It ran for a number of years, did it, the factory?*

All during the War, all during the War. They had one in Sanquhar as well, but they closed them down. The McGeorge's was, Ah think, retired and it was taken over and they just kept the one main factory.

Before the advent of the National Health Service, doctors attended to the medical needs of the townsfolk from their own premises in the town. The next two extracts give an insight into how this worked.

### Tom Allan

*And what about services? Ah mean you mentioned Dr Wilson, in Bruce Street?*

Dr Wilson. He was in Bruce Street at Lake House. Dr Campbell had his surgery down at the lochs at the Victory Park.

*Oh aye, down there. So that was a doctor's surgery at one time?*

Aye, Dr Campbell. He was the Provost as well. Then before that there'd been Dr Gilchrist, which was where Dr Frost stays now. That was, surgery was in there.

*And if people needed to go the hospital, I mean, what happened? Did they get picked up by ambulance or what?*

Ambulance usually picked them up, aye. Ah remember ma mother taking appendicitis. Ah'd tae run in ma bare feet doon tae Dr Gilchrist's and she wasnae a happy woman.

*No, no.*

She wasnae talking to me. Gave me a row for disturbing him.

*Oh, and your mother had appendicitis?*

Anyway, wee Tommy Gilchrist came and 'Ah,' he says, 'Mattie, Ah think ye've appendicitis. You'll have to gaun tae the infirmary. Ah'll gaun an phone for an ambulance'. But ma dad wis bowlin on the green up at the hospital so Ah had tae run up the field an tell him. Ah says: 'Ma mum's gaun tae hospital, Dad.'

He said: 'Aye, Ah'll be there in a minute. I'll jist finish this end.' What a man (laughter).

*Yea, yea.*

### Paul Roxburgh

Aye, both ma brother Stuart an I were born at 29 Bruce Street, in Loch-maben of course; 29 August 1934, Ah was born, Stuart was born about six

years later. We were both delivered by Dr Gilchrist, quite a character, he
attended to many medical problems, I remember even
him pulling out ma mother's teeth.

Roy Thorburn and Hal McGhie have both successfully run their own businesses
and when interviewed, recalled the hard work and risks that were involved. In the
following extract Roy talked about serving his apprenticeship with a joiner and
undertaker in Lochmaben. He then went on to work in the joinery business his
father had established in the town which, due to Roy's ambition, became the first
to supply and erect timber frame houses in Scotland.

## Roy Thorburn

*And obviously you had to get work so how did you go about getting work?*
> Well, ma father was hell-bent on me staying at school, Ah don't know what
> he wanted me to come out as, Ah think it was architecture he was thinkin
> about. But Ah was struggling at school an Ah left when ma father was in
> Rhodesia [now Zimbabwe]. Ah found great difficulty in getting a job
> because normally apprentices either started when they left school, well, they
> did start at 15 year old. Ah was trying to get a job coming 17, as an appren-
> tice, and nobody would take ye because ye were too old. Anyway, Ah went
> to the local joiner, Charlie Graham, Ah went to him about three different
> times an he wasn't for starting me because he already had four apprentices
> an they weren't too happy with him. Ah volunteered tae work for nothing
> for six months, so he thought, he said 'Ok', so he took me on an Ah worked
> for six months an after six months Ah went to him and said: 'Look, what's
> ma future, am Ah still here?'
> He said: 'You stay where you are an Ah'll give ye another threepence a week',
> so Ah knew Ah was goin in the right direction when Ah got that increase in
> wages.

*You mentioned that you had offered to work for nothing but you, in fact, got paid.*
> Ah did get paid.

*What was your pay?*
> Ma pay was 26s [shillings] a week and ma mother took £1. And she was
> good to me, she let me keep 6s and 6s went quite a long way in these days.
> But the thing is, Ah was now in ma 18th year an Ah needed, really needed
> more than 6s .

*If we were translating it to pounds and pence I think that comes to about £1.50.*
> £1.50, aye.

*Which Ah think the people listening will be gaping at probably.*
> Well, £1.50, would be, aye £1.50, that's right.

*But Ah mean that's not taking into account inflation and everything. But, in 1953,
you nearly went to Rhodesia but that didn't happen.*

No, Ah left my job an Charlie Graham wasn't too suited with me leaving
because Ah'd only been there what, about nine months, a year. Ma father
sent for me to go out to Rhodesia. Ah was flying out on the Sunday night;
however, Ah got a wire on the Saturday morning, saying 'Stay where you
are, there's trouble'. So, Ah went back to Charlie Graham on the Monday
morning and asked him for ma job which he was glad to take me back,
which Ah was glad he did take me back. Ah got on exceptionally well with
Charlie, he was the local undertaker and Ah used to make coffins.

*How long did it take you to make a coffin?*

Well, you were allowed eight hours. Ah mean some were easy and some
were difficult because if they were hardwood, they were more difficult. If
they were softwood, an it was for a kid, well, they were quite simple, you
could knock these out in about four or five hours. But eight hours was the
recognised time, the same as making windows, you got eight hours to make
a sash and case window, glaze it and paint it. You didn't waste much time.

*So, it was all handmade?*

Everything was handmade.

*Not machine?*

We only had a morticing machine which, again, it wasn't electrified an it
was hard work but work that Ah enjoyed

Roy's working life was interrupted in 1957 when he was called up for National
Service until he returned in 1959.

*So, you returned to Lochmaben in 1959 and went to work for your father, Hugh,
who'd started a joinery business.*

Well, ma father started the business just prior to me going to the RAF,
when he came back from Rhodesia. He was in a small, jist a shed at
Bereflats, known as the Bereflat, where Ah'm staying at this present
moment. Him an I started together and we went into timber framed
houses. It was a thing Ah'd always wanted to do an Ah used to send tae
Australia and New Zealand an all these places for brochures an Ah copied,
Ah must admit now, Ah copied quite a few o them. But it took off and we
were quite successful, actually, for a long period of time, till we had the fire.

*You're being very modest because you were the first firm in Scotland selling timber
frame houses.*

We were, we were the first firm in Scotland to manufacture timber frame.
The first one Ah built Ah was a bit apprehensive about it, because we're on
a building site in West Linton an Ah thought, *Well, if we went up there and
this house doesn't fit or marry in*—. Ah mean this was only the very first, so
Ah assembled it, actually, in the back yard, which today seems a bit foolish
but at least when Ah went onto the site Ah knew that it went up very rapidly

an everything would fit, to the surprise of the local contractors.
*That was in West Linton Ah think …*

That was West Linton.

*… which was the first one and you designed and built your own frames.*

From then on. We built our workshops down at Marjoriebanks, there. We were stretched because we didn't have much money, but we built the work-shops an we manufactured houses. And we wis putting them out quite rapidly for a number of years and we were doing exceptionally well until the next disaster came along.

*You were working 24/7, Ah think, at that time, with Margaret in the office?*

We were workin, Ah was away from home sometimes for four weeks at a time jumpin from one house to another an Ah had a very small squad of men, but they were excellent men, but, as Ah said, we were doing excep-tionally well an the fire was the next.

*Yea, you now come to an important event in your life. The 19th of June 1977, can you tell us what happened then?*

Well, it's never been established to this day to what caused it but a couple of our joiners had a small heater which Ah'm quite sure was for heating their pies, just like a kind of microwave thing they had. And Ah'm quite sure, on two occasions, Ah used to go in, maybe on a Sunday when they weren't workin, and that had been left on from the Friday night, an on two occasions, well obviously Ah put it off. But on this particular weekend on the 19th of June, it was the Gala Day in Dumfries, Ah was playing golf, Margaret was playing golf at the time as well, an we seen this great smoke rising from the area an Ah knew that it was quite close but we had about maybe 300 or 400 tyres which were going to be used for the Jubilee, we were going to be building a fire an Ah thought the tyres had caught fire some way or another, however a chap came runnin down the golf course shouting that ma workshop was on fire. So, by the time Ah got up to home the fire was an inferno, the fire brigades couldn't get out of Dumfries because of the Gala. They got here eventually and when they did get to the workshop the fire hydrants had no water so they had to then to divert down to the loch and pump it from the loch, which is about a quarter of a mile away, probably a wee bit more. And by the time they got the water going, the two houses, the windows in the two houses adjoining the workshop were startin tae melt, the glass was starting to melt, so they had to concentrate on the houses, one of them which was mine. Then, of course, everything was burnt to the ground. On the Monday morning we were in dire straits. Ma father came down about seven in the morning and said: 'What are we going to do? We can only pack up, we havenae got money to carry on or rebuild.' So, there were 15 men standing out there wondering what to do, an he said: 'Are you going to tell them?' So, Ah went from ma house across the road to tell them that we were folding up an we couldn't carry on. However, on the way across Ah changed my mind and thought, *Oh well, what's the point of folding up, Ah'll give them a chance.* So, Ah said to them if they wanted to remain with us there was a job for them but times would be tough and very hard for the next six months, a year, an if they wanted to leave there'd be no hard feelings. However, I gave them two or three minutes to make up their minds an Ah went back to them and every one of them stayed with us, which I really admired them for it. Unfortunately, we had an architect an he came out at nine o'clock and he decided to move on.

*And you'd lost, as you say, everything, records, everything.*

Everything, the office went, everything went. And unfortunately, Ah had a map up in the office of Scotland, northern England and Ah had pinpoints on this map, the map was about six feet high and about three feet wide, of every job and every house we'd done an of course we lost all of the records of it.

*But, as so often happened, out of this massive tragedy there were some terrific acts of goodwill.*

Oh, no doubt about it. The local builders, two of the local builders, who are the biggest builders an Ah was direct opposition, not in as large a way as they were, McCall Wells, he came up and he offered me half of his workshop to operate in until we got back on our feet, which Ah thought was a very great gesture. An then the following day Robison and Davidson, Bob Robison came out, an Ah mean they were a big concern, an he offered me his workshops as well. An Ah thought, that was one thing that inspired me to keep going, it just lets you see that there's good in a lot of people.

*That's a great tribute to you. In 1977, another obviously tragic incident, your father died.*

Six or seven weeks after the fire ma father died on the golf course, so that was another blow.

*One of the nice things is, if you don't mind me saying it, is that the name of the firm still is H. K. Thorburn & Son.*

That's right and Ah mean it's been known as H. K. Thorburn & Son and the first van we had we put the name on it, we wrote the name on it ourselves, which wasn't very pretty like, but everybody knew who we were, well, nowadays we run about with six or seven vans. But that was the start.

*Can you maybe just let people know how far afield you built these houses?*

Well, we done a lot in the north of Scotland. We went as far of John o' Groats, up on the west coast, sorry the east coast, Aberdeen, Stonehaven. We done a lot in that area … an on the west coast we went up as far as Ullapool, was as far. An Skye of course, we done quite a few on Skye and on the islands. An Ah mean Ah got a reasonable reputation on the islands and we done quite a lot of houses up in there, follow-ons that Ah was getting, which Ah still get to this day, young Roy's still building up on the islands. We went as far south as York, on the Midlands, we were down to Wakefield and then on to the Isle of Man, so it's a pity to this day we don't have these, a record of all these places, but we don't.

*The other outstanding thing, as far as Ah'm concerned, is that you are still going strong in this deep recession at the moment.*

Well, they are, and they're very, very busy at the moment and they've got into one or two, they're building at Stonehaven and they're building at Filey and Southport, for the Caravan Club, and they've got a good reputation with them. They do, obviously it's winter work because these buildings have to be ready for the summer, for the summer work that they have, and a lot of winter work which suits them fine because the wintertime's usually the hard time in the building trade. But on the housing side they're still going very, very strong. And they're building two houses at the moment on the island of Coll, and one of them's worth £750,000, well that's the price of it, and the other one's worth £500,000 so they're in a good line.

*That's good, and of course, since 1977 there have been a few changes, such as Kenny Bell joining the business, in 1993, and Margaret, your wife, retiring from the office, in 1994, and then yourself retiring from the business, in 1995, but Ah don't think retirement is a suitable word for what you do now.*

Naw, it didnae appeal tae me, the thing is Ah started working away on ma own again, Ah do quite a few contracts. Ah don't work directly against them but I do quite a few contracts.

*Right, can we maybe, is there anything else you want to say about work?*

Not really, no. Kenny Bell came into the business, Ah'd done the under-taking for a period of, what, 30 years. Ma father started it but Ah was quite knowledgeable with it. Charlie Graham was the undertaker and Ah had to do quite a bit of undertaking with him. Kenny Bell come in and Ah taught him the ins and outs of the undertaking, he's makin a great job of it, now.

In this next extract Hal McGhie tells how he worked for his father in the family dairy and milk delivery business and how, over time, he took over the reins, expanding it geographically, as well as taking on other business challenges. He was a founder member of the Dumfries Chamber of Commerce, has been a member of the Dairy Trade Federation and was involved with the running of Auchincruive Agricultural College and Dumfries and Galloway College.

### Hal McGhie

*You said that McGhie's dairy started in 1938. Why did your father change from being a farrier to being a milkman, ... do you know why?*

Well, in 1938, ma Aunt Mamie got married, that was ma father's sister, and she had delivered milk round Lochmaben. There were six milkmen in

Lochmaben at that time and ma father took over. It was a very much a part-time job. He would go to Halleaths, we bought our milk from Hunter, at Halleaths, and bottle it there, or Ah think by the time we took over we'd started bottling. It was the old 44 millimetre bottles with cardboard tops, which were very unhygienic, because if ye put … the dust would settle on the cardboard top, when ye opened the cardboard top, all the dust fell into the milk. So that was how it started, and he was still shoeing horses all through the War because there were still working horses right through the War. Ah think he wouldn't stop his farriering till well into the 1950s, maybe 1960, he would still be doing a bit of everything. Ah can't remember exactly when we took our first round in Dumfries but it was before Ah had a driving licence.

*When did you actually start helping him?*

Oh well, you were helping him from whenever you were old enough to do anything. We'd go down to Halleaths in the morning, deliver on a Saturday or the weekends we'd work, but Ah left school at 16 to be a milk boy and graduated to a milkman a year later when Ah was 17.

*What were the deliveries done in, was it a horse drawn vehicle or was it a motor or van?*

No, Ah gather at the start it was a makeshift part of a car at the back with two cans on it and it got crates and it developed intae vans. Just after the War he bought WD [War Department], ex-WD, rescue vehicles which had been cars converted into a rescue vehicle, cut the back off them and they were just glorified pickups, not exactly ideal for delivering milk, but they did their job and it was very difficult to get a hold of vehicles then. …

*Now, from sort of 1965, McGhie's dairies started expanding, would you like to say something about how that happened.*

It expanded gradually until 1965 and, in 1965, Ah managed to negotiate to take over the Co-op [dairy work] in Dumfries, where we originally just bottled the milk, pasteurised and bottled the milk for them, and then eventually they gave it up and we honoured their token system, they ran a token system. You bought tokens from the local Co-op store and if ye put a token out ye left a pint, and it was a pint for a token. That was quite a big step forward because they had a fairly big share of Dumfries [trade] and then, in 1967, in January '67, we bought Northern Retail Dairies which was a branch of Express Dairies. They had, Northern, they actually owned the cheese factories at Lockerbie and in Sanquhar. I think they were called IMS, Independent Milk Suppliers, that owned the cheese factories then, it was part of Express Dairies. And that left more or less ourselves and Scott [UNCLEAR] [who] were the only two milkmen left in Dumfries. And then Ah think about two years later, about 1969, we bought Kinnaird's, who were in Dalbeattie and Kirkcudbright, and so we had, without having a monopoly, we had a very big share of the milk market in Dumfriesshire, Dumfries and Galloway.

*I mean all the six branches [were] a result of you, you and your family, moving to Dumfries. So, were you in charge of the Dumfries operation then?*

Well, it was, Ah was really quite involved in purchasing it and it was considered a bit of a handful so Ah actually stayed in the dairy house at Redheugh, in Glasgow Street, in Dumfries. And Ah stayed, Ah lived, Ah actually slept there for nine years although, apart from working there, Ah had to come home, had to come back to Lochmaben most days because, particularly when ma mother died, because Ah had to go in charge of the office side of it a bit, as well, so it was quite, it was quite a busy life.

*Well, it certainly sounds it and Ah know when we came here, in 1969, McGhie's dairy was a big operation in Lochmaben and further afield.*

Yes, we were quite a big employer, we actually wholesaled in Carlisle and Cumbria, supplying Allied Suppliers who are Morrison's now, I mean there have been so many changes in the supermarket side, that was what eventually, that was why eventually we sold, because the market was moving away from doorstep delivery to shop delivery then to supermarkets delivery. And the supermarkets were taking a bigger and bigger share and if ye wanted to supply a supermarket chain they said: 'Right, you'll have to supply the whole of Scotland or not at all.' Or, you know, it finished up there was only three suppliers, supplying the whole of the milk in the UK for the supermarkets.

*You actually expanded outwith Dumfries and Galloway too, didn't you? You took over firms in the central belt.*

We took over a company in Dumbarton and one in Largs. That was to try and get into the Glasgow market, and there was a consortium set up, six dairies in Scotland, with a view to supplying the supermarkets, taking the Scottish trade, but there were some weak links in it so it wisnae just quite as successful as it should have been.

*But it must have been quite difficult running a business at that distance too.*

Yes.

*Unless you had sort of good local managers on site.*

Well, it was the owners that were running it and they couldn't run it for themselves, so it was very difficult to run it for somebody else, so it was quite hard work.

*During all this expansion and so on, you managed to find time to start Border Travel Services, in Queensberry Street.*

Yes.

*Would you like to say something about this?*

Well, Ah was originally brought in as a shareholder with ma father, then he brought in two of ma brothers and he brought in the third brother and ma mother, an Ah was a bit unhappy about—

*This was in the dairy?*

79

In the dairy, in the dairy business, Ah was a bit unhappy about this so Ah was thinking of leaving and eventually the agreement was that Ah would, the firm would guarantee a loan of [£]2500 for me and Ah started off Border Travel. When Ah started Border Travel it was from scratch, there was only one travel agent in Dumfries, Grieve's, and their principal business was, Ah suppose, shipping business or rail because in 1963/64 there was very little air business, very little inclusive tour business. So, Ah bought premises in Queensberry Street, 73/75 it was, it was on three floors and Ah bought the ground floor first and then the top floor and then the middle floor and then Ah spent a bit o money on it and converted it into a reasonable office shop, which it still is. We rent it out now to a company called Alternative which sells these trinkets and things.

*Yes, Ah know the shop.*

So, that was where it all started and I advertised and a bloke, Peter Mason, came down, he had been working in Edinburgh. So, he came down and started it off and he would be there until 1969, Ah think. Not Peter Mason, he was David Mason, sorry, apologies, and it was reasonably successful, we managed to get our IATA [accreditation] fairly quickly which is International Air Transport Association and we had quite a few successful years and then we went into tour operating in the early '70s. We started a company in association with Anchor Travel, in Glasgow, but we went in just at the, when there was a battle going on between Clarkson's and Thomson's, so the prices were getting so tight and the margins non-existent, that we had to come out of it, lost a wee bit o [money], a few quid on that. About the same time, we opened a branch in Hamilton, in leased premises, which kept us going, which was fairly successful too, although it was another string to your bow, if you want, but another problem, because it was another 60 miles up there and 60 miles back and Ah eventually sold it to Nairn Travel. That was in 1974, Ah think, this was about the time we got involved in various types of diversions, if ye want, one of which was operating to South Africa and various places selling tickets. In those days there was, IATA regulations were such that you couldn't undercut the fare but ye couldn't, there was no such thing as cut prices, the prices were all regulated, but the way around it was you could buy what they called an IT fare, Inclusive Tour fare, which was quite a bit cheaper, so you sold that along with a package which was hotel rooms and that entitled you to the Inclusive Tour fare so then you had, you sent them out on a, without any Inclusive Tour, but you have to have an arrangement at the other end, an inspector went out, he had a voucher and he handed the voucher in and ye had tae put him into the very basic accommodation. That didn't happen very much so it was pretty successful except I got involved with a company in London which I think didn't run their books very well so eventually they were owing us [£]34,000 which was a lot of money. And we went to court, won our case, it cost [£]10,000 for a week in court down there, in 1974, and we won our case. [We] barely got all our money back and then it went bankrupt so that was gone. So, [it was] around this time that Ann Rafferty came in as a partner, well in theory to look after the accounting side of it.

*You were obviously far-seeing to go into the travel business when you did, when you think of what's happened.*

Well, it was obvious it was gonnae expand, there was talk of, they were just starting to operate charter flights, people had more money in the late '60s and '70s. You know, they were starting to get more money about them and instead of going to Blackpool or Northern Ireland, we did a lot of tours to Northern Ireland in the '60s to Portrush, bus tours, which was huge business, but that all stopped when the problems started in Ireland in '68, '69, and the business started to go to Majorca, well it was the Costa Brava, Barcelona was the first one. That was the first place to take off, Spain is obviously still the biggest market.

*You also managed to diversify your portfolio during this period.*

Well, there was a lot of things happened. In 1972 we bought the Station Hotel, that was a nice big acquisition, if you want, after starting Border Travel, that was the family firm. The dairy bought the Station Hotel on the 7th April 1972 from British Transport Hotels and Catering, and we've still got it, it's actually ma daughter's now because Ah gave it to her. It's been quite a successful venture.

*Well, when you think of Border Travel that still is a highly regarded firm …*

Yes.

*… in Dumfries.*

Still going, we had our 50th anniversary not long ago. So, it's still going quite strong.

*That's good but you also, you went into some other lines at the same time.*

Well, quite a lot. Border Travel bought Southerness Holiday Village which had about 60 acres of land that was in a not a very good state of health, if you want, but still had a nice location. We bought it from a London company and over the years we spent quite a lot o money on it, all the profits were ploughed back in, built a swimming pool, built toilet blocks. They were mostly static caravans, and all these had sewage in and then ye started putting electric in. And then eventually we started putting electric points in the touring [area], so that a touring caravan could stop, plug into the sewage, plug into the water, plug into the electricity. It changed quite a lot, it was very successful, we maybe shouldn't have sold it but anyway we were given a good offer in, Ah think it was in 2004, and we took it and it's kinna set us up a bit.

*Aye, you diversified into the building industry as well.*

Well, that was a sort of, an accident, if you want. It was very difficult to get a hold of builders, at one time, to do odd jobs and we actually started looking, we had talks with Carruthers and Green, the nephew or something that was running at the time, and he was thinking of selling. And, in the meantime, Crombie Construction, who were based in Carrutherstown, near Annan, got into big trouble and approached us and we took over Crombie Construction which expanded a bit, it grew quite a lot. We've also taken over Border Construction, which we based in Carlisle, and McCall Wells at another time, so the construction side was very big at one time. We did quite a lot of private housing, some quite big contracts, in fact we've just parted company with that this year.

*That's a long time too.*

Yes.

*Now, during all this time you also had links with the dairy industry in being part of various organisations. Would you like to say something about that?*

Well, I always said I was a milkman and that was the only trade Ah knew, really, was being a milkman, whether it was the processing the milk or delivering milk and I was elected on to the, on to the Dairy Trade Federation, in 1969, and Ah was on that for, until 1988, when I retired from the dairy trade industry. Ah was Chairman of the Scottish Dairy Council for one year. Ah was President of the Scottish Dairy Trades Federation, I had two sessions of that. I started the Scottish Milk Distributors Training Scheme, because there was a serious lack o training in the dairy trade and [was] first Chairman of that. Ah was Chairman of that until Ah retired.

*And you were also a Governor—*

Well, I was appointed by the Dairy Trades Federation, I was a governor at Auchencruive, at West of Scotland College, and a governor of the Hannah Food Research Institute, which was quite a prestigious organisation.

*Where was that based then?*

It was very close to Auchencruive.

*Auchencruive, aye.*

Very close to there.

*Now, as well as these links with the dairy industry you also had other interests in Dumfries and Galloway, and in, particularly in education and business. Would you like to say about what organisations you were part of there?*

Well, I was approached, the Dumfries Shopkeepers' Association had had some problems and they thought they wanted a stronger body to represent them. I was approached by Douglas Barbour and someone else to set ... to see if we could set up a Chamber of Commerce. And Eileen Breck and Robin Braidwood and I did all the donkey work and started it off and I was the first President. Ah think Ah was President there for five years, for six years, which has got stronger and stronger.

*Yes, it's still going strong.*

Still going strong, it's got stronger and stronger. We used to meet in the Station Hotel and we got a very good lobby going to try and help things although, needless to say, the local authorities didn't always listen to us. One of the strongest lobbies we had [was] when they built the bypass. They also decided they were going to pedestrianise Dumfries [town centre] and we fought quite hard with them and said the Loreburn Centre was taking it too far, that pedestrianisation was too much. And there was a Grosvenor House, who were [a] very successful operation, had approached Dumfries [Council] and they came to see us and I've got it in their scheme there which was to buy Woolworths then, and Ah think it was Littlewoods next door to them at the time and they had already had a deal with them and they were going to develop a scheme right over the Irish Street and down to the markets. It would have made Dumfries very strong but they said they needed time to put it together but Dumfries councillors hadn't enough time. They jumped on to Scottish Metropolitan who were starting this scheme down in the, what is now the Loreburn Centre. Ah think it cost them £30 million, they put it together and they finished up taking about £10 million for it so that didnae help the Scottish Metropolitan, Ah don't know whether they exist now or not, Ah don't think they do. If they got into too many ventures like that, they wouldn't exist.

*Well, I mean, I think that you've been proved correct in that the town centre was over-pedestrianised, which is a shame.*

Yes, it was extended too far, it was over-pedestrianised and the big fight we had was about car parking provision, because the Loreburn School was closing and, opposite the drill hall in Rae Street, between Rae Street and Newall Terrace, and it was ideal for car parking. And they had the money, and they had the planning, and everything was going ahead but the councillors fought very hard and well, we didn't get it. That's another thing that would have made Dumfries a much more accessible [town centre] and much more of a centre. Instead of that they've got out-of-town centres that-are, because they've got plenty parking, people go there.

*They've not progressed on the parking issue in Dumfries since that time.*

No, they've not progressed. They insist that people won't pay for parking, but people pay for parking if it's reasonable and it's available and if you want, you'll go shopping if you know you can get your car parked.

*I mean, I draw the parallel with Carlisle, you know, who didn't over-pedestrianise and they ringed their pedestrianised quarter with car parks …*

Yes.

*… five minutes you knew you'd get into the middle of Carlisle.*

Yes, and get your car parked. And their prices are reasonable.

*Oh, I know, Ah'm with you on that one.*

Yes.

*And I remember, as a councillor, having to listen to Dumfries councillors trying to sell Dumfries as a free parking centre and they didn't appreciate that people go to a place because there is an attraction, and they don't think about parking …*

No.

*… paying for parking.*

As long as parking is affordable, but everybody's idea of affordable is different. But they'll pay a reasonable amount, there can be a little, there can be free parking for up to two hours, if you want in [the town] centre parts but there's nothing wrong, people will pay for parking.

*You also were connected to Dumfries and Galloway College; would you like to say something about that?*

Yes, Ah first got involved with [Pickup], Ah was approached by a person from the Scottish Office because Ah had been quite involved with the Scottish Office in my negotiations with the farmers, when Ah was in the Dairy Trade Federation, and we started the [Pickup]. Now Ah can't remember what the abbreviation's for but it was tae work with the College and to make sure that the College produced courses that were actually of some use, that there was a job at the end of it. [May have been SWAP, the Scottish Wider Access Programme.] That was my first time Ah met Jim Neil, who was the Principal of the College, and we had quite a few rows, if you want, and then the Scottish Office told me 'You don't need to ask him, you tell him.' So that was my first step into education, if you want. And then Dumfries, the College was run by Dumfries and Galloway Council at that time and it had been agreed that they would become an autonomous body to move away, so there was a new Board of Management to start up and Ah went into it, went to the meeting expecting, Ah said Ah was willing to be a member of it, and come out as Chairman (*laughter*). And Ah was Chairman of that for quite a long time, Ah can't remember, it'll tell ye on there how long I was Chairman.

*Hal, has just handed me the presentation watch, or clock, that he got in recognition of his service as Chairman of Dumfries and Galloway College from 1988 to 2000. You'll not be surprised to know that, in light of what Hal has said about Dumfries and Galloway College and the Chamber of Commerce, that he was given an award for services to business and education. Could you tell us about the award and where you got it and who gave it to you, Hal please?*

It was the OBE [Order of the British Empire], Other Bugger's Efforts, Ah think they call it (laughter). It was given at Buckingham Palace, by Prince Charles, Ah think it was 1999, Ah could have a look at it and see but Ah'm pretty sure it was 1999.

*Yes, you said 1999. What are your memories of that day then?*

Well, the award's a very simple thing, I mean you go in and sit and wait along with a few others, Parkinson was there, and …

*Michael Parkinson?*

… Michael Parkinson, aye, and Ah think it was Lulu [who] was there, the one who's married to a hairdresser. And then you were just called through and Ah had a kilt on, the last time Ah had a kilt on, and so it was mentioned that you were wearing a kilt but it was very straightforward. Ma sister went down and ma daughter and we went and had lunch after that. Then we went on the London Eye, and then we went out for a meal at night and went to a show. So, it was quite enjoyable.

*Good.*

But the presentation itself is nothing.

*Over in a flash, was it?*

Over in a flash, yes. Quicker than a flash.

*Still, it'll be a nice memory to have that.*

Yes.

*Well, these are all the questions I have, Hal, I don't know if you've anything you want to add at all.*

Well, Ah could talk for a long time, Ah mean Ah've had adventures into, Ah had the Queensberry [Arms] Hotel in Annan, for a short period of time. The biggest disaster Ah have was Ah was talked into taking over a golf factory in Heathhall which was a total disaster. It was a, it had a, huge, made big losses, enterprise company suggested that it could be successful and instead o doing ma homework before Ah went in, Ah did ma homework after Ah was in. And it's a world market, it's a world [?] product, golf balls are made all over the world, and unless ye had millions to spend and get it totally mechanised, Ah don't think it's practical and so we hung on to it for a while and then had to eventually close it so that's probably the worst venture Ah've been in.

*You've fortunately had more successes than failures.*

Well, Ah'm still alive, Ah'm still alive after 82 years and still manage to keep body and soul together.

# 4

# Childhood

The extracts used in this chapter give an insight into the interviewees' experience of childhood in the town. Schooldays at Lochmaben Primary School – or 'A Guid Wee schule' as one elderly resident had it – are recalled with memories of the physical layout of the premises, teachers, lessons taught, playground activities and the school garden. A pupil's performance in the eleven-plus examination, which took place in Primary 7, determined how their education progressed. Some would continue their learning at Lochmaben for longer while others would move on to schools in Dumfries or Lockerbie. This move from the local primary school to secondary education in a larger town was not a particularly happy experience for some and there are recollections of this here. Free time spent out of school, playing outdoors, and often away from adult supervision is recalled as well as participation in organised group activities in the town. The chapter concludes with some childhood memories of family, friends and events in the town such as the first cars and television sets in Lochmaben.

George McCall remembers his time at Lochmaben School and then moving on to Dumfries High School. In later life, his trade as a plasterer took him back there when it had become a college, and he taught the skill in one of the classrooms that he had been taught in.

## George McCall

Ah went to school in Lochmaben. It … wis a secondary school then.
*But you started when you were five, did you?*
Ah started when Ah was five and we went through the primary school. The primary school, which is still there yet, the old primary school. That's the house as ye turn up, it sits on the left-hand side as you go up Castle Hill.
*Behind the golf course?*
Yea, that was the primary department and the other bit, across the road, it wis the drill hall and a lot of entertainment was put on there for Lochmaben as well.
*In the school drill hall, aye.*
Upstairs was the woodwork room and the science room.

*You mentioned, George, ... something about a garden, there was a garden across this side somewhere, was there?*

The school gardens was behind the new Centre that's built in Lochmaben, where these houses are now. Have ye been up that vennel?

*Yes, aye, up the vennel.*

Up to the Centre, up from the High Street, aw that was school gardens. They had plots, an being a secondary school, they had aboot two [pupils] tae a plot actually an they grew some lovely vegetables. An ... when they were ready, at certain times o the year, they used tae take them round and sell them. But they used the manure frae the sewage and it was ... they stopped it because [of] ...

*Health and safety.*

... health and safety.

*You said that you finished at Lochmaben School and then you had to sit an exam or something before you went on?*

The Control Exam.

*The Control Exam, aye.*

Aye, it consisted o, it more or less consisted of English and a wee bit mental arithmetic. If Ah remember right, Ah think there would be aboot 120 questions on mental arithmetic and ye got a certain time to do it; that was the exam. An that qualified ye, eether, ye could eether stay in Lochmaben School because, at that time, it was still a secondary school....

Or ye could get a chance to go tae Lockerbie [Academy] or the High School [Dumfries High School] or the Academy [Dumfries Academy]. Now I don't know how it was selected, whether it was according to how ye done in your exam or no, Ah don't know, on yer marks, you got marked then in yer exams.

*An how did you travel to Dumfries or to Lockerbie if you were going there?*

The bus. ... Ye got a bus pass.

*An you chose to go to Dumfries, is that right?*

Ah chose tae go to the High School. Ah got intae the High School, Ah was kinda sorry that Ah had taken the wrong course because Ah think that Ah realised that Ah was more o a practical man, or a technical [man], than theory. Ah enjoyed the schooling in Lochmaben because they were good teachers, really good teachers. In fact, they really drummed it intae ye. An Ah didnae do so well when Ah went tae the High School, but that was a good school too. The High School, at that time, was on George Street. ...

*That became the college that, or something didn't it?*

It became part of the college, aye, but it's still, the new part was Loreburn Primary School. Now, the funny thing is, when Ah went tae the High School when Ah wis eleven, twelve, after [the] Control [Examination], Ah started there, at the High School. An Ah finished at the High School. That's where my workshop was. They made the workshop in 1986 for tae start off a plastering course.

*So, at that time you were teaching people then, you were teaching them how to be plasterers?*

Ah was teaching plastering, aye, Ah was teaching plastering. Ah had a classroom as well, Ah done the theory as well as the practical, more practical than anything else, of course. An the old science room at George Street, Ah had it as a sort o classroom. It wis a workshop for doing cornice work and that sort of thing.

Isabelle Gow enjoyed her time at Lochmaben school and had a memory of her first day there. She also recalled the physical layout, some of the subjects she was taught and each of the teachers who taught her. School outings and time spent in the playground were also remembered.

### Isabelle Gow

*Isabelle, can I ask you, where did you live about, when you went to primary school?*

Well, Ah lived on the farm, so Ah had to come into Lochmaben to school. Ma Dad would drive me into Lochmaben in the morning, but at night, because he would be milking at half past three, four o'clock, Ah can't remember when we left school, he couldn't come down for me, so Ah had to wait an get the school bus. And the school bus went through Templand and up to Nethermill and then back along past Elshieshields and then dropped me off at Esbie the last drop, an it was always that route. An then Ah had a mile to walk home after that.

*Did your Mother meet you?*

Yes, ma Mother met me and she had the pushchair with ma baby brother in it as well, so they had two miles each day to walk.

*Can you tell me what year you started school?*

I started Lochmaben Primary in 1958.

*And where was the school situated?*

The school is where the new houses are now, beside the church. Some o the buildings have been knocked down since then but some o the buildings remain.

*Is there any recollections of the school playground or any of the buildings within the school?*

Yes, the drill hall was, it's still in existence, it's flats now. We had a hall at the bottom and that was for PE [physical education] and when we got photographs taken and that sort of thing, parties, school parties, things like that, school dances. An upstairs was the Primary 3 room and Primary 5 room, when I was there. The other building that remains was the infant room, the Primary 1 room, an Ah remember that quite well, a big open fire an big, big tall windows. Some o the other buildings have been demolished but the main part of the school with the offices, the Primary 2, 4, 6 and 7 classrooms, headmaster's office, and the bell tower [remain]. And underneath it was all the, where they stocked the coal and kept things under there. We had two playgrounds: top playground, bottom playground. Bottom playground was a huge area, a great big tarmacadam area an a great big grassy area right up to the walls that adjoin the church. There also was, well it wouldn't be a permanent building, but that was the cafeteria, not the cafeteria, it would be a school canteen, basically a school canteen, Ah think the food was bought in. Ah remember in, Ah think maybe Primary 6 or Primary 7, we had got monkey bars installed at that time, and that was great fun.

*What are monkey bars?*

Like a climbing frame, big climbing frame, we used to climb on it and somersault over them and swing on them. We used to do all sorts of things like that in the playground and, against the big walls, we used to do handstands.

*I always thought monkey bars would be in the gym themselves. That's most unusual.*

No, Ah don't think there were anything to climb in the gym, Ah can't remember that. Ah think we did have things like the wooden horses and beanbags and hula hoops.

*Can you remember your first day at school?*

Yes, Ah remember ma first day at school because ma mother had knitted me a brown hat with a button on it, an it was sort of fluffy wool, it must have been like a mohair, and Ah couldn't get the thing unbuttoned. An Ah remember the teacher, Miss McLellan, lifting me up on top of the desk to undo the button for me. That's ma first memory of primary school. An Ah remember, I went with the Easter intake because ma birthday is in April. And Ah remember, in the summer, Miss McLellan asking me, it was two boys, two Wilson boys, which one was my cousin. Because it was ma cousin David, who used to live at the bungalow at the farm, his birthday was May an he didn't start till then. And the other Wilson was Alistair Wilson, Dr Wilson's son, an his birthday was May as well an Ah remember her asking me: 'Which one's your cousin, Isabelle?'

*Can you tell me the names of all the teachers you had at primary [school]?*

Yes, Ah remember them all. Primary 1, Miss McLellan, a lovely woman, grey haired, sort of very granny-like, jist really, really liked her, can't remember much about the lessons at all. Primary 2, we had Miss Blacklock, and thinking back she must have been quite forward thinking with her teaching, because Ah do remember having things like wee slates to record money and having shops, with, oh I don't know, it would be cornflake packets and biscuit packets and shopping. And fishing with magnetic ... fishing for numbers. An Ah remember a big tank outside the school with water for measuring, it would be capacity, pints and gallons an things in those days. Ah remember all that. Primary 3, we had Mrs Turnbull, she was the headmaster's wife, can't remember too much about the lessons, the only lesson Ah do remember is she brought in a big stuffed heron which we had to draw. Primary 4, we had an elderly lady called Mrs Richardson, an she had taught ma dad and my uncle and their cousins, she knew them all. She had grey hair pinned up and Ah remember her havin a, like a big kinna overall on. An two things Ah remember in her class, this was Primary 4, was all of us knitting, and learning to knit a hot water bottle cover and one day her saying: 'Right, now's the time, some of you are going to learn how to do long division.' Primary 5, we had Mrs Martin and she liked nature study an she would take us up along Greig's Road, picking flowers and lookin for tadpoles. Growing beans, Ah remember growin bean plants in water. We used to have pressed flower competitions, used to collect flowers an name them an put them … in a big scrap book, and there was a prize at the end o term for it. Primary 6, I was in with part of Primary 7, it was the two top sections and we had Mr Turnbull, the headmaster, can't remember that much about the lessons then but we were the two top groups taught together. An in Primary 7 I remember we had Mrs McGhie and Ah thought she was wonderful … a very elegant lady, very kinna 50s-style with sort of blonde curls and spiky high heels and straight skirts sittin on the desk an reading us *The Scarlet Pimpernel*. Ah remember that vividly, it was the end of the day, it was great. An Ah remember doin the Control Exam and we'd had the Intelligence Tests in Primary 6 an earlier in Primary 7. And then we got the results in P7 an Ah remember we got all the results an a lot of people were in tears, the people who had failed, Ah remember that. Because it depended, that depended where we went to at Lockerbie, you know, which classes we were in. Ah remember doin a wee bit of the exam, there was a lot of things like sequences, but the writing, Ah remember we had to write a story an Ah remember writing about a visit to St Andrew's Castle. I also remember, in that class, being given biros for the first time, other than that we must have been using pencils.

*Did you have any favourite subjects?*

Well, Ah always liked history. Ah was always interested in history, and Ah remember some o the games we used to play had a historical slant … it was either Robin Hood and Maid Marion or Mary Queen o Scots and Lord Darnley. An Ah remember Billy Howatson and I were both really, really, keen on history and we were always vying to get the most points. And Ah remember, Ah think it was Mrs McGhie, letting Billy give a lesson an it would only have been about five minutes, probably, on the blackboard, but Ah remember and Ah can't even remember what it was about, it was some sort of history lesson.

*And your least favourite subject?*

Ah can't remember, at primary school Ah think Ah liked everything. Ah remember, Ah mean later, Ah kinna went off maths. ... Ah remember tables at school, you know, you had to stand up and do your times tables and if you couldn't … you were allowed to sit down once you'd done them. And Ah remember what craft things Ah enjoyed, Ah remember makin, with a cane, you know, wettin cane, soakin cane, an trying to wind it round an trying to make trays and baskets and things like that. Ah remember the school broadcasting, we used to get geography lessons on the radio *Look Around Scotland*, something like that. Ah remember things like Dundee for jute, jam an journalism. We had singing with that as well, we had a singing teacher from the secondary [school]. Ah really didn't like singing, Ah used tae sit at the back an Ah didn't like to sing. Ah think that was about the only thing Ah didn't really like. Ah didn't particularly like PE but I did do some netball. Netball was okay, quite enjoyed that, but Ah wasn't very good at PE. An Ah remember sports, egg and spoon race and sack race and things like that, but Ah was never any good at it. Ah cannae run, and Ah couldn't run then either.

*When you were at school, you'd be in the era where you sat exams on a yearly basis and would have positions like First, Second, Third, last in the class?*

Yes, Ah remember all that, Ah certainly remember. Ah've got this vision of P5 class where we had to sit in order of merit in the class, the top person sat at the back, left hand side, and it went right down to the people at the front. Ah never even thought about people at the front really. Ah do remember gettin upset when people got the belt, and sometimes it wasn't for bad behaviour. Sometimes it was just because they couldn't do their sums. We did have prizes at prize giving. I was most often in the top three, there was me and two other boys, Ah could never get first and Ah wasn't the Dux, Ah think Ah was second that year, Ian Beck and Ian Macdonald and me. But it went right down, first, second, third, fourth, fifth, whatever. An there was prizes, Ah remember a girl in the class havin a prize for perfect attendance, there was prizes for the wildflower collections … probably singing prizes and so on, as well. Ah remember classes being big though, big classes.

*How many would you say were in a class?*

Ah think in the P7 class, it would probably be about 40, maybe mair. Ah don't think the population in school has changed much, I think it was about 240 when I was at school.

*So, what kinna playground games would you have?*

Well, Ah liked marbles, but it tended to be the boys that played wi marbles, Ah played wi the boys. Ah loved marbles, great fun. Other things, when Ah played wi the girls it was classes, teachers [we played at], an Ah was the teacher. The other things we did though, we did have hula hoops, an we did do kinna handstands. Ah mentioned that earlier, Ah think. We used to play that and just play throwin the ball and catch the ball against the wall, that sort o thing. A lot o the boys played football, but some o the boys who didn't play football played marbles.

*Were you allowed out of the playground at [lunch] break time?*

Ah can't remember, Ah don't think we did, but maybe the people who lived in the town probably went home for their lunch. Oh, yes we did, Ah remember now. People who had their lunches at home, obviously went home and some of us had packed lunches. We either ate them in the shed, there was a shed that was partly covered, or we went up Greig's Road and sat outside and ate them.

*That would be near the Bruce's Castle* [Lochmaben Castle], *the motte and bailey castle, did you go there at all?*

Yes, Ah remember that, Ah remember one really, really, really cold winter, the golf course, well it wasn't called the golf course at that time, it was covered in snow, and we were mucking about in the snow, just at the motte of Bruce's Castle, sort of trying to make igloos and things like that.

*Was there any school trips?*

Yeah, Ah remember going out to Prestwick, to the airport, a trip to the airport, an Ah think, maybe it was the same time, to Burns Cottage. I don't think we went anywhere else, there was no overnights, not like nowadays, and no foreign trips, nothing like that. Ah think that was it, can't remember anything else, as far as Ayr and Prestwick, that was it. Maybe Edinburgh, maybe we went to the zoo, I'm not sure.

*Thank you. Do you have anything else to add?*

Ah really enjoyed primary school, Ah think it was a good school. Ah made a lot of friends there, a bit confused when Ah went to Lockerbie, because we were in … separated up and there was only a couple of folk [from Lochmaben] in my class. I missed quite a lot of friends that Ah'd had at primary school.

This transition from primary to secondary education in Dumfries was a daunting experience for some people as recalled by Betty Hutt.

## Betty Hutt

*Now, you went to Lochmaben Primary. Can you tell us anything about your education there?*

Ah loved Lochmaben Primary. Mr Fraser was the headmaster and he had a belt an he kept it in the third drawer on the right-hand side of his desk. An Ah felt so important when he asked me to go down to his office and bring up 'James Black'. He was going to belt some boys. So, it was good. But I did get the strap twice maself. …

*Any other memories? Ah believe you were in the same class as Paul Roxburgh?*

Yes, Paul and I went through school and we were in the last group to go to Dumfries Academy and the High School. After that everybody went to Lockerbie for the first three years but we went to Dumfries Academy.

*And what about your time at Dumfries Academy?*

Oh, Ah hated it. Ah loved it when the holidays were on but Ah didnae like it. Ah used tae hide behind the Town Hall an miss the bus.

*And one of the reasons you said was that it was just a bit too big?*

Oh, it was too big, compared to Lochmaben, [where] you knew everybody, an everybody knew you. We had tae get the bus there and the bus back an Ah didnae like it.

*At that time Dumfries Academy would be taking pupils from all over Dumfriesshire?*

They were, even Langholm. And then it was fourth year they came from Langholm.

*The school hall was an excellent hall though, wasn't it?*

It was super. It was.

*They used to play badminton in it as well, did they not?*

I don't know. Aye, they did. They did because I used to try and play but I was never very good at it.

*That was one of the sad things about when the new school was built, that the fine facility like that went from the community.*

Aye, that's right.

Tom Allan was apprehensive when he moved to Lochmaben School from a much smaller school where one teacher taught all the pupils. At Lochmaben, morning assembly was led by the headmaster who would choose someone to recite a passage from the Bible which they had been given to learn. School lunches and the heating system are also recalled.

**Tom Allan**

*And you went to Lochmaben School from there?*

Oh aye, Ah remember it wis a big step, actually, because Ah'd came from a small country school where the teacher taught from the infants right up tae finishing, you know, then coming here tae a school, where they went right on tae they were 14. It wis a big school and it wis, kinnae felt a bit …

*Frightened, aye?*

Aye, a wee bit apprehensive. But, Ah, once I got in tae know people, ye're an incomer, of course, Ah wis nine and Ah wasnae born and bred in Lochmaben.

*And do you remember any of the teachers, or anything like that?*

Oh aye. Mr Freer was a, he had assembly every morning, Ah remember everybody … had tae learn a bit piece of the Bible, you know, a tinkling

cymbal an aw that. An everybody used tae stand petrified in case he pointed
at them ... cause maybe they hadnae learned it. But he was a big, hefty man
with a quiff, you know, an glasses. He was Provost as well in Lochmaben.

*Oh, that's the same man, aye?*

Aye. An there wis Miss Carmichael, of course, which everybody went
through her class an she was a great teacher. Ah liked her. An Mrs
Richardson. An there was a piano chappie taught music, Papa Inglis, he
came fae Lockerbie. Ah liked singing and music, Ah liked music. Then the
dinners were made up the stairs in Lochmaben old school where it's a bit
house now wi a balcony, Mr Thorburn converted it. There was woodwork at
one ... side and the girls did cookery in there. But the dinners were made
there as well by Mrs Fraser and a Mrs Trotter.

*They were local ladies, were they?*

Local ladies, they made the dinners. An a pattie on a Friday wis a great thing.

*A great thing, aye.*

An it was great to be sent for the pies, if you were, kinnae ending your time
at Lochmaben, you went for the pies wi the basket. And Baggie Broon, the
butcher, used tae put [in] what pastry was left, was baked, and you always
got a bit of this pastry (laughs).

*A treat, eh, a treat, aye.*

Aye, Ah used tae enjoy it.

*And did you get milk at that time, in the mornings?*

Yeah, a third of a pint. ... Ah've seen it sitting with the ice coming oot the
top, when the bottle tops were removed.

*Did you have heating in the classrooms then?*

There was heating, there was a boiler room underneath an, as Ah say, it wis
coke, fired by coke, an in the classroom above the stokehole the fumes used
to come through the fire when ye opened the, down the bottom, when ye
opened up, out it come, an the fumes come up through the floorboards.

*It wouldnae be allowed these days* (laughter).

No, Health and Safety would be up in arms. But aye, Ah enjoyed ma
schoolin at Lochmaben, Ah did, immensely.

*And you left there when you were what?*

Aye well, Ah would be comin eleven plus, you know, an Ah went tae
Lockerbie.

*And then you went to Lockerbie.*

Which was, but again, ye know, you're startin tae move fae class to class
then.

*And you'd meet a lot of different people there?*

Oh aye. Ah've still got friends yet that Ah made when Ah was there.

The Three Ladies spoke about having to show respect to teachers, both in school and out. They also recalled some of their teachers and discipline being administered with the tawse, as well as the school garden and school sports.

**Three Ladies**

*We wondered about school days. Anything in particular, any teachers or lessons, games, sports, punishments at schools, anything that comes to mind?* (Laughter)

Ah once got the belt. Ah got another belting at home for getting the belt (laughs).

Ah don't know, Ah think we sort of respected oor teachers. We were sort of frightened to dae any wrong.

Oh, aye an if ye met them on the street ye were frightened, the boys had to salute and the girls had to curtsey. The only one Ah can remember is Miss Carmichael from the farm up there.

On a bicycle.

…

She used tae cycle down to the school. Aye, but was it: 'Edinburgh, Leith, Portobello, Musselburgh and don't forget Dalkeith.' That was, she used tae say that.

*Was that primary school?*

Uh huh.

*About the school sports, you mentioned that, earlier? Anything in particular?*

We had school sports every year.

*And where were they held?*

The school field.

*Where they still are.*

School field. Auld school back then. It was in a field next to the church, was it not?

Oh, Ah cannae remember that.

It was the auld school then.

Ah, but we always came up tae the school field where they had the school gardens.

That's right.

The boys had the school gardens there.

Yes.

Where Mr Penny lives, that was the schoolhouse an they had a school garden, where the boys used tae come up and do their gardening.

On a Friday

On a Friday afternoon.

And beyond that was the field.

That's right.

A playing field and a garden.

*And what was in the garden, can you remember that?*
> The boys used to have vegetables an pull them up.
> They used to have lovely flowers and that.
> Did Mr Martin take them [to the garden]?
> Ah can't remember.
> Ah think it was Mr Martin that took them to the garden on a Friday.
> Remember Mr Martin?
> Aye, Ah can remember Martin.
> Aye, because Bobby, ma brother, he got prizes for his. They had to have wee plots.
> How neat his was, and things like that, this school garden.
> Aye, he stayed where Ian Munro stays now, Mr Martin.
> Aye, the auld Bank House?
> Aye.
> He took us for science.
> Wis it science? Aye, he was a science teacher. What was Mrs Martin, she was a teacher as well?
> Ah cannae remember.
> Oh, Ah do remember her.
> Ah don't know.
> I don't know if she worked at Lochmaben School.

*And would that be round about, what you were saying earlier about 1940, early 40s, when the gardening was done?*
> At the school?
> Would it no be a wee bit later than that?
> Because Bobby's older than me. My brother would be about what? Bobby was about four years older than me. He was already at school.

Another interviewee who clearly remembered her first day at school and who later enjoyed her transition to secondary education was Wilma Twidale.

### Wilma Twidale

Ah went to school in Lochmaben, Ah can remember ma first day at school very clearly. Ma Aunt took me, she didn't take me till aboot ten o'clock, Ah don't know why, took me at ten o'clock, an Ah [was] faced with this class-room full of children, most of whom Ah think Ah knew vaguely. An the teacher said: 'Where would you like to sit?' An Ah could see Moira McGhie, who lived near us an was a friend, so Ah said: 'Ah would like tae sit beside Moira.' An the girl that was beside her was shifted, an Ah'm sure that didnae make a very good feeling. However, it was okay. So, Ah came up through Lochmaben school and then, when it was time to change, Ah went to Dumfries. For some reason Ah chose to go to the High School, Ah think it was ma mother really who suggested it, although Ah probably should have gone tae the Academy. But, anyway, Ah went to the High School an Ah enjoyed it there, it was good.

*And how did you get from Lochmaben to the High School?*

Bus, service bus every day. You got a season ticket, you got [it] supplied from the Education Authority. An Ah made a lot o friends at school, Ah suppose. And then when Ah finished at the school, Ah went on to a, well it was called a, what was it called? A commercial school, a business school, really. Which was in Irish Street, it was the De Vere School. An Ah went there, an learnt the skills an when Ah finished, after Ah'd started tae work, Ah still went several evenings a week to teach, because they asked me to, so Ah did that for a wee while.

Paul Roxburgh recalled the physical layout of the school, teachers, discipline and some of the lessons he was taught. He also explained why his schooling ended abruptly when he was required to work in the family business.

## Paul Roxburgh

*So, what age would you be when you started school?*

Five years old.

*And what memories do you have of being there?*

I was at Lochmaben School from 1939 to 1945, Ah found it very enjoyable, we had tae walk back and forward every day, of course, no matter what the weather was like. An Ah even walked home for lunch and back, which didnae leave very much time. It was a rushed job. There were many play-ground fights at Lochmaben School.

*Ah remember them too!*

Aye, at least one good one every week! There were cold outside toilets an they were often frozen up in the winter, but the classrooms were well heated. Some o them had coal fires in them, of course. There were aw the separate buildings at Lochmaben School, you know, what we used to caw the drill hall, where ye had music lessons and physical exercise and there were workshops upstairs for the joinery classes and then you had the separate Infant School.

*So, you talk about the joinery classes, these would be for the children that stayed on at Lochmaben after eleven …*

Aye, yes, aye.

*… to leave school at 14. I remember ma wife taking PE in the drill hall.*

Aye.

*It was a fine hall.*

Oh, it was a good hall.

*It was a shame that we've lost that, Ah think, in the community.*

97

Aye, we used to play badminton in there as well.

*Have you any memorable teachers, or that?*

Yes, well, a memorable teacher was a Mr McIntyre, the art teacher, and once again, Ah'm back tae art an Ah really liked him. We used to have visiting music teachers and visiting PE teachers. The PE teacher was a Sergeant Kirkwood, he still kept his Army title, he was a typical ex-Army PTI [Physical Training Instructor]. [REDACTED] visited from Lockerbie, Ah think he taught music at Lockerbie and Lochmaben, but Ah didnae get on particularly well wi him, because Ah used to deliberately sing off-key (laughs). Aye, Ah remember him giving me a right good thrashing and it must hae been in the morning because Ah managed to cry aw the way home to let ma dad see how he had upset me. But Ah got no sympathy at all, he said: 'Oh, you must have been askin for it.'

*You mentioned the word thrashing. Now, a lot of younger people won't understand what you mean by that.*

Well, Ah wouldnae hold ma hand out for the belt an, of course, we had short troosers on, so he took me intae the changing room beside the drill hall, an gave me a good thrashing roond ma legs, ma bare legs, with his belt, which would hae been at least a criminal offence nowadays.

*They talk about these being the good old days.*

Aye, oh aye.

*Ah think we've made progress on that.*

Aye. There was one o the teachers, another teacher Ah remember well, a Miss Carmichael, fae Lochbank Farm, she cycled back and forward, Ah remember her old-fashioned bike. She used tae bring apples for her favourite pupils. An, David Hewitson was on about this tae me, an she had brought Davie an apple one day, he was one o her pets. Later on she caught him talking and it's: 'Hewitson, bring that apple back.'

'Ah'm sorry Miss Carmichael Ah've eaten it!' (laughter).

*Now you mention Miss Carmichael, she was related to Isabelle Gow, Ah think?*

Aye, that's right.

*An you mention Lochbank Farm which is adjoining to Esbie isn't it?*

Aye, it is, aye. Ah remember her wi her cane keeping time to what she was saying on the blackboard. She'd: 'Edinburgh, Leith, Portobello, Mussel-burgh and Dalkeith.'

*Well, my subject was geography and that was all jingles.*

Aye, uh huh.

*It was terrible because you had all these coastal towns and then two or three inland.*

Aye, these were the teachers that Ah remember best.

*What about equipment, you didn't have any computers.*

Oh no, no.

*What did you use?*

Well, in the early days we used to use the slate boards [in the] infant class; paper was very, very scarce. As Ah said, Ah could never get anything to draw on, an paper was very, very scarce at school, so we were limited in what paper ye got.

*So, did you draw with the slate?*

No really, no, you might have drawn an apple, 'A for apple, you know, something like that but not to any great extent, no.

*Were there any characters amongst your school group?*

No, no really, Ah had ma own wee bunch o friends, but for wild boys, no I wouldnae say sae Tom.

... In 1945, I sat my Control Examination, otherwise known as the eleven plus. The results o this determined which school you went tae. Perhaps you stayed at Lochmaben, where the trend was to the technical side, leaving at 14 to start work on an Apprenticeship or some other job, or you went onto Lockerbie school, until ye were 14, or ye went to Dumfries Academy. The people who went to Lockerbie school, if they wanted to continue on because ... you were only taught at Lockerbie until you were 14, they then joined you at Dumfries. So, a lot o yer old friends arrived aged 14 at Dumfries Academy and continued there.

*And that arrangement lasted, Ah think Lockerbie Academy only became a sixth-year school in 1966. So, you arrived at Dumfries Academy, what are your recollections about being at Dumfries Academy?*

Ah didnae like it, no, Ah wisnae particularly well at the time, an Ah remember Ah hadnae been at Dumfries Academy very long an Ah had tae get ma tonsils out, they reckoned that the tonsils were causing part o ma troubles. Ah think it was a convenient reason or excuse, at that time. If ye werenae well, oh, it would be your tonsils. Anyway, Ah went intae Dumfries Infirmary and a Mr Devery took ma tonsils out. Now Davie Shankland tells me that they pulled your tonsils out, they virtually tore them out, and he could describe the instrument that they used to pull your tonsils out, so it was no wonder that they were pretty sore.

*Ah can even remember in my youth it was a pretty common occurrence for tonsils to be extracted.*

Aye, Ah remember that we went to Dumfries Infirmary, of course, and there would be about ten of us. And we went into this wee waiting room beside the theatre, an the ten of us were in there an taken, one by one, through the door into the theatre to get our tonsils oot, it was really quite primitive.

*So, is that what we call Nithbank now, the Dumfries Infirmary.*

Aye.

*There was one highlight, though, of your time at Dumfries Academy, Ah think?*

Aye, there was, there was Tom.

*You excelled at something.*

Aye, Ah excelled at art, actually, Ah won the Junior Gordon Art Prize an Ah got on extremely well with Mr Mackay, ma art teacher, Ah even managed to fiddle my classes an avoid woodwork an ironwork to get extra art classes, until they found out where I was.

*Your time at Dumfries Academy was determined by an external factor, Ah think, wasn't it?*

It was, aye, it was Tom, when Ah was 16 the manager of the family business, the shop, walked out and ma mother asked me if Ah could go in the next day, temporarily, until somebody else was found. But nobody else was ever found so Ah was kept there for quite some time. Ah didnae particularly like the job, but Ah suppose it was necessary.

Paul had memories of severe winters when he was a pupil at the Academy.

Ah remember, too, walkin to school in a tremendous snowstorm, roond aboot, in the 1940s, Ah think it must have been aboot, must have been nearly the end of the War and the snow being almost impassable.
… I wis going tae remark about going into Dumfries Academy in a tremen-dous snowstorm, and they had the soldiers from Halleaths Camp at Torthorwald wi their lorries cutting the snow up in huge blocks and takin it away in their lorries to try to clear the roads.

*That wouldn't be in 1947 would it?*

Aye.

*That was, Ah remember that was a terrific snowstorm.*

It was, aye. An the Lochar Moss used tae flood, an several times we couldnae get through the Lochar Moss. It's aw drained now of course an it disnae flood but it was quite a common occurrence.

*So, did you just travel on the service bus?*

Aye.

Fights in the playground and the disciplinary consequences of them are remem-bered by Roy Thorburn. Roy was a proficient football player who, when he was a pupil at Lockerbie Academy, played for the school team as well as local juvenile teams.

## Roy Thorburn

*You started at Lochmaben Primary in 1940. What are your memories of Lochmaben Primary?*

One that sticks out in my memory is the schoolmaster who was very, very strict, a disciplinary man, well respected, an Ah had a great admiration for him. He also taught ma father. By the time he was teaching me he was getting on in years but there's a few stories which would take a long time tae tell.

*His name was Mr Fraser. Were there any other people you recollect? Or did you manage to avoid any fights in the playground?*

No, unfortunately.

*That was quite a regular occurrence, wasn't it?*

I used to help out with these, unfortunately, but Ah don't know whether it was unfortunate or not. But Ah was involved wi one or two of them and they all used to gather roundabout ye in a circle and you'd no way of getting out. If you weren't winning, you had to face up to the consequences. I was pretty good at it though. Mr Fraser used to watch the ongoing fights from the school window an immediately it was finished he would take you both in and give you six or twelve of the belt, depends, but you couldn't win.

*The current youngsters won't understand what the belt was.*

No, the belt was obviously leather and it was probably about two feet in length an he used to carry it in his hip pocket all the time, just for convenience. An he didn't hesitate to take it out and he'd belt ye in front of other pupils, it didn't matter where you were. If he thought you deserved it, you got it.

*They were known as Lochgellys because that's where they were produced.*

He would make you put your hand out and he would put your other hand underneath it so that ye got a bit of support but obviously that was going to make it worse. But ye got six, Ah did anyway, you got six on each hand, he thought it would learn ye not to get it again, but it happened once or twice.

*It was a regular occurrence in my day as well.*

Well, aye, an Ah really admired the man, he was a great man. It's a pity he's not around nowadays.

*Aged twelve you moved to Lockerbie Academy. Have you any memories of Lockerbie Academy?*

No really, Ah went to Lockerbie when Ah was twelve till Ah was 15.

*You excelled at something at Lockerbie Academy.*

Aye, Ah played in the football team. Ah got intae the football team in the second year. We won the South of Scotland championships on ma third year at Lockerbie, and funnily enough there was one or two Lochmaben boys, there were four Lochmaben boys in it, Bobby Armstrong, Willie Edwards, maself an Ah can't remember the other boy's name now. Unfortunately, they're all dead now, there's not one of them left. No, Ah enjoyed ma years at Lockerbie, Ah progressed physically and mentally an Ah went from there to Dumfries when Ah was 15.

*An you stayed about 18 months at Dumfries Academy and, again, football played a big part on your life there.*

Yes, aye, Ah went to Dumfries Academy an Ah got intae the football team there, the first eleven, which was the under 18s and Ah done quite well. Ah recollect, as Ah said, Ah played three games in the one day. Ah played for

Greystone Rovers in the morning, at ten o'clock, it was a juvenile side at the
time, a Dumfries team. Then Ah played for, no, Ah played for the Academy
at ten o'clock in the morning, an in the afternoon, at three o'clock, Ah
played for Greystone Rovers. And then, in the evening, Ah played for
Kinnel Rovers, at Thornhill, in the final of the Thornhill Cup, that night,
and Ah still felt fit.

*Ah don't think there'll be many people listening will have played three games of*
*football in the one day.*

I don't think so, no, and yet they complain nowadays about playing two
games in a week. And they are professionals.

*No comment.*

No comment (laughter).

*An Ah believe you had some future internationalists in your Academy team, as well.*

We had, in Dumfries Academy, Billy Little, he was an internationalist. Ah
don't know, he didn't get many caps, but he was, an he played for Aberdeen.
The other lads, Ah don't recollect their names at all, but there were some
good players at the team at that time.

*Aye, Dumfries Academy had a pretty good reputation as a footballing school.*


A visit by an expert on birds and animals was recalled by Ian Tweedie.


## Ian Tweedie

*Ah take it you went to school in Lochmaben?*

Yes, correct.

*And do you have any memories of school there?*

Oh yes, aye.

*What kind of … did you like the teachers, or what do you remember?*

The teachers, aw, the teachers, aye, Ah can't remember them now. …

But there was quite, it was different altogether from today. Ah mean Ah can
remember some of the boys coming jist wi a jersey on, an the thing was they
didn't have anything to blow their noses [on], they went (laughs).

*Wiped it on their sleeves, aye, aye. Aye they were different days then, weren't they?*

Aye, they were, aye.

*Was that in the old primary school building, round by the golf course?*

Aye round there, aye. The one as you go up off from the church, up that
road there, this one here was the first year.

*Okay. So, you started in that building eh, that's where you started?*

Yes, that's where Ah started, an Ah just went on from there.

*An apart from lessons in the classroom, Ah mean, did you do any, was there PE or*
*what other things did you do at school?*

Oh, aye there was. We did gym and stuff like that, an Ah remember the, oh
what's his name? Ah remember the day that David Scott came, aye, came to

talk about birds and animals an whatever aye.

*Oh, that must have been a big day for you at the school.*

Oh, aye, the first month.

*And then you stayed there until Primary 7, did you, at Lochmaben?*

Aye.

*And what happened when you were ready to go to the big school? What did you do then? Did you go to Lockerbie or—?*

Lockerbie Academy, aye, that's right. An we used to get … the bus used to take them, Matt Green's bus used tae take us.

Some teachers and gender differences in the lessons taught and the games played when they attended school were remembered by James McWhirter and Isabel Wells.

## Isabel Wells and James McWhirter

*Can you tell me a bit more about the school in the '50s? Can you remember any particular teachers you were fond of or—*

JMcW: Fond of (laughter). Well, they were awright.

IW: Ah wouldnae say fond of, they were awright.

JMcW: Miss McLellan, she was the Primary 1, she kept ye in line and then, when Ah was there, it was Miss Shankland.

IW: That's the yin Ah can never mind.

JMcW: And then you moved up intae the hall, the gym was on that level, an in the hall, an the classroom, it was Miss Blacklock?

IW: Yes.

JMcW: Then if ye come down there Primary 4 would be Mrs Richardson.

*Ah remember her.*

JMcW: And then ye moved through, it wis Doris Clark and then it was Doull his self.

*Headmaster was Doull at that time?*

IW: Aye, it wis.

*An what subjects did ye like, Ah mean did ye enjoy school or was it just something you had to do?*

IW: No, Ah did.

*You enjoyed it?*

IW: Ah enjoyed school, an ye jist got a variety of things really, didn't ye? You got writing, arithmetic, geography, whatever, just ye got loads o things.

JMcW: Ah think Ah wis jist a typical boy, a lot o nonsense in ma head.

*Oh dear, did you get the strap?*

JMcW: Quite a few times (laughter).

IW: Ah think the girls would maybe get sewing or knitting or somethin an the boys maybe went for football, didn't they?

JMcW: Aye, we played football, we won the thingummy cup. Ah was playing. What cup was it again? The Houliston cup or, no the Houliston, they made up a cup for all the primary schools round about.

…

JMcW: What dae ye call it? Hergarth or something.

*Oh, Hecklegirth, Hecklegirth.*

JMcW: Hecklegirth, aye, Beattock an aw them places. They run a competition an the year Ah played they had the final at Beattock and we won it 2–1.

*Oh good.*

JMcW: Ah think Ah've still got the photograph.

*Oh, well that would be interesting to see, so who coached you?*

JMcW: Well, Doull always came up himself, Mr Doull.

*Oh, he did.*

JMcW: But Sam Jardine had a lot tae dae with it.

IW: Aye, Sam.

JMcW: You'd always gaun doon an ye would say to Sam: 'Say tae Doull that we need some practice.' (Laughter.)

*To get off lessons?*

IW: An aw the time the lassies were shoved in gettin knitting or sewin or somethin o the kind.

*Did ye not dae netball?*

IW: No.

*That must have come in a wee bit later then.*

IW: It must have, we didnae really, other than jist havin yer ordinary gym an then ye got yer sports on sports day, kinna thing, ye didnae, there was nothin really.

*So, when you were out in the playground, cos Ah remember things like marbles and things.*

JMcW: Yeah, we used tae play marbles. But the square, the tarmac square, that's where all the boys went tae play football.

*Yes, that's right, football, that's right.*

JMcW: Ye had an arch there an that's where the boys went tae play football.

*Well, that didnae change, cos Ah remember that.*

IW: Aye, but then ye'd seasons for your chestnuts.

*And conkers, aye.*

JMcW: Conkers, Ah used tae play a lot o conkers.

IW: Lassies used to play skippin.

*Can you remember any skipping games, the names o them?*

IW: Oh, no.

JMcW: Ah cannae, but—

IW: Sometimes, when you were skippin, it was jist a case o ye were running through [the rope], an the next yin gaun through.

*Aye, that's right.*

JMcW: But then there was yin where ye stood in the middle [of a circle] yourself an everybody else was shouting …

IW: Aye, that's right.

JMcW: … an then ye came oot, an the next yin came in.

IW: Aye, that's right.

*Ah remember ye yaist tae dae skipping an ye would go in an it was like boys' names and things an ye were in love with so and so.*

IW: Aye, that's right.

…

JMcW: We used tae play kiss catch.

*Yes, Ah remember that.*

IW: We used to play the … when you kicked the tin can.

JMcW: Oh aye, the tin can aye.

IW: Used to dae that at Castle Street, didn't oo?

JMcW: Aye, [jaking?], caw's it k-i-n-g-king.

*An what, did ye ever, did ye leave the playground at all at break time or lunchtime.*

JMcW: No.

IW: Lunchtimes, well, Ah went home.

JMcW: Lunchtime, aye, lunchtime, ye could go home if ye wanted but in the small breaks nothing happened like that.

IW: No, no, you just stayed in the playground.

JMcW: Ye had tae be goin home, ken, when you were in the lower classes, like, if ye mother wasnae there to meet ye, tae take ye home, ye didnae get home.

IW: Aye, that's right.

*So, they were still quite strict about that. So, what did ye do when you were at school and you didn't go home, where was the food served then or did you—?*

IW: In the dinner hut.

JMcW: Dinner hut.

*They did have the dinner hut then.*

JMcW: Oh, aye.

IW: Oh, aye.

JMcW: It wis jist a big, long kind of ammunition hut.

IW: Aye, it wis like a munitions hut.

*Well, Ah remember that, so when was that set up?*

JMcW: Well, it was there when Ah was there.

IW: It was there when Ah was there.

*Oh, Ah remember it, there was a long, long hut, yes, like a Nissen hut sort of thing.*

IW: Concrete looking.

JMcW: And ye got your wee pint of milk, you know, yer wee bottle of milk.

The crates o milk.

JMcW: That was at playtime, Ah think.

IW: Playtime, aye.

Bill Gibson recalled walking three miles to school from Thornithwaite Farm with his siblings and the children from the farm cottage. For breakfast he would have porridge with salt and the cream that his mother had skimmed off the milk. At school the pupils were given a third of a pint of milk mid-morning and soup was served at lunchtime upstairs in the drill hall. Bill particularly enjoyed working in the school garden, near where the community centre now is. This was also the location of the football pitch and where the school sports were held.

Born in the 1970s, Allison Laurie recalled the move from the school buildings that the previous interviewees attended to the current one. She also remembered the introduction of the first computer at the school. The differences between the schooling that she experienced and which her children were experiencing were also observed by her.

## Allison Laurie

*So, did you got to school in Lochmaben?*

Ah did, yes, Ah went to the old Lochmaben Primary School for two years and then Ah went to the new one when that was built. That was in Primary 2, we moved there.

*How did you find the change, did you like the new school?*

Ah did like it, yea, from what Ah can remember. Yea, it was modern, it was new, it was warmer. Ah remember the old school, having to go from building to building for PE and from the classroom to the dinner hall and ye'd to go outside whereas in the new school everything was in the one building, so Ah think that was the biggest change.

*When Ah was at the school we had outside toilets, was it still outside toilets in your day?*

Yes, yes, Ah do remember the outside toilets, yes, Ah just remember them being really cold.

*Frozen over.*

Yea, and the tracing paper toilet roll (laughter).

*Exactly, so they hadn't changed that in 20 years.*

No (laughter).

*So, it would be quite nice in the new school when you had inside toilets.*

That's right and underfloor heating in the gym hall. ...

That was quite modern for the time and, yea, that's what Ah remember the most about it.

*And how did the move take place, I mean how did—?*

Well, Ah believe, in fact it was, I'm sure it was Miss Aldridge, the Deputy Head, who retired a few years ago, and she said that now if a school is moving then they would have a week off, or something, to move everything.

But she said at that point, what they done is, they done it in a weekend and they asked for parents to help move everything. So, I didn't know about any of that because I was only six at the time, or seven, but yes, it must have been quite an upheaval for the parents and the teachers.

*What about the playground? Was that better do you think, in the new school?*

Probably, yea, Ah've got good memories of the playground. It was different then from what it is now because Ah think a bit was added on, even from when Ah started at the primary school. So, yea, Ah just remember playing in a whole load of trees because there was, [in] part of the playground there was a few trees and [UNCLEAR], yea, it was a good size of playground. Ah remember in Primary 1, at the old school, chasing after somebody and falling over and skiffing ma knee and Ah've still got the scar there now and so it seems like in the new playground there was less tarmac and maybe a wee bit more grass than at the old school.

*I remember from the old school it tended to be, we talked about the top playground and the bottom playground. The bottom playground was mainly for boys' football. Would that be the same?*

Ah can't remember that, no, Ah remember the monkey bars an Ah remember a wee sand area.

*The monkey bars had been there a long time then because I remember when they came in, so that would be in the sixties* (laughter). *And the old dining hall, can you remember much about that?*

Yea, just, remember having to pray before [lessons], which Ah don't remember doing at the new school, and prayers before we had our lunch. And just school dinners, Ah remember the dinners being warm, Ah can't really remember what we ate and Ah don't even remember if Ah particularly liked it or not. But yes, certainly remember the hustle and bustle of the busy dinner hall and yes, it seemed massive at the time.

*And do you think [there were] any more facilities in the new school? What sort of computers, would you have computers then?*

Ah remember, Ah think it was when we were in about Primary 6, that we got one computer for the whole school and it was put in the hall, in the main hall, and each class went to have a wee go on the computer. And it was very basic, the program was very basic, whereas now they've got computers in the nursery and they've got a computer suite and computers in every classroom, whereas back then it was one for the whole school and that was a big, exciting thing to happen.

*Do you think there was other changes, Ah mean in subjects, and even in your own kids' time? What changes have there been?*

Goodness, Ah think there—?

*Certainly, when I was at school it was much more, you had a history lesson, a geography lesson and we had craft, and knitting. Knitting was popular when Ah was at school. What about [that], was that still popular?*

Ah think there's probably less kinna gender separation now than there was. I remember in P7, the girls done sewing and the boys went to football and Ah remember being quite angry about that and thinking we didn't have a choice and maybe I would like to have done football, whereas now I think it's definitely better that way. So, Ah suppose that's a big change.

... Joe's, he's in P2, and he's started French, which Ah think's fantastic, which we never done any languages until S1 at the Academy.

*Yes, that was the same with me.*

And Molly has been doing French as well, from about P5, Ah think, so yea.

*So, that's new.*

They're introducing modern languages earlier.

*What about use of, would you use the television? I mean we had television programmes and radio programs we used to listen to, schools' programmes. Was that something you remember?*

Yes, yep, Ah remember getting the telly wheeled in and watching TV for educational programmes. Yea, Ah remember that.

*Now, of course, it'll be on the computer.*

Ah would imagine so, yea, Ah don't think there's much radio now (laughter).

*What about playground games?*

Yea, Ah remember we used to just, aye, just the usual, chasing each other and skipping, hopscotch, Ah don't think that's changed much now, Ah think my children play those things as well.

*They still do that?*

Yea, yea, I suppose skipping when they were younger, Molly used to.

*We used to play marbles.*

Marbles, no.

*That's changed then, quite a bit, because that was a big thing when Ah was at the school. And doing things like handstands against the wall and things like that we used to do.*

Yes, I think there's still a bit of gymnastics in the playground, [there] was when Ah was there as well, yea.

*Good. And what about the teachers, do you think they're maybe more sociable with their kids now?*

Not sure, Ah think there's still a kinna respect for teachers, Ah would say, certainly at primary school level. Maybe they're less strict than they were, certainly there was no corporal punishment when I was at school but ma partner, he can, he's 50, he can remember getting the belt, etc.

*Yes.*

But Ah think it's better now because it seems to be more of a reward rather than, you know, more carrot and stick now than there used to be, yes.

Andre McCrae found the Scots language a challenge when he started at Loch-maben Primary after moving to the town from Manchester, when he was seven years old.

## Andre McCrae

*What did you feel about going into school? I mean, how different was that?*

I couldn't really understand anybody but, you know, you sort of get used to it. So, I picked it up quite quickly because I was around everybody that was speaking just Scottish.

*Did you feel quite welcome?*

I did, actually, everybody was fine with me, with the way I spoke as well. And they'd help me out more with my speaking, you know, they'd encourage me to say other things that I wouldn't usually say, like more Scottish things.

*Uh huh, can you give me an example?*

There's quite a few. For instance, there was 'weesht', and the first time that was said to me, my dad had actually said it to me and I didn't understand what he was saying. I said to him: 'What do you mean when you said that?' and he said: 'It means, you know, to shoosht, be quiet.'

*Be quiet, uh huh.*

It was good and another one's 'aye' as well and when I said 'yes' they understood but when I was asking them a question and they'd say 'aye' in response, I wouldn't know what they were saying.

*You didn't understand that.*

So, you know, '*What's that?*' and then, eventually, one day, one of my friends said, 'Oh, it means yes'.

*So, you'd learn it. Did you think it was just like another language?*

Ah did actually, yea, because there's so much to it that's so different. But I found it quite easy to pick up as I went along, you know.

*Your dad's Scottish, isn't he?*

Yes, he is.

*So, would he use a lot of Scots at home?*

Yea, he did and when we were in Manchester he'd still, his accent hadn't changed, but he'd been there for ten years. But, you know, he just sort of stayed with the same accent so it was a bit hard to understand him but he sort of got used to that with me so he would speak more non-Scots to me.

*He would adapt to you?*

Yea. And then when we come up here, he would start speaking more Scots to me so that I got used to it easier. So, it was around the house as well as outside.

*Good. And what about your teachers, how different were they from the teachers you had in England? Any different?*

Well, speaking-wise, the teachers that I got, they weren't really too much different because some of the ones in primary school, when we were here, they didn't really speak Scots or anything, they try and speak more formal with you. So, they wouldn't say things like 'Aye' and 'Weesht'.

*But what about in the playground, do you think the language in the playground was quite different from the language in the class?*

Very different, yes, yes. And another word was 'ken'.

*Oh yes, 'ken'.*

You know, the meaning, know, ye know. And one of the things we loved to say was, to someone that wasn't Scottish, was 'Dae ye ken Ken, Ken that kens another Ken'.

*Ah, that's a good one, yes.*

It was good and we used to say that to people. Yea, it was good fun, we used to like, say [that] a lot.

*So, what else was different from Manchester schools?*

It was a lot calmer here because in Manchester, being in the city, I'd be in fights a lot and it was mainly with my best friend as well.

*I see.*

I've got scars in my ear, there's one going across there and one across there from where he dug his nails into to me and gouged out my ears.

*Oh! Are you sure he was your friend (laughs)?*

Yea. I mean we got on really well, you know, we just liked to fight a lot.

*I see, play fighting.*

But in, yea, but it turned rough, pretty quick. But then we just, you know, later on in the day, we'd end up saying 'that was a good fight' or something.

…

*Did you find a big change when you went from Lochmaben Primary to Lockerbie Academy?*

Not really, it was just the amount of people and the amount of things you got to do. Because when you get to the Academy, you can then, you know, there's the likes of chemistry and stuff you get to do. And their facilities are quite well kept, especially with it being a new school as well. So, it was really just the amount of people that was the difference.

*And meeting other people from other schools.*

And that was pretty easy because your registration classes that you were put in was from, wasn't just from your school, it was from all the other schools mixed in as well, and everybody was friendly. Obviously, you get the one or two idiots that, you know, [but] it wasn't really much of a difference to the primary.

*And you enjoyed it.*

Yea, Ah do.

*And you still enjoy it.*

Yea, Ah still enjoy it now, yea.

Another young interviewee, Beth Corrie recalled her time at Lochmaben Primary and moving on to secondary education at Lockerbie.

**Beth Corrie**

*Beth, can you tell me a little bit about yourself, please?*

Well, I've lived in Lochmaben for 17 years now, down at Marjoriebanks, so I've been to Lochmaben Primary and then moved to Lockerbie Academy, throughout my school years.

*And have you lived anywhere else?*

No, just always in Lochmaben.

*So, can you tell me a wee bit about your primary days?*

Oh, my primary days, I loved my primary days and that's what really made me want to become a primary teacher.

*Right.*

It was—

*Yea, if you want, tell me about it. What subjects did you like?*

Oh, I loved drama, it was Miss Aldridge who was my teacher at the time, and I just recently saw her, yesterday, as well, so it was nice to catch up.

*She's still acting.*

She is.

*Yes.*

Uh huh, so she really made me want to become, do drama in my Academy years.

*Excellent. Anything else that you enjoyed? What about sports and things, did you have?*

We had lacrosse.

*That's unusual isn't it?*

It is, definitely, for Scotland, but we were part of a big team and we went to this place outside London to do a competition. ... and it was really good, it was a really good opportunity for Lochmaben, because it's such a small place, but it was, like a really big competition.

*You had great opportunities, then?*

Definitely.

*Good, and how many people play lacrosse, is it popular?*

Yea, there was kind of a group where you just got to play for fun and then there was a more serious competition group. And a lot of people get involved in it, it's still happening just now. And when I went to do work experience, I did like a, what is it, I kind of taught them it, when I was there. So, I did an after-school club, so that was nice, just going back and doing it again.

*Oh, that's good. What other sports were at Lochmaben?*

I liked gymnastics, there was an after-school gymnastics club, and there was trampolining. There was, what else was there? Football and stuff like that.

They've brought in rugby as well, now, but not when I was there....
*We're looking at how people speak and their language and the use of Scots. Do you think that's, it's still here in Lochmaben, the use of Scots?*

I think so, I think, I went to Norway the other week and I was, like, talking away and she was like, 'I have no idea what you said'.

*And of course, their second language is English.*

I know, but they learn American English, as well, so that's a wee bit different. But yea, we still, a lot of the teachers at the primary still use Scots language and they'll encourage it.

*That's good.*

And you do a big project in Primary 6, about Scots language, so they're definitely trying to encourage it among children.

*That's great. What about the changes from going from a small primary school to a big secondary school?*

That is a big jump. You're going from a safe environment with 30 people you know, or something, and then you're going into a class of 100, it's a big jump. But, as long as you have the people around you that you grew up with, it's nice to kind of move up together and see everyone grow.

*Yes, there's still strong links with Lochmaben.*

Yes, I'm still really good friends with all the people in my primary. I still meet up and all that, so it's nice.

In the next selection of interview extracts we learn how older interviewees amused themselves when out of school. The youth club, Girl Guides and Boy Scouts offered organised, supervised activities. Other organised activities included dance classes and the church choir. The early days of the boy scouts, in the town, are recalled. Skipping, beds, and group games were played out in the street, mostly by girls, while boys were keen on bird nesting, guddling for fish and trapping rabbits. There are recollections here too of the scrapes that some of them got into while collecting rosehips, along the railway line.

### Betty Hutt

We had a youth club and it was held in the school hall and there was the headmaster, Mr Doull and his wife, who ran it, and it was on the Wednesday night. We also had the keep fit and it was a Sergeant Kirkwood who taught PE at Lockerbie Academy. He used to come over. I think that would maybe be a Monday night. And on Friday night we had the choir practice and that was held in the church hall.

*You also mentioned Jackie Proudfoot.*

Yes, he used to cycle from Hunterhouse and every week we would hide his bike and he had to find it. But we didn't hide it too far away. It was part of the fun. He was a bit older than us.

## Three Ladies

*How would you spend your time in the evenings before television became such a big part of life? What sort of pastimes do you remember as a child?*

We listened to the wireless, *The McFlannels*. That sticks oot in my mind, *The McFlannels*, on a Saturday night.

Aye, the wireless.

And you were saying about just playing out in the street?

Aye, we made oor own entertainment.

Aye, we jist made oor own entertainment.

We went for walks, we walked a lot an went through the woods gatherin wood and that, for the fire.

Aye.

We used to walk for miles.

Aye.

*And were there any games that you played, like organised?*

There were a hall.

We had hoops.

Templand Hall.

*Ye had hoops?*

Aye.

We used tae have carpet bowling for the men an that.

Well, we would go down and watch them playin it an things like that. I can't remember ever goin anywhere.

*So, you had hoops and skipping ropes?*

Skipping ropes, rubber tyres, rubber tyres, uh huh. Old tyres, the boys gave us.

Beds. Aye, just flat stones, and ye'd put them on a number, throw a bet.

*Was that just the girls or did the boys play that as well?*

No, they'd be away on their own, Ah think. Ah think the boys would be away on their own.

Oh aye, we didnae bother aboot boys then. Maybe in oor mind (laughter).

## Roy Thorburn

I spent most of my time, although we were in Marjoriebanks, spent most of ma time at Kinnel Bridge with my grandparents, particularly weekends. I learned in these days to guddle fish, trap rabbits, I was more or less a loner, you could say.

*Can I just stop you there, Roy? Maybe you should explain the word guddling to the listeners because a lot of them will not know what that means. If you could you explain guddling.*

So, guddling was a means of catching fish which you lay on the banks, on the grass, deep burns and you had to be very, very patient and at times the fish would come along and you'd tickle them and that's what you called guddling, and we managed to catch them, Ah was quite successful at that.

*What kind of fish did you catch?*

Trout, mainly [it] was trout in the burns. You didn't catch salmon, salmon were too large but trout was the main fish we caught. Other things Ah did was ferret. I had a ferret an ah could catch rabbits. Ah used to do all this on my own.

*You mentioned in the conversation that you snared.*

Yes.

*What, again, did you do to snare rabbits?*

Oh well, the snare was a wire, with a timber post, a small timber post, which ye drove into the ground and ye put the wire snare over the access to the rabbits' burrows an of course when they came out, supposedly, they got caught up, ye'd snared a rabbit. An Ah used to sell these rabbits, Ah didn't get very much for them in these days but it always gave me some pocket money.

## Ian Tweedie

*Who do you remember about that time? I mean, did you have pals?*

Och, aye.

*Who do you remember?*

Who can Ah remember? Oh the Duffs.

*The Duffs, aye.*

Aye, Sheila Richardson, she was in the same class as me, och there are lots o them.

*Aye, that's okay. So, who was your special pals then at that time?*

At that time?

*Who did you play about with in Lochmaben?*

Well, jist, well, Roy Thorburn was one o them, an Jim Stewart. Och, there's a lot o them.

*But you knew Lou Crolla at that time?*

Yes, Ah did.

*You knew Lou Crolla, uh huh.*

Yes, Ah knew him, yes.

*And did you know Jimmy McWhirter that we were talking about?*

Yes, aye.

*Is he ages with you or was he younger?*

He would be, Ah would be a wee bit older as him, definitely.

*And do you remember any of the special adventures you had?*

Adventures?

*Round the Castle Loch or ...*

Aye.

*... Mill Loch?*

We used to, when Ah was at, when Ah stayed at Townhead, we used to go away with the boys, we used to go tae the castle an play about there an then we discovered there was a wee sandstone bit an it was for the people that came and looked at it, you know jist visitors or whatever, put money in this bit (laughter).

*So, you found where the money was* (laughter).

We used go with the Scouts, aye he started it.

*This was with Mr Gibbs, the—*

The minister.

*Right, so he started the Scouts in Lochmaben?*

Yes, aye.

*An how many boys would you have in the Scouts?*

In the Scouts, there would be, what? There'd be about ten.

*About ten.*

Ten, aye there was, uh huh.

*And did you ever go away from Lochmaben, camping and things?*

Uh huh, yes.

*Where to, where did you go?*

We went to Derwent Water.

*Oh right.*

This tent had been kept from away, away back, so off we go to Derwent Water, right, put the thing up. The next thing, through the night, the rain come on an the thing came down because nobody had put the, where the—

*The pole in.*

Aye, it landed right on top of us.

*Didnae hold the tent up, right. So that must have been quite good fun, yes.*

## Anne Hills

*An were there areas that, like play areas, swings and—?*

There were. The grass bits are still there. Some of them on the front of the houses have been taken away for parking cars and there were some on the centre circle. On each of the quadrants there was a grass area and there were the flowering cherry trees and there were crab apple trees and there was hawthorn trees. It was beautiful, it was green and, in the springtime, all the flowers. An as kids we played on the grass areas, we just ran riot. When the grass cutter came we used to collect up all the grass and make nests an play around and there was a swing park down at the bottom end which, Ah'm not sure whether it's still there now.

*No, Ah don't think it is.*

That's gone, because it used to back onto the coal yard, where the coal yard was. There was a swing park in there where we all used to gather.

*And can ye remember what kinna games and children's activities there were?*

Well, we played on the grass an we also played on the streets because there was no vehicles. There was never any vehicles so we used to play, furthest back memories are playing on the grass next to our house, because we had a grassy bit there, and we used to play circle games, singing games, party games, round and round, that kind of thing. We used to play those an we used to play marbles and then we played skipping on the street. We played beds, peevers.

*Yes, I know, I know, Ah've had this conversation with somebody before.*

We used to have the beds, uh huh, we used to have the hopscotch: the six beds, we used to have aeroplane beds and we used to have great big house beds. The aeroplane bed was one, two three then four and five, were like the wings, six and seven were like that.

*Oh yes, Ah see what you mean, yes, Ah remember, that.*

Well, we called them aeroplanes, and then there were the skipping games, all the different skipping games but everybody played together, it was very open.

*Yes, boys and girls as well.*

Well, the boys, Ah don't think they played so much with us, they'd be playin football down— We were never allowed to play rounders because it caused too much bother.

*Broken windows* (laughter).

We used to play rounders at school in the big playground.

*Oh, Ah mean that playground's huge, huge.*

An the top one as well, up at the [UNCLEAR].

*Yea, yea. Any other things? What about Brownies and Guides?*

Yep, Ah went to the Brownies. We used to go to the, what do you call it, the school hall.

*Oh, the drill hall.*

Yes, the school hall.

*There were Cubs as well.*

That was the woman who used to live next to the police station, who lives in Janeville, she used to do the Brownies and the Guides. And Frances Martin used to do the Guides, then after the Brownies you flew up to the Guides.

*The Girl Guides in Lochmaben?*

Yes, Ah was a Guide as well, both Brownies and Guides. Yes, it was definitely in the hall, Ah remember it now.

*Was there any other activities organised?*

Dancing but you had to pay for it, that was in the town hall. We used to go to highland and barn dancing when Ah was small, Ah would go to that. Ah can't think of anything else. There used to be the tent that came once a year to Annandale Crescent, a religious tent, used to come every summer, and set up down next to Charlie Stewart's house. Which number was that, cannae

1. Tweedie's shop at Townhead.

Photograph by kind permission of Lochmaben and District Community Initiative

2. Original Barras Church and Manse. Barras Church was used as a cinema in the 1940s. It no longer exists, although the manse is still inhabited.

Photograph by kind permission of Lochmaben and District Community Initiative

3 and 4. Between 1897 and 1901 there were more than thirty businesses, like these shops, including drapers, grocers, bakeries, butcheries, chemist, coal merchants, blacksmiths, cobblers, a stationer, a post office and two banks. There was a police station as well as doctors who worked from their own homes. Many of these existed into the 1960s.

Photographs by kind permission of Lochmaben and District Community Initiative

5. Miss Carmichael, who lived at Lochbank Farm, was a popular teacher at Lochmaben School from the 1920s to 1950. Many of those interviewed were taught by her.

Photograph is by kind permission of Isabelle Gow, her great niece.

6. Malachy McCruddin and Tommy Mitchell with horse and cart.

Photograph by kind permission of Lochmaben and District Community Initiative

7. Lochmaben Church, Church of Scotland, is now the only church in the burgh. It was opened in 1820. Upstairs there were boxed pews with the names of the local farms for the use of their families. It also contains the oldest working bells in Scotland – the Bruce and the Pope's bells – from the fourteenth century.

Photograph by kind permission of Isabelle Gow

8. Elshieshields Tower House is situated about 2 miles north of the burgh and was the ancestral home of the Johnston family for 500 years. The oldest reference to the place is in 1245. The house was bought in 1966 by Sir Stephen Runciman who was a well known historian of the Crusades. It has since been renovated by the present owner, Stephen's niece and has been continuously inhabited for over 600 years.

Photograph by kind permission of Isabelle Gow

9. The town hall is in the centre of the burgh. It was the venue for council business, but now houses the library. There are stained glass windows commemorating two of Scotland's heroes William Wallace and Robert the Bruce.

Lynne Kirton, Wikimedia Commons

10 and 11. In front of the town hall is the Victorian statue of King Robert whose family's twelfth century motte-and-bailey castle was situated where the golf course is nowadays. (The motte can still be seen clearly today.) Originally iron railings surrounded the statue.

Photographs by kind permission of Isabelle Gow

12. Kirk Loch was used for curling bonspiels as recently as January 2010.

Photograph by kind permission of David Mair

13. Mill Loch is the deepest loch in the burgh and was home to the vendace fish.
There was a flax mill situated at the north of the loch.

Photograph by kind permission of David Mair

14. Castle Loch is the largest loch in the burgh and the Castle, built by Edward 1 of England at the time of the Scottish Wars of Independence, sits on a promontory jutting into this body of water. Mary, Queen of Scots visited the castle in 1565. An archaeological dig recently found that the castle would have been just as strategically important as Edward's castles in Wales. Evidence of Crannogs have been found in the loch.

Photograph by kind permission of David Mair

15. Castle Loch Walk. There was a very successful community buyout in 2014 of the Castle Loch. Volunteers have built, and maintain, a three-mile walkway around the loch. There are several beautiful wood carvings (by world champion chain saw carver, Peter Bowsher) and brass plaques for brass rubbing along the sculpture trail. An outdoor classroom has also been built and the Loch has the benefit of a Ranger.

Photograph by kind permission of Lochmaben and District Community

16. Lochmaben Bowling Club was established in 1890 and is still popular today.
Photograph by kind permission of David Mair

17. Lochmaben Tennis Club. Next to the bowling green and Castle Loch is the
thriving tennis club.
Photograph by kind permission of David Mair

18. Coaching session with young players at Lochmaben Golf Club. The Golf Club was established in 1926 and designed by James Baird. It was extended to 18 holes in 1995.

Photograph by kind permission of David Mair

19. Annandale Sailing Club. The sailing club is one of the town's most popular clubs. It has its HQ on the Castle Loch.

Photograph by kind permission of David Mair

Lochmaben participated in 'The day of the Region' in 2016. It was an extremely popular event which allowed people from far and near to try out the activities the town has on offer.

20. Scottish Country Dancers perform at the school hall. The dancers are members of another popular Lochmaben club.

21. Sailing a GP14 at Annandale Sailing Club.

22. Young boys learning the drums, perhaps auditioning for the town Pipe Band which has since merged with Dumfries Pipe Band.

23. Art display with artists John Lethbridge and David Rose.

Photographs by kind permission of David Mair

remember? Down the bottom end, just as you go down to Whitehills, there was a piece o grass there. An they used to set a tent up there every summer an we used to be spiritually renewed (laughs) but us kids used to go, they used to do something for kids.

*An this was a company that came?*

Oh aye, Ah can't remember what the church group, Ah mean it was one o these weird and wonderful ones. They set a tent up there most summers. An we used to have to organise tattie howking.

*Aye, yes.*

Farmers would send round a thing to do tattie howking but ma mother would never let me go.

*Do you remember the rosehip collection?*

Oh, yea, Ah remember that at school. Ah remember Shirley Arnold and I were collecting one day, so Ah must have been Primary 6 and Shirley would have been in Primary 7 and we were on the railway line because us kids in Annandale Crescent played down in the fields, and down the back, an we played on the railway line, an we played in the marshes an we played in the woods. In Annandale Crescent we just raked everywhere and Shirley and I were on the line collecting. At that time the line was officially closed an, all of a sudden, we heard this noise and vibration and the pair of us, we jumped into these rosehips, (laughter) because it was a train came past. And that reminds me that when Ah was a child ma father used to work with the railways in Dumfries, but he brought me, on his bicycle, on the bar of the bike, up to the railway station and there was an engine in, a steam engine in, an ma dad knew the driver so ma father and I, we got onto the footplate of the engine and the driver took us along the back of Annandale Crescent and then back, on the foot plate.

*That sounds good fun.*

Now, Ah must have been, Ah don't think Ah'd be at school then, that would have been before Ah was at school. But in Annandale Crescent, I think, up until secondary school, we all just ran wild.

*Well, Ah remember being at school and walking up and down the High Street an there was no problem at all, even at lunchtime, in Primary 7.*

We used to go down to the loch side and play down there and up and down the street.

*Ah remember when it was heavy snow, it must have been that year, '63 probably, an going on to the golf course, where the golf course is now, the snow there, there was huge piles of it and trying to make igloos and things like that.*

No, it was different, we had great freedom in those days.

## Isabel Wells and James McWhirter

*An can ye remember, Ah mean Ah remember collecting rosehips at school?*

    JMcW: Yip.

    IW: Mm, mm.

*Ye did that as well?*

    IW: Aye.

    JMcW: That's where we used to go right along the railway, that was great for rosehips up there. Up the railway.

    IW: Ah yince went wi Moira Thorburn up the Watchhill Road …

    JMcW: Oh yes, aye.

    IW: … an Ah dinnae ken what Ah wis daen on top o the dyke an Moira was at the bottom o it but Ah fell off backwards and they had barbed wire.

*Oh, no.*

    IW: An Ah was hinging, wi ma legs stuck in the barbed wire, an she's shoving it doon, she says, 'Push your leg oot,' she says (laughter).

    JMcW: An think Ah've telt ye, Ah can mind the time wi Billy, Billy Wells, we were away bird nesting, walkin, ye ken, an we were up by the Blind Lochs, where there were a crow's nest away up there. Ah says: 'Ah'll gaun up an get it, away an get a couple o eggs oot of it.' So, Ah wis droppin them doon tae Billy but every yin o them broke, so we couldnae hingmy, Ah says: 'Listen I'm gonnae bring this yin doon in ma mouth.' So we were coming doon and ye had tae kinda swing a wee bit to get ontae the next branch, Ah swung an fell down an Ah came right down on ma shoulder an the egg was broken. An the last thing Ah can mind o sayin tae Billy, Ah says, 'There's something the maiter with this airm o mine,' an Ah passed out.

    IW: Billy, can mind that, Jimmy.

    JMcW: And the next thing Ah can remember is this bloody black horse coming tae me an, ken, yer no thinking, Ah'm gaun. It wis Billy on his horse, aye, it was Billy on his horse.

    IW: He wasnae gonnae throw ye ower the saddle wis he, take ye hame?

    JMcW: No, he went hame an telt ma faither and ma faither had got the ambulance, Ah can remember Nutt was the—

    IW: Oh, Nutt frae Lockerbie, aye.

    JMcW: Aye, frae Lockerbie, so they had tae cairry me aboot three mile.

    IW: Billy minds that like, he says, 'Ah mind when Jimmy felt oot and he broke his shooder'.

*So that must have up by Lochbank then?*

    JMcW: Aye, away up there, aye.

    IW: Aye, away up in through there, aye.

*And clubs or anything like that, did you, when you were young, you know, what did you do in the evening?*

    IW: Hung aboot the Cross likely.

JMcW: They had a pole, if ye gaun doon Princes Street they had a pole at what we used to call Maggie …

IW: Mrs Maitlands's, aye.

JMcW: … Maggie Maitlands, she was never done oot chasing us away fae there and we used tae dae aw oor games fae there like.

IW: Aye, that's right.

JMcW: Whether it was kiss catch or knocking at somebody's door and runnin away.

IW: Oh aye that's right, we used tae dae a lot o that but then later on, well when we were teenagers there was the youth club.

JMcW: Aye, the youth club that's right, aye.

IW: That was the Reverend Carmichael, Ah think, that got that gaun didn't he Jimmy?

*What did you do there?*

IW: Oh just, well table tennis or whatever, they had an odd dance an aw.

JMcW: [UNCLEAR] disco and that there aye.

IW: And well, Joe Crolla, he had the billiard room, doon [the small] vennel, well maybe some of you boys would gaun tae the carpet booling an aw.

JMcW: Aye, we did, aye.

IW: When you got a wee bit aulder.

*So there was plenty to do you, ye didnae have to go anywhere else out of Lochmaben, no?*

JMcW: No, no.

IW: Och you made yer ain entertainment, its no like nowadays they dinnae seem to want tae.

JMcW: Very few people had televisions, very few, there was an odd one here and there.

IW: Aye, that's right.

*It would be the radio.*

J McW: Aye, radio, aye, very few people had televisions, so you just got out.

## Hal McGhie

*Now you mentioned that you were involved in one or two activities in Lochmaben, as a youth.*

Yes, there was a youth club in the church hall and Ah can't remember how often it was held but it was a fairly busy youth club, doing handball and Ah can't remember everything. And the boys, somebody, we got a Scout Master who started off the Boy Scouts, that must have been in the 1940s and Ah joined the Boy Scouts. Because we were a very new organisation, there was three of us made platoon leaders and then, three weeks later,
they picked a troop leader and Ah became the troop leader of the only Boy Scouts that Ah've ever known in Lochmaben. Ah don't think it's been resurrected again.

*Well, Jack Wades ran them for several years but there currently aren't any unfortu-nately, which is a shame for the youth here.*

Yes, it was good discipline.

*Yes, you also mentioned that you had some musical talents.*

Oh, Ah could sing, Ah've no musical talents but apparently Ah was a fairly good singer because Ah would sing in the choir, Ah sang a solo, Ah think it was 'The Road to the Isles', in Lochmaben church hall, and Ah sang a solo in the church. And then things all went wrong, and Ah remember, by ma sister, being told to 'shut up' because there were some peculiar noises coming out of ma mouth, when ma voice broke. And Ah've never really, Ah've never really been any good at singing since then. Ah suppose if Ah'd worked at it Ah night have been reasonable.

The Three Ladies remember the games played and the food treats provided at Sunday School picnics.

**Three Ladies**

*Right. You mentioned earlier about the Sunday School and Sunday School trips. Can you fill that in for me? Where did you go and what did you do?*

Sandyhills, well, Sandyhill first time though, Sheila. No, at Powfoot and then we went up to Markie's, up tae Markie's Farm to the field for the sports an everything.

*And what age would you be then?*

...

Ah don't know how old, we, must have been about, what, eight or nine?

What age would we be about?

Nine?

Nine, ten, eleven or something

Ah was born in '33 an the War started in '39 so Ah must have been six when the War started.

*And what were the sports like, what kind of races?*

The three-legged, egg and spoon race.

An aw the bags, put yer feet in the bags.

The sack race.

*The sack race.*

Aye. We had oor tea in the field, it was good, that.

*Now, you mentioned that the last time something about your—*

Aye, Paris buns. Getting up tae the farmer. And then they'd the cartons o milk, not like they have now.

Ah think then they sort of depended on farmers and that then, to giving free gratis and that.

An ice cream, we used tae get, did we no used tae get ice cream?

That was Crolla for the Gala.

For the Gala, that was it?

Wilma Twidale remembers a weekly treat that she was given by a local lady.

## Wilma Twidale

*Right, Wilma, could you tell me a little bit about your early days in Lochmaben and childhood?*

Well, Ah was born at 28 Barras, so I've kind of come back home to live, which was ma grandmother's house, because ma mum an dad were living with her at the time. So, that's where Ah was born. Early days, we moved to Welldale Place very soon after Ah was born and that's where ma early memories are, as a very small child, in Welldale Place. Ah can remember sittin on the doorstep as a very little girl, you know, Ah would sit there an folk would come by and talk to me.

*As they did in those days, aye.*

And there was one old lady who lived in Lochmaben, ..., but Ah don't know what her right name was, she, a Mrs Wilson, Ah think? And she, every week when she came by, she came and talked to me and gave me a sweetie. And it was a conversation lozenge. Do you remember them?

*No, for your throat was it?*

No, no they were flat sweeties with a little motto or something on them.

*Oh, a bit like Lovehearts, that sort of idea?*

Yes, but they were oblong or square and they had writing on them, an every week she gave me this conversation lozenge. She had it held in her hand, it wasn't very clean, Ah don't think, but Ah ate it an enjoyed it (laughter). So, we lived there and then ma brother was born, Edgar, and then Johnny, an then Nancy, quite a long time later.

Betty Hutt recalled wartime rationing and some of her mother's coping strategies.

## Betty Hutt

*Betty, would you like to tell us where and when you were born?*

I was born in Lockerbie in 1935.

*And when did you come to Lochmaben?*

We came to Lochmaben in 1940 and we stayed at 8 Castle Street, Lochmaben. Ma father was a baker with McMichael's, in Queen Street, and he must have got an increase in earnings and he earned about £2 10s. a week an ma mother made the baker's apron out of flour bags because everything was rationed.

*Right. I believe your mother was at the centre of an interesting story when you were a child?*

She went to a sale at Old Bank House in Lochmaben. Then, you needed tokens for everything an she came back with three doormats and six hens. We had nowhere to put the hens, so they were put up in the box room until ma dad and brother made this kind of a shed, until we got a proper henhouse. And the feathers, they produced eggs for us all during the War and when they stopped producing, then we ate them.

*Nothing wasted.*

Nothing wasted, Tom.

*And Ah believe you had a pet white mouse?*

Ah had a pet mouse an it was called Toby an ma dad was reading the paper one day an Ah couldn't resist putting the mouse down his back. Ah tried to resist it but it was too strong, jist couldae do it.

*So, your sense of mischief was there at that age?*

Well, maybe (laughter)

Childhood neighbours are recalled next by George McCall.

## George McCall

*George, Ah believe you were born in Lochmaben, is that right?*

Yes, Ah was born in Lochmaben, 12th April 1929.

*And you were one of quite a big family, were you?*

Ah was one of four of a family.

*Four of a family.*

Well, that was counting maself.

*Aye, that was three boys and a girl was it?*

Three boys and a girl.

*Three boys and a girl, aye.*

Yes. Father was a postman, he was a local postman. He done a lot of work in Lochmaben, he done a lot of work being in the council and aw that sort o thing. He was very keen on Lochmaben and he was born in Queen Street, of course, 59. In fact, Bill Miller, he's retired clergy, Church of Scotland clergyman, he stayed next door to where he stayed in 59. That was Queen Street, Queen Street was a, quite a good street to stay in, you know. It changed quite a bit, where Ah stayed, next door was a joiner's shop, belonging Quinn's. Ah spent quite a bit o time in there when Ah was a kid because Ah got well on. George Quinn was a joiner but his dad was Deputy Chief Constable for Dumfries and Galloway and his brother was a sergeant. He was on the Maxwelltown side, at that time. Although they were joint, they were was still the separate police forces.

Paul Roxburgh's grandfather was a grocer with a shop and a mobile shop who still had time to breed pedigree dogs which he exported abroad. Paul's love of drawing used to get him into bother with his mum when he drew on books in the house.

## Paul Roxburgh

Ma father had only had one arm [and] because it was never mentioned, I suspect it was a fault at birth. He was an only son. Ma grandfather started a grocer's shop in the front room, in 1884, but his main interest was in rough collies, you know, the Lassie-type, winnin many national awards, an even exporting them, pre-war, for £100 a pup tae, several o them, tae America. Later he built a proper shop next to the house, an had a horse and cart mobile shop, an covered Annandale from north tae south, summer and winter, wi that. So that's my memories o ma pre-school days. I remember somebody, Ah never met ma grandfather, he died before I was born, but somebody, in fact several people have told me he had dogs runnin in kennels all the way fae the back o the shop up tae the church hall, there were no houses built there then.

*How did you occupy yourself before you went to school, then?*

I cannae remember, Tom, but Ah think Ah was even starting to draw then. I remember ma mother being very annoyed because every book in the house that had an empty page in it, Ah drew on it. Dictionaries, cookbooks the lot, an Ah suspect Ah started that before Ah went to school. Ah had ma eye on the family bible but, luckily, she managed to stop me drawing on the family bible.

*Do you still have the family bible, then?*

Ah think Stuart has it.

The first cars and first television in the town are recalled here by Roy Thorburn.

## Roy Thorburn

*You mentioned that some of your earliest memories were of the first people in Lochmaben to get a car and the first people to get TV, can you tell us a bit about that?*

What I recollect of that is that Dr Campbell and Peter Smail, who was a local contractor, they were the first two cars in Lochmaben an in these days you could play football on the street, there was no vehicles at all except them. The first television Ah remember was, Peter Smail had it, who, Simon Smail, his brother, who was in the Crown Hotel, he had the first television set an Ah recall looking through the window and Simon callin me in to watch Scotland play Uruguay. What year that was I can't just remember.

*I think it might have been 1952.*

1952, aye possibly, aye. Ah remember the screen an all ye could see was jist black figures goin to and fro and you got an odd vision of the ball but it wasn't very great, but that was the initial televisions Ah remember.

*So, there would be no parking problems in Lochmaben at that time?*

There certainly wis no parking problems whatsoever, no.

# 5

# Working Life

This chapter gives an insight into the working life of the interviewees and employment opportunities that were available locally. To gain employment on leaving school was important. Tom Allan recalled his father insisting that he served an apprenticeship when he left. George McCall – during a period when work was scarce – remembered being sent to Dumfries by his father and being told not to come back until he had found a job. The extracts suggest that there was a variety of employment opportunities available nearby and that it was possible to move from one employer to another. Three extracts are of the work experience of women, two in offices and one in nursing and these show that, at that time, women were expected to leave their employment on marriage, despite being qualified and experienced. George McCall recalled soup kitchens, one in Lochmaben and one in Dumfries, which operated when work was scarce. He also referred to 'parish money' being paid out to those in need during these times.

Bill Gibson spoke about his childhood and early life living on Thorniethwaite Farm and gave a glimpse of the contribution that children often made to the family's work routine. Thorniethwaite was a mixed farm with livestock and a dairy. His older brother went to Lochmaben and the surrounding area selling the farm milk and had installed a water wheel which provided electricity for the threshing mill and bruiser. Potatoes were sold for seed and wool was taken to the station in Lochmaben to be sent further afield. Bill's early contribution was to fill the paraffin lamps when he got home after school. He also helped with the milking and his father could collect him from school early to do this. He recalled the potato harvest with children being employed daily to help at this. It seems that they often had to be supervised, as the lengths of the drills were measured with sticks and some children shortened the sticks to make it look as if they had done more than they had. As well as being paid for their work, the children were given a meal at the farm.

Bill Carrick also worked on a local farm and later he started his own coal merchant's business.

## Bill Carrick

*How old were you when you used to go to the farm at Kirkmahoe.*

Ah wis aboot twelve … jist afore the War broke oot.

*Yes, 1930s.*

Aye, '39, was it?

*Yea, that's right. It broke out in '39. An how did you get there?*

Ah jist stayed like. Yince Ah wis there, Ah jist stayed.

*Oh, I see. How did you get there though … did you used to walk along the railway line?*

Walk along the railway, aye.

*Through, past Amisfield?*

Aye. Yist tae go up the lane at Amisfield an walk up across the field.

*Aye, an you used to stay there, then?*

Uh huh.

*For the summer or—?*

No, no, Ah volunteered for the Airmy. The auld fellow, ma stepfaither, fell oot aboot it, he created merry hell.

*Your stepfather did?*

Aye. Oh, he got it, we had a scrap like an Ah still stayed at the ferm, like, ye ken.

*Oh, I see. He wouldn't let you go from the farm.*

No.

*Was that your uncle at the farm, at Kirkmahoe, was it, or your stepfather?*

Ma stepfather. …

*You worked with horses, you used to like that, didn't you?*

Liked the horses.

*Ploughing?*

Ploughing, aye. …

*Dae you mind the first tractor coming on the farm at Kirkmahoe?*

First tractor?

*Ye'd horses you see, I wondered when they started working with tractors.*

Well, the brother, he got a tractor, was it a Major?

*Fordson Major.*

It wis yin o thae yins, onyway, he got, but, aw, Ah didnae like the McAlpine.

*Metal seats.*

Aye. …

*You told me about, there was a cart there, a special cart somewhere and you brought it across the fields. What was that about? A big horse. Or somebody did, they bought a cart, or something like that, and they couldn't get it across the field. Ah think it was coming from Johnstone's or somewhere like that. You told me about it a while back. And how many butchers were there in the toon then, quite a few weren't there?*

There was Broon, the butcher, and there was, oh heavens, maybe it was Broon, they had vans on the road.

*Uh huh. There were other butchers. There was a slaughterhouse in the town, was there not?*

No, that wis Lockerbie.

*It was in Lockerbie. Always in Lockerbie, was it? And then you would be a coalman from when, Bill? How old were you when you started carting coal?*

Oh, Ah'd be aboot 30, Ah started to carry the coal.

*And had you been on the farm till then? Till you were 30?*

Aye. Came back tae Lochmaben and having got a lorry, sterted hauling coal roond the doors ye ken, selling it roond the doors.

*Aye. You'd be that a long time.*

Aye. A bag of coal was about 30-odd pence.

*A bag of coal?*

Aye. Think what it is now.

*Exactly. Pounds and pounds.*

Aye.

*You wouldn't have difficulty getting your money, did you?*

Pardon?

*Did you have difficulty getting your money in those days?*

No, really, no, Ah didn't have. What maybe helped wis me being born in Lochmaben and that, ye ken, they kent is.

*Everybody knew you. And you'd go round every how often, every week, fortnight?*

Every week.

*Every week?*

Aye. An some o the country, through the week ye ken, Nethermill an up roond that wey through the week.

*Did you get your coal from the station?*

Aye.

*And you had the bags to fill?*

Aye, it came in trucks and Ah had tae fill the bags oot the wagons.

*That would be hard going?*

Aye, an stoor galore.

*Where was that coal coming from, Bill, was it coming from Sanquhar and places like that, or not?*

It came fae, aye, it came fae aboot Sanquhar somewhere.

*Or Cumnock, somewhere up there.*

Cumnock, aye.

*And you were selling it for 30 pence a bag. How much did you pay for it a ton?*

Pardon?

*Can you mind how much you paid a ton for it? Were they hundredweight bags or half hundredweight bags?*

Hundredweight.
*Hundredweight, 30 pence?*
So, it was well spent storing the pence while ye were gaun.
*You'd have to weigh them though, didn't ye.*
Oh aye.
*On the scale?*
The scales, atween *50* an *60* in them.
*Aye, that's right.*
And ye'd tae cairry them on the lorry.
*So that someone could ask you to check them?*
Oh aye.
*Did they come round and inspect those?*
Oh aye, the inspectors was keen. Ah think they'd been getting narked by [REDACTED]. He'd been on the fiddle and making mair bags oot o his load an they, aye, they were gey keen up there.
*So, was he fined for doing that was he?*
Pardon?
*Was he fined?*
Possibly would be, likely. No, they said tae me, efter a wee while, that it's no worth checking you. Ah just said: 'Well, when ye're working for yersel ye cannae afford tae dae anythin that stupid.'
*You'd lose your customers.*
You'd lose all your customers. He says: 'Aye,' he says, 'but there's a lot o folk dinnae see it that wey.'
*So, would you go to all the farms as well, Bill? Did you go to the farms?*
Aye, well some o the farms wis ten hundredweight or a ton at a time like, ye ken.
*Fill the coal place.*
Aye. They used a 'black dip' they cawd it, or a draughty cellar, ye ken, an ye'd tae cowp them into [it].
*Aye, down below. Because you, jist was a, was there just two of you doing that or just you yourself?*
Aye, Ah wis masell, jist, at the coal.
*You went round, what kinna wagon was it?*
A Commer Carrier.
*Was it a good starter?*
Oh aye. It was that. Ah could cairry what? Ah could put fower ton on it and it wis only supposed tae carry three ton, something.
*Aye.*
But Ah aye had a further ton on it, ye ken, and yae nicht they stopped is, an a fellow coonted the bags on the larry, you see. He says: 'Ye've mair bags on here as what ye're supposed tae have.'

'Well,' Ah says, 'If Ah'd got 50 yairds up the road there. ... Ah'd have got rid o some o them there, there's a customer up there. ... Ah'd hae got rid o them.' An the fellow was humming and hawing an aw that an he says: 'Ignore that,' he says. 'Anyway,' he says, 'if everybody's lorry was kept as good as this yin,' he says, 'Ah'd be oot o a job'.

*Probably.*

Aye, Dick, the mechanic, he always made a good job o always doing it up like, you ken.

Before serving his time as an apprentice motor mechanic Tom Allan worked with a chimney sweep.

## Tom Allan

Ah left school, well, the first thing ye did wis get a job. An the first job Ah had wis as a chimney sweep. We had a fireside, fireplace company in the Main Street in Lockerbie.

*In Lockerbie, yes, aye.*

An when Ah got there in the morning, aw rigged up wi a boiler suit an what have ye, an a piece bag, the foreman an the yard man come out and he said: 'Look son, the gentleman you were meant to be working with—,' he didn't call him a gentleman, he said his name, but he said he was off ill so Ah'd work in the yard for that day.

'Oh, but Ah'll find ye a wee job, son. You're John Allan's boy, aren't you?' Ah says, 'Aye'.

'Oh, Ah ken yer father fine.'

Ah says, 'Oh'.

He belonged to Kettleholm seemingly, an ma faither belonged Kettleholm. Anyway: 'Get ye a job. Now, see a these bricks across there? These facing bricks?'

'Oh, the facing bricks, yes.'

'Now Ah want ye tae build them in straw.'

'Oh, right.'

So, when Ah got home at night ma mother said: 'Well son, how did ye get on wi your first day at your work?'

'Oh,' Ah says, 'Well, it was awright but Ah'm no very happy aboot it'. Ah says, 'Ah'd nae hands left'.

These bricks were rough, facing bricks an they tore the skin clean off ma fingers (laughter). Anyway, Ah started on the chimney sweeping and it was vacuum and brush, a big vacuum on the back o this lorry, ye know, and you cart aw the hoses up. An Ah had some fun wi that, Ah can tell you, ye ken. Dalswinton big hoose an Station Hotel, Dumfries, up on the top, dropping stanes doon the chimney tae see that ye've got the right yin. Ah remember

129

there were a Dr McLaughlin ower Lockerbie. It's a home now for elderly, if ye gaun intae Lockerbie and turn at Eskbridge.

*Aye. Dryfehome, it'll be.*

Aye, Dryfemount, is it?

*Dryfemount.*

Aye, an we're in there and we were tae sweep this chimney. Well, [we] gits aw rigged up an there was a Persian carpet on the floor, a white Persian carpet, you know. Put their sheets doon, put the cover in front o the fireplace, connected up the hose for the suction, opened the wee window and put the brushes in. Jim gets them tae the top. 'Gaun ootside an see if it's oot.' Oot Ah goes, has a look, comes back an Ah says, 'Aye, it's oot, Jim'. So, tae get it doon through the, ye've tae get a really good heave at it. Well, Jim took a great heave at it, of course, it caught the underside o this big fireplace an the whole fireplace came off the wall, plus aw the soot went fleein up in the air. Well, as a boy, Ah seen the funny side but he didae see the funny side.

*Oh, the Persian carpet, aye.*

Oh (laughter). Aw, that was one experience.

*But you didnae, ye didnae spend too long there, did you?*

No. Ah had tae have an apprenticeship, Ah was told.

*Right.*

You always done as you were told.

*Who was it that told you?*

Well, your parents, right.

*Yer parents, right, your dad was saying, 'You've gotta have an apprenticeship'.*

So, Ah got a job as an apprentice mechanic, like, at McCall Wells, which had a wee garage o their own, that was doing some work as well.

*That was in Lockerbie was it?*

In Lochmaben.

*In Lochmaben?*

Jist behind the Railway Inn.

*Behind the Railway Inn?*

Up through 28 Barras entrance, there's a wee garage wis in there.

*Right, right, aye.*

Aye, Ah wasnae terribly keen on being a mechanic really.

*No, no.*

Anyway, Ah had a lot of experiences there. Ah got gassed, doin a petrol engine on a four-cylinder Albion engine, [it] had been decoked an it was a hard, hard frost. An we were tightenin the head down, ye know, started it up and warmed it up and were tightenin the head doon and this fellow, that drove the lorry says to me: 'I dinnae feel too well.'

'Oh, what's wrong Sam?'

'Ah don't know. Maybe something Ah had for ma breakfast?'

Just by that, he fell down between the lorry and the bench. Adam, who wis the mechanic, he was ootside at another lorry. Ah went tae pick this fellow up but, oh, Ah felt funny as well. Ah just let him go an Ah flattened his nose on the flair. Next thing Ah ken, Ah was ootside and this doctor was there, sitting on a cuddy. Dae you ken what a cuddy is?

*Aye.*

For sawin sticks. Ah wis sittin on a cuddy an he was soundin ma chest. So, Ah got the rest o the day off for being unwell. But that, as Ah say, it was a very, very hard frost an Ah remember there must hae been aboot 50-odd rinks curlin on the loch that day. Mr Boyer and Mr Notman had been marking oot the rinks on the ice an, oh, it was covered with people. It froze for aboot seven weeks, Ah think.

*Oh, is that right?*

Aye. There was ice on it for aboot seven weeks. But that was an experience. ... . So, as Ah say, Ah got married an huntin for a house, of course, but Ah got yin in Princes Street in Lochmaben, 67 Princes Street. It was jist a cauld water tap, a swey at the fire, the kettle on it. But we were happy enough.

*Aye.*

Aye, ma daughter was born in 67 Princes Street. Ah had tae shift the job because Ah needed a wee bit mair money when Ah had a family so, Ah shifted for another 10s, which ma wage would be aboot £7 a week then. An Ah was bagging coal for Willie Noble, two or three ton of coal a day. Ye were tired at night.

*Oh, I'm sure, I'm sure aye. Back-breaking stuff, eh?*

Aye.

*Aye, they've got machines to do it now, of course.*

Aye. But of course, as Ah say, there wis different grades of coals, an aye, it was interesting, but it was hard work. Ah left, Ah had a disagreement with the chap Ah was working wi, an Ah left an Ah got a job on the dual carriageway at Lockerbie, building it wi Carmichael.

*Oh, right.*

An it wis good money but, ye know, if ye got bad weather ye could get paid off. So, Ah was gang tae the doctor's one day, Dr Wilson worked in Bruce Street then, at Lake House, that was the surgery then. An as Ah wis goin by, Mr Noble came out and he said: 'Do ye fancy working on the petrol?'

'Aye,' Ah said. 'Well we could discuss terms and what have you, if ye're happy enough about me coming back.'

'Aw, aye, it'll be fine,' he said.

Ah said, 'As long as you dinnae put me on the coal again'.

'Aye, right then.'

So, Ah started on the petrol an there wis four grades then, Esso, Esso

Mixture, Esso Plus an Esso Extra and then there wis Esso Golden an aw, ye could get Golden, Esso Golden, which was 101 octane.

*So, what were your duties there, then?*

Just general. Going out, serving the petrol, blowin tyres up and jist generally helping the public.

*And you were there for quite a while?*

Ah was there for 38 years and to see the price o petrol when Ah started off at aboot 4 and 5 pence a gallon, which was about 22 pence, so that worked out at aboot what, 4 ½ pence a litre to what it is now?

*Changed days, eh? Changed days.*

Aye. So, ma wife wasn't well so Ah retired two years early tae help at home because, Ah've a handicapped daughter and Annie wasnae feeling jist too great for a while. So, as Ah say, Ah took early retirement. Ah had a couple of wee pensions o ma ain.

George McCall's father sent him to look for work when he had been unemployed for a while.

### George McCall

Ma grandad, he was a builder, an as Ah say, ma father was a postman. But when they were building, this industry was very good at that time because we had Robison and Davidson, which was quite a big firm in these days, an it employed quite a lot of local men, a lot of them used to cycle tae Dumfries.

*And you got a job down The Vennel [Friars Vennel, Dumfries] or something, didn't you? For a plasterer?*

Ah got a job as a plasterer, aye … . Ma dad said to is when Ah wis off work, Ah think Ah wis off for aboot six weeks after I left Robison and Davidson. I was kinna sorry for it, after it, like, because work was scarce. An ma dad says, 'You've been long enough off now,' he says, 'Ye can go to Dumfries and don't come back till you get a job,' an of course when Ah went down The Vennel there were these plasterers workin and they jist laughed at is.

Ah says: 'Ah'm looking for a job an Ah've got tae get a job before Ah go back because ma dad says Ah've got tae get a job.'

'Well, Ah don't know whether tae take ye on or no like? Dae ye think ye could manage it? It's hard work.'

Well, Ah done it 50-odd years, 55 years working non-stop, bar maybe the odd times when Ah had been sick or something like that.

Lynne McNeish's nursing career, which started at Lochmaben Sanatorium, covered a variety of specialities.

## Lynne McNeish

*Lynne, can you tell me a wee bit about your schooling and where you went to school and where you were born?*

I was born in Cresswell, in Dumfries, although all my life and childhood was in Lochmaben. I went to Lochmaben Primary School and then went on to Lockerbie Academy School.

*So, when did you think about nursing?*

Nursing, Ah think, has always been at the back o ma mind, quite a few of my female relatives were nurses in their time and it was something I always wanted to do as a child.

*So, what, did you go straight into nursing from school?*

No, when Ah left school Ah went into, and Ah worked in, McGeorge's factory, in the production office. And then at the age of 17½, that's when Ah started ma training.

*Was that because that was the age to start training or …*

Yes, it was 17½.

*And where did you do that training?*

I actually started at Ballochmyle, in Ayrshire, but due to homesickness, I really was unwell and the Home Sister wrote to my parents advising that being away from home was just 'not for Lynne at this time'. So, we managed to get, I managed to get a transfer back down to Dumfries, so it was the South West of Scotland College o Nursing.

*Oh, right, ok. And that was attached to the Infirmary?*

Actually, at that point, the Infirmary and the Crichton had merged together and that's when the South West of Scotland College of Nursing came about. So, it was a whole, you know, rather than just having the Infirmary training and the Crichton training, they joined up.

*Right, ok, ok. So, did, what sort of exams and things did you have to pass?*

You had to pass an entrance exam and that was all you needed to pass at that time, for the enrolment.

*And did you do more training when you were nursing, I mean not just practical but—*

Yes, uh huh. I did, actually, do all ma practical training at Lochmaben Hospital but [for] any theory you went to Crichton Hall, to South West o Scotland College, to do your actual theory and things like that. So, you would have different blocks, like just being at university, you would go out, you know, that type of thing.

*Right, ok. And did you, what was your uniform like at that time?*

It was just a plain white dress.

*Plain white dress. No hat?*

No hat at that point, no. Oh, there was, I beg your pardon, there was a hat, it was later on that we did away with the hats and it was just a plain white hat and then once you qualified you got a coloured band, whether it be a blue band for Registered or green band for Enrolled nurse. Black shoes, American tan tights (laughter).

Lynne undertook her practical training at Lochmaben Sanatorium and her recollections of this experience are included in that section of this publication.

… And then, Ah think it was roughly about the beginning of 1974, Ah went up to the Western, in Glasgow, and Ah worked in the Intensive Care then.

*Oh right. And how different was that?*

A big shock to the system, although a lot of it, the medical side put me in good steading for it but a lot o it, the surgical intensive care unit, so it was another good learning curve. Because at first Ah thought Ah had walked into the Tardis with the machines and all the rest of it but it was, Ah thoroughly enjoyed it and as Ah say, I learnt quite a bit at that stage.

*So, you had to stay, obviously, in Glasgow at the time.*

Yes.

*Ok, so after Glasgow what happened?*

After Glasgow, Ah moved back down to Dumfries and Ah got a post in Accident and Emergency, which, at that point, was at, well what is now classed as Nithbank, the new infirmary wasn't opened at that time. So, I worked there for nine months and then moved up to Dumfries and Galloway, the new hospital. I think it was July '75.

*Right, ok.*

And I was eleven years working in Accident and Emergency. So that, again, I think if I was to, if you were to ask me what part of my nursing did I enjoy the most in ma career, I would have to say Accident and Emergency.

*Really?*

Uh huh.

*Because I think nowadays people would say. 'Oh, that's a terrible thing to do'.*

Uh huh, but at that time, well eleven years, Ah think that proves a point in itself doesn't it?

*So, you were dealing with accidents—*

We were dealing with, oh we had quite few big accidents. Well, a couple of major incidents, you know, it covers the time when we had the bad bus crash and then we had Lockerbie as well.

*Of course. You were there then?*

Uh huh.

*So, you just had your usual admissions and things like that, and overdoses.*

Yes. Oh, a variety of everything.

*Some things that have never changed. I presume ye'd drunks and things coming in as well.*

Yes, that's right and I believe, well, drugs, not so much drugs in that time then but certainly drunks. You always had your usual people came, you knew them whenever they come through the door.

*So, that's no really changed.*

No.

*Right, ok. So, then?*

Well, after that I got a post as the Occupational Health Nurse in the Gates Rubber Company.

*Oh yes.*

Again, it was a different type of thing, you were dealing wi medicals and you were involved wi the Health and Safety, welfare of the staff, so that was interesting as well, very interesting.

*Because that was a big company at the time.*

Yes, at the time it was very big. So, that was good, I enjoyed that as well. I was only there a year because at that point my husband had a promotion up to Ayrshire.

*Ah, so that's why—*

He worked wi the Ambulance Service and I got a post in Crosshouse Hospital and at that point, for five years, Ah worked in the Plaster Room, in the Orthopaedic Clinic, also in Casualty, the three places over the five years.

*That was in Kilmarnock.*

That was in Kilmarnock.

*And then you came back down to Dumfries.*

Then Ah came back down to Dumfries, again through ma husband's job, and that is when Ah went into Learning Disabilities.

*Yes.*

Working with people, to begin with it was adults and it was like a respite unit but in the latter years it was children up to the age of 18, so Ah was 19 years [there].

*Yes, that's a long time with—*

So, again, that was a different type of nursing.

*Yes, I can imagine.*

You know, completely different to the general side but I enjoyed that as well, it's all learning.

*So, it's been a career where you've changed, you know, but you've learned.*

I've learned quite a bit, you know. And then that was it, retired.

*Well, you've said, looking back, you've enjoyed the Accident and Emergency. Well, maybe not 'enjoyed' is the best word but that's the time you thought was best.*

Uh huh.

*What, how, I mean you hear all these stories now about hospitals and real problems with staffing and so on, I mean, do you think that things have changed much, or a lot?*

Ah think the staffing is a big problem now. Even prior to me retiring, staffing was a big, big problem. When Ah started nursing Ah can't say Ah was ever aware of real staffing problems, we seemed to have more staff then or whether, Ah don't ... no Ah think it has definitely got worse.

*Do you think it's anything to do with the fact that so many folk are living longer?*

Ah think that has a lot to do with it. Personally, Ah also think, when Ah did ma training, you did your training on the wards, anything you learned was on the wards.

*Yes, yes, practical.*

Yes, your practical side, where it's all done in university now. And Ah always went into nursing because it was a middle of the road profession and it was something Ah thought Ah could do and Ah like to say, or think, Ah have a lot of common sense and forward thinking, can see things. As an outsider, now, I think some of these things are missing.

Isabel Wells worked until she was married and then went back to employment when her daughter was two. James McWhirter served in the Army and had to look for employment when he returned to civilian life.

## Isabel Wells & James McWhirter

*Can you tell a little bit ... what did you do when you left school, Isabel?*

IW: Well, when Ah left Lockerbie Academy Ah went to the Tech[nical College] at Dumfries, which was down the bottom o George Street, Ah went there for a year an, when Ah finished there, Ah went to work with M. R. Rodgers, he was a surveyor, building surveyors.

*Oh, yes.*

IW: Quantity surveyors, so Ah went to work there until Ah was married, basically, and when, Ah think it would be Gail was maybe two or something Ah went tae work for John McCall Wells, an Ah was there for 18, 20 years ... and when Ah left there, Ah went tae Graham's at Langholm an Ah was there for 22 years.

*Oh, right.*

IW: Ah havenae got a fantastic working life, Ah've worked a long time. Ah worked, well Ah was 65 when Ah retired.

*Uh huh, so James, what about you, what did you do when you left school?*

JMcW: Ah served ma time as a brickie, wi Carruthers & Green.

*Oh, yes*

...

*So, it must have been quite difficult to settle back in Lochmaben after being, you know, touring [Army service] and being—*

JMcW: Oh it wis, aye, especially working in a factory, cos Ah went tae Uniroyal, Ah wanted tae be a Security Office but there were two o us in for it and he said Ah was too young for it but he says: 'Ah'll offer ye another job.'

So he taen [me] to this new place they'd built, Power Transmission, how Ah lasted 25 years, Ah don't know.

On leaving school Wilma Twidale worked for an insurance company and would have had to leave when she married. However, her new life took her away from the area.

### Wilma Twidale

… when Ah started tae work, Ah got a job in the Royal Insurance Company in Dumfries, which was in Buccleuch Street, quite a well-known insurance company at that time. But there was only the Manager and me, because the men weren't back from the War, so there was just the two of us, but we seemed to manage okay and then somebody did come back, a Mr Robertson, an he joined us an there was the three of us then so Ah was sort of, Ah did everything, really, in that place and, well, Ah was there until Ah got married.

*You gave up your work and got married?*

Well, you had to, the insurance companies didn't employ married women but Ah remember them saying to me, an Ah said, 'Well, Ah'll have tae leave?' an they said, 'Oh no, we would have made an exception'. Ah said 'Well Ah'm goin away tae Elgin,' and actually, they had contacted the place there but it never came to anything.

After returning to Lochmaben and having a family, Wilma was given the opportunity of working again.

Yes, well, it kinda started when Ah lived in Annandale Crescent, one winter Ah had a really bad dose of bronchitis. It was ma own fault because Ah knew Ah had this cough an Ah knew Ah wasn't right an Ah didn't go to the doctor's. You know what you were like, Ah'm still the same, but when Ah was young Ah was worse, and one morning when Ah woke up, it must have been the Christmas holidays because the kids were at home, an Ah woke up an there was this note beside the bed from Jim saying *Ah'm phoning the doctor and askin him to call.* So, Dr Jack Wilson duly came and he was attending me and during the course o this he said tae me: 'How would you feel about doing a wee bit of typing for me?' Ah had been actually helping out at McJerrow and Stevenson's – not all the time, now and again they would phone and say 'Could ye come in an give us a hand?' An he knew this an he said to me: 'Ah don't want you travelling on the bus for the rest of the winter'. So, Ah said: 'Well, Ah wouldn't mind but Ah don't have a typewriter'. He said: 'No, but Ah'll bring ye mine'. So, he brought me his wee portable and Ah did a wee bit of typing for him and that was how it wis started.

*For his books and so on?*[1]

For his books, uh huh. Yes, well yes, it wasn't so much, well Ah think Ah did do some of the history too, but some of it was medical stuff. An then, oh well, it was a good number o years later, Ah was living up here, when they decided tae buy that house and build the surgery between them and he sort of came and said to me, 'Would you be interested?' Ah was working by then, Ah had got, Ah was working at the cheese factory at Lockerbie, in the office there, they'd come an asked me and Ah worked, Ah was wi them for two year, it wasn't great, it was okay, but it wasn't a very nice place to work. The folk in the factory were fine, it was somebody we had in the office that caused problems. Anyway, Ah'd been there two years and he came and Ah said, 'Yes, Ah would be interested,' so eventually Ah was asked, well it has tae be advertised, of course, so Ah had tae apply an Ah went an started in the surgery in 1970 and was there for 22 years.

*It's a long time.*

Ah mean, Ah never even thought about that when Ah went, but 22 years later Ah was still there. So, and that was my ideal job. It really was.

*Yes, meeting lots of people.*

It was the job Ah'd always sort of wanted and you were with people and you felt you were making a difference, so Ah did that. So, Ah retired in 1992, an that's me, Ah've been retired for all that time, Ah can't believe it.

Two essential jobs in the neighbourhood, that of the county roadman and the refuse collectors are recalled here by Paul Roxburgh.

### Paul Roxburgh

In these days, the local waste collection service was operated by what we cawd the scaffies. The scaffies later became burgh officers, Ah don't know exactly what ye caw them now, refuse collectors.

*Aye, roadmen.*

Aye, Ah well, no, the roadmen wis a different thing, the roadmen wis responsible for keeping the culvert clean. The roadman used to have his own wee territory and wi the shovel tied on the bar o the bike and kept that territory up tae scratch. But the scaffies, then, had a horse and that horse was quite a character, the horse used to stop ootside the shop looking for a slice o bread, an sometimes it was reluctant to go on until it got its slice o bread. The two men Ah remember first operating the cart were a Mr Trotter an a Mr Moffat.

*That's quite an interesting name to have a horse-drawn cart, a Mr Trotter* (laughs).

Aye, that's right.

*An actually, on ma way here this morning, Ah passed what we would call the local scaffie. … With his barrow an his two bins an his brush for sweeping the rubbish.*

Aye.

*He does a good job, that chap.*

Oh, he does, aye, but Ah don't think he would be too pleased to be called scaffies because it's just an abbreviation of scavenger.

*Yes, but it is such an expressive word.*

Oh, it is, aye, aye.

*One of the good Scottish words.*

Aye, but probably no acceptable nowadays.

Paul worked in his family grocery business, on leaving school, but this hadn't been the case for his father.

## Paul Roxburgh

Ma father had never, for some reason, never involved himself in the grocery business, he had several jobs, several good jobs. He worked at the Arrol-Johnston for a while in the clerical department.

*Could you tell people what Arrol-Johnston was?*

Arrol-Johnston was a vehicle manufacturer, Ah don't know what, they must have made something else in addition to cars but they were known for their cars in their day, that's where the rubber works is, now.

*You can see Arrol-Johnston cars in the transport museum in Glasgow.*

Oh aye, aye.

*What else did he do then?*

He worked in the employment exchange, worked in the factory at Gretna, during the War, I don't know how he got back and forward, but there were an awful lot of women from Lochmaben were employed in munitions at Gretna and Powfoot

*This is post Devil's Porridge?*[2]

No, the same time, the same time as the Devil's Porridge, aye Ah had two cousins who worked in the munitions. Ah think it was more or less they could make ye work there, it was compulsory.

In the following extract George McCall recalls a soup kitchen operating in the town when jobs were scarce.

## George McCall

An Ah also told ye aboot the soup kitchen, that was a new one on me, the soup kitchen. But ma older brother, he remembered it as a soup kitchen, an Ah remember the hard times, the unemployment. There were no work at all really, and all the workers, all the unemployed, used to stand jist at, round the Bruce [statue of Robert the Bruce in the town centre]. It was quite busy.

*How many of them would there be?*

Ah would say there could be anything up tae a couple of dozen, maybe.

But Ah can remember them standing there, round the Bruce. The Bruce was fenced off at one time, but it was … the fence was cut down during the War for tae get the metal to make munitions.

*Munitions, yes, aye.*

Also, the church had a fence round the church wall.

*A metal fence?*

A metal fence, yes, an it was taken down, Government law[3] …

*And that was at times when there wasnae a lot o work going? There wisnae much at all.*

There was no work at all. In fact, the general foreman told me that he remembered sitting on a dyke waiting on somebody dying, tae get his job. That was in Dumfries.

*In Dumfries, aye, goodness.*

He was the general foreman, of course, wi Wells, an he wis a real gentleman like, you know? But he told us how hard times it really was and it was hard times.

*And the soup kitchen was an example of that?*

The soup kitchen, well, what happened on a Saturday night, when the butchers closed, if they had any surplus meat or anything, they took it to the soup kitchen for to make soup. An Ah cannae remember the soup kitchen in Lochmaben working but the one in Dumfries, Ah remember it working. It was on Munches Street jist big urns, like, an anybody that wanted could go in an get a plate of soup.

*And were these local women that made the food?*

I think just local volunteers.

*Just local volunteers?*

Aye.

*And how many people would turn up for something to eat at that time?*

Well, food was plentifu if you could buy it, but if there were no, when there were no work, Ah mean, ma cousin, Davy McCall, he was a stonemason. As soon as a touch of frost came, roon aboot September or October, ye were put off work and they didnae get started again tae March. There were no money bar Ah think there were an allowance, now Ah don't know how this allowance worked. We talk aboot it nowadays, aboot 'the social' but these men went down tae Annie Clark's, Annie Clark was the registrar, that was the house next to Balcastle and they used to get money there. They cawd it 'parish money' but Ah'm no, Ah'm no sure how it, how the system worked, or how they got paid. Ma dad was, he was a postman, he hadnae a big pay but it was great tae have a good—

*Regular job, eh.*

These were good jobs, these were good jobs in these days.

# Leisure

The extracts in this chapter tell us how the interviewees spent their leisure time. Over the years there has been a variety of sporting activities available in the town for residents to enjoy. There are recollections of big sporting events which attracted participants from a wide area, such as the Waterlow Cup curling bonspiel, the national quoiting championships and the Lowland Games. Other sports enjoyed in the town over the years include football, golf, bowling and sailing. In their early life, the interviewees enjoyed visiting the local cinema to watch the latest films. Regular dances with music from local dance bands were another popular activity. Solitary pastimes and personal hobbies such as angling, horse racing and collecting ornaments are also recalled here.

Curling on the lochs, during winters which have been recalled as being more severe than nowadays, are recalled in these first four extracts.

**Three Ladies**

*You mentioned earlier about the curling and the lochs.*

Aye, the Waterlow.

*What can you say about that?*

Well, Ah asked Wilma Twidale about it and she thought it wid be the seventeenth century when it started. Ye're gaun back a long way then.

*You could remember them using the car headlights?*

Aye. And they'd whisky at either end o the—

Oh, it was a big thing, the Waterlow. Farmers used to come fae all over the place.

Aye.

An there wis the hut where they kept the curling stones in.

That's right, there was a wee hut in there. Ah wondered what that was.

They kept the curling stones in there.

It was in there for years, wasn't it? Was it a wee green one?

Ah think it was, Nell, because Ah remember Alex saying that he'd skipped the school and he'd went ontae the ice and he'd got absolutely soaked so he had tae go in there an get dried off, an played truant.

Paul Roxburgh recalled the special halt on the railway provided for the Waterlow Cup competitors.

### Paul Roxburgh

The curling in Lochmaben used to be, not on the Kirk Loch, but the Castle Loch an there was a drop off point … on the railway, just beside the wee cottage there, we cawd it Paddy's Cottage.

*Oh yes, yes.*

And the train used, frae Lochmaben, the Lockerbie train used to stop there and aw the curlers got off an went on directly to the Castle Loch, Ah don't know why it was changed fae the Castle Loch to the Kirk Loch, actually.

*Well, I suppose, I mean the Castle Loch would take longer to freeze, a bigger area but it was shallower.*

The bonspiel was also recalled by Roy Thorburn who could remember seeing the event take place.

### Roy Thorburn

*You also mentioned some events that used to take place in Lochmaben, for instance the Waterloo Curling Cup.*

Yes, Ah vaguely recollect that. The train used to stop at Paddy Marshall's, which is about a mile out of Lochmaben on the Lockerbie Road, an the curlers used to stream off that train onto the loch. It was the Castle Loch that done all the curling, they played the Waterlow, what they called the Waterloo, at that particular time and there were various ladders all over, they laid ladders flat on the water, obviously for any, if there had to be, if there were any accidents or ice breaking. But the ladders were strewn all over the loch. As Ah say, Ah just vaguely recollect that.

*So that was a health and safety measure?*

Exactly, aye, aye, they probably had to do that.

Another local curling competition is mentioned in this extract.

### Isabel Wells and James McWhirter

JMcW: As a matter o fact that used tae be the curling hut.

IW: Yes, that's' right.

JMcW: An they held the curling aboot every year, it Well's, was it no Well's tournament or something?

IW: Aye, something like that Ah cannae remember, but the loch froze ower a lot in thaim days.

JMcW: Oh, that's right.

*So, the winters were maybe colder.*

JMcW: Ah can mind o a car being on it.
*Can you mind that?*
JMcW: A car aye.
IW: Can you mind of Wullie Edwards being on wi his motorbike?
JMcW: Aye.
*On the Kirk Loch?*
JMcW: It was the only loch where yer mother and faither would let ye go
and it had to be passed by the authorities, ken, drilled and passed.

Castle Loch is now used for sailing and it was here that the Annandale Sailing Club was formed, as recalled by founder member, Paul Roxburgh, who also spoke of his love of fishing.

## Paul Roxburgh

*Have you any other memories at all?*
Well, Ah was a founder member o the Annandale Sailing Club.
*When was that? Do you remember when that was formed?*
Well, it must have been about 55 years ago.
*And what kind of boat did you sail then?*
A GP14, there were only GP14s[1] on it then. Jack Wilson was a founder
member as well [and] Sandy Smith. Ah shared a boat with a chap cawed
Bruce Beveridge, who used to have the Crown Hotel.
*That's right, in Lockerbie?*
In Lockerbie, aye, but it was a very active wee club, an of course it's thrived,
an even more so now.
*Yeah, well they draw people from a wide area.*
… Fishin was always ma great interest. Ah started off … Ah remember
Mother, ma mother, takin me to Mill Loch. She was very patient; an Ah
started the fishing in the lochs in Lochmaben. There wis coarse fishin for
perch and roach, even pike at times. And fishin the rivers, starting off with
the Ae and the Kinnel and graduating to the River Annan, catchin quite a
few trout an creepin back home at night on my bike, withoot any lights.
*Did you eat the fish that you caught from the Mill Loch?*
Oh, no, no Tom, no.
*Just put them back?*
Aye.
… Ah mentioned ma love of fishing, Ah would jist like to say that my
closest fishing companion has been Davie Shankland, we've fished for over
60 years tigither fishing the lochs an rivers an what a sad deterioration in the
quality o trout an sea trout fishing there has been in that time.
*Do you know why that is?*
Well, acid rain seemed to start it off in the Galloway lochs and there were

several times when there was disease in the River Annan that affected the trout an salmon. They blamed overfishing in the seas. The latest thing to blame is contamination from the farmed salmon, the sea lice coming off the farmed salmon an affecting the natural fish. Ah don't know whether that's true or not.

*What were some of your favourite places, then, for fishing?*

Halleaths, I liked Halleaths, and Davie an I used tae fish the Galloway hill lochs, Lairdmannoch, a wee loch called Lochinvar, up near Dalry.

*Loch Kindar would be one of them?*

No, Loch Kindar has happened in the last ten to 15 years.

*And did you ever go up to Orkney with Davie?*

No, I didnae, no.

*So, what other memories have you got of Davie then?*

Oh, Ah used tae play badminton wi Davie up at the sanatorium as well.

Another two sporting events which attracted a big following from outwith the district were the National Quoiting Championships and the Lowland Games.

## Roy Thorburn

*Another event you mentioned was National Quoiting Championships.*

Aye, the quoiting, Ah remember that quite well. It used to start, again the train used to stop, well it was just next to the station where the piece of land that they played in [was]. It looked as if hundreds of people used to get off there. And they used to start around whenever daybreak [was], probably eight in the morning, and they were they till ten o'clock at night when they were playing the finals. And it was quite an occasion that as well. Obviously, the local publicans had done exceptionally well.

*What were the quoits made of then?*

The quoits, the same shape as a horseshoe, a bit larger like, they would probably be about nine inches in diameter, and they were made of steel and they had an open end on them. An of course they used to throw these to a pin which was about, Ah'd just be guessing, it looked about 30 yards away, which they had to be pretty skilful to hit the pin. And they used to get guys that used to hold a piece of paper behind the pin which they were brave boys, so that the, what they called a marker.

*To get a better sight of the pin?*

A piece o white paper behind the pin. They used to throw these quoits and the blokes that were holding the paper never seemed to waiver but they'd obviously ... they had a lot of confidence in the competitors.

*It's a bit similar to the French boules.*

Exactly, well, aye but Ah mean—

*But they didn't roll?*

No, they were thrown through the air, like, and they were going quite a distance, Ah'd say aboot 25, 30 yards and they had tae be very skilful to hit the pin.

## George McCall

*And then there was the Lowland Games too?*

The Lowland Games, they were brilliant, they were [the] top games in the south of Scotland, they were the main games in the south of Scotland. Kirkconnel, they had them as well, they were quite good, but Lochmaben was the place and we had really top sportsmen coming and competing. It was a great affair and in fact, it was a big day out for Lochmaben, something like the Gala but it was aw sport. They had greyhound racing, M'Ghies, they had greyhounds and they had the greyhound racin. They used to have the rabbit and the greyhounds and they used to run on the tracks. And the runs, they had them stringed off for the 100-yard runs and that sort of thing. And cycle racing, country dancing, highland dancing; they had a platform and they had the highland dancing and they used to bring top pipe bands as well. Aye.

*So, who organised all that?*

Well, they had a local committee.

*Committee, aye.*

It was actually for the Lowland Games, a Lowland Games committee. Ma dad would be on it as well. He was in everything, like. Like Wilma's dad, Wilma's dad was a great worker for …

*For the community.*

## Paul Roxburgh

*You mentioned some other activities, Ah think, the Lowland Games.*

Ah remember games being held up at Riggfoot Farm, don't remember a lot about them but Ah think there were pipe bands there, but the Lowland Games were held in Stanedyke Park, off the High Street, and it was quite a big event, there were athletic meetings and even horse racing. Jim McGhie, the milkman, had a horse entered, that's one that Ah remember.

*So, it wouldn't be a milk horse?*

No, no a milk horse, no.

## Roy Thorburn

*What can you remember about the Lowland Games?*

Well, Ah recollect they used to have quite a lot of stalls in the old school playground, which is just adjacent to the church, the present church. They had horse racing, they had foot athletics, but again that was, that would probably, Ah only seen one year of that. That would be 19—, just immediately after the War, 1945, and then for some reason or other it ceased which was a great pity, like, because it was one of the, Ah believe, one o the best events in the whole area but it disappeared from the scene.

*The athletics and the horse racing, they were held in Stanedyke Park, weren't they?*

The horse racing was in Stanedyke Park. So was the athletics, of course, everything was held in the Stanedyke Park.

## Hal McGhie

*… did you have any experience of the Lowland Games before the War, in Lochmaben?*

Ah remember vaguely the Lowland Games but Ah've no experience of them. Ah'd be very young.

*Because seemingly there was horse racing in it.*

Oh, that was after the War, there was horse racing. In the Stanedyke Park.

*Yes.*

Because ma sister, Moira, fell off in one race.

… Sheena, ma oldest sister Sheena, was a good horsewoman.

*Did they still call them the Lowland Games then?*

Ah don't know what they called them, Ah can't remember, but probably.

*But they had athletics.*

Athletics, yea.

*Did they have cycling?*

Ah can't remember cycling.

*No.*

Ah remember running.

*Aye, running and the horse racing.*

Horse racing, long jumps, high jumps, whatnot, it was, aye, that was very good.

*When did that, these games stop, then?*

It must have been in the 40s, Ah can't remember them when Ah came back from the Army, no.

*That's what Ah thought, it was sort of pre-war.*

No, it was post-war.

*Was it the First War as well?*

Aye, it was post-war too.

*I mean Ina Boyer's the only person that's been able to, she gave me a photograph of the crowd, that she's in.*

Yes.

*At that time because it was a big event.*

It was, aye, it was quite a big event. I have notions that it used to be held up near Marjoriebanks, Tom.

*Ah've heard that, was it not Riggfoot?*

Yes, it was held at Riggfoot, Ah can remember ma Uncle Wullie, who thought he was a sprinter, but when the gun went off, Ah think he got a bit of a fright, he was, he didnae manage to get off his mark, he got left at the start and got beat (laughter).

*You have no other recollections?*

No, Ah just, Ah remember seeing Dyke Park and that must have been, Moira wouldnae have been riding before the War. It was after the War they had the Lowland Games, as you call them, and it was a big fun day, big, with a lot o horses.

*Yea.*

A lot of, it was a lot of events, it was a full day.

The following extracts offer a varied collection of football memories. Tom Allan recalled matches played by the local team against troops stationed at Halleaths Camp during the Second World War. Some of the soldiers had played professionally for English teams so some matches were quite a challenge for the local team. Ian Tweedie enjoyed playing football with his school friends and Bill Carrick recalled playing in the summer league and the rivalry between local teams. Five-a-side tournaments were once popular in the area and Roy Thorburn recalled the ones that he used to organise as part of the children's Gala Day festivities. Maitland Pollock played as a schoolboy and eventually chose a career in professional football. The availability of open spaces in the area providing the opportunity to play are recounted by Andre McCrae, one of the younger interviewees.

## Tom Allan

*You also mentioned that the Halleaths Camp had a football team.*

Yes, aye, they had a very, very good football team. There was about four or five players there that were actually English internationalists and of course they used to play Lochmaben regularly. But the only thing Ah was really sorry for was the Lochmaben goalkeeper, because he done nothing else but exercise, taking the ball out of the back of the net. On one occasion we went down there and it was 15–0. It wasn't a competition at all.

*It wasn't rugby, it was football?*

It was definitely football, aye (laughter).

*That was Lochmaben Rangers.*

Lochmaben Rangers, aye. Joe Lockerbie was the goalkeeper. He was an old worthy as well. He had a hard day.

*We've got photographs of Lochmaben Rangers on the web site, in fact, with Ernie Boyer in it and the Richardson brothers.*

Ernie was an exceptionally good football player. In fact, he played professional football in England, Ah don't know who for, but he certainly did and he was an exceptionally good player. An he played for Lochmaben for quite a number of seasons. When Ah was startin tae, jist aboot playing maself he, Ernie, departed from the scene o the football.

*Davie Hewitson, Ah think, was another.*

Davie Hewitson, Duncan Rankine, they formed a football team up at Kinnel Bridge, what they called Kinnel Rovers and, of course, that was a pretty competitive match when Lochmaben and Kinnel Rovers played.

## Ian Tweedie

*You played football.*

Ah played, well, during the summer holidays an that, we used to go in the morning, go back an get oor dinner, come back again and then play till about four or five o'clock.

*Before you went hame to yer tea. An where was that about, Ian? Was that at Grummel Park, was it? You played at Grummel Park, did you?*

Grummel Park, yes.

*That's right beside the school, the new school, or maybe it wasnae there at that time.*

No, it was— Aye, we played football, the pitch was just off the High Street.

*Aye, there are houses there now, of course, Ian.*

## Bill Carrick

Oh, Ah used tae play, Ah used tae gaun oot tae the Riggheads Ferm for the fitbaw.

*Riggheads?*

Summer League fitbaw, ye ken? Ye ken the summer league fitbaw, dae ye, can ye? Ah never yet saw a gem between Lochmaben an Lockerbie Accies, Ah never saw a gem feenished, never.

*What happened to them?*

Oh scrappin'.

*Really?*

Aye (laughing). Ah never saw a gem feenish, never.

*How lovely. Did you play? Did you play with them?*

Ah didnae play. Ah didnae like playin fitba. Too soft a head. Half-battered when Ah heided the ball. It pit it richt doon below ma lugs (laughing).

## Roy Thorburn

*The name Roy Thorburn's connected with two gala events, Ah think, in particular, first of all, was the football tournament. Would you like to tell us about the football tournament?*

There used to be five-a-side football tournaments in various areas, Lockerbie, Lochmaben, Johnstonebridge, they used to, all the small places used to have … five-a-side team competitions. An anyway, we decided to start one in Lochmaben, which we did, and it become quite a success.

Teams used to come from as far as Penrith an Thornhill an Dumfries, an, in fact, one particular time we were struggling tae accommodate them all. But they were very, very successful, the five-a-sides, an Ah don't know what happened but it died a death as well.

*And at its height it lasted for a full week?*

Two weeks it used to last for, aye it lasted for two weeks, an we had to limit the amount o teams. But, as Ah say, it was a great crowd-puller as well, an it's a pity it didnae continue, but well, it hasn't.

*Aye these things come in cycles.*

Exactly....

*In sport, am I right in saying that football was your main life and you mentioned briefly you've played for Glenafton Rovers? You could maybe tell people who they were.*

I played for Armadale Thistle, in Edinburgh, when Ah was 16 year old an there were two players then which were far above me, Joe and Gerry Baker they called them, Ah don't know if you ever heard of them.

*Hibs.*

Hibs, aye. Well, they were with Armadale at the time Ah was with Armadale. Ah used tae leave Lockerbie Station at six o'clock on a Saturday morning and it would be midday before Ah got to Edinburgh an Ah had tae wait till three o'clock till kick-off an then invariably Ah wasn't in the team. An Ah probably played four or five games that season for them, Ah was jist young enough, but Joe and Gerry Baker, at that particular time, both played for Armadale. An then after that Ah come home, Ah signed for Glenafton, Glenafton Athletic, which is New Cumnock. An, at that particular time, Ah was gettin £4, well just under £4, a week an ma wages were £3.

*So, you were getting more playing football for a day?*

Aye, Ah was getting more playing football. It must be a great incentive for boys nowadays. That was the comparison then, Ah mean Ah was getting this extra £4 which helped to build our first house down at Marjoriebanks, Lochmaben, there. Ah had a great passion for horses, of course, an when we were building that particular house, this £4 for the football, was keeping the thing going but Ah was really struggling. Ah put ma weekly wages one particular day, £4, on a horse called Presidium, which won the Derby at 66/1, so it was all hands go from then on....

Roy then went on to recall an occasion when he was asked, by Davie Shankland, to play in the sanatorium team against the local police team, in an annual friendly match between the two sides.

*Well, Ah think we've run through most o my questions, Ah don't know if there's any other characters you can think of.*

Well there's Davie Shankland was the other one. Davie, Ah was a great friend o Davie. We used to play football together, believe it or not, an Ah remember one year, Ah'd be aboot 19, 20, jist about when Ah was playing wi Glenafton, an Davie approached me an asked if Ah'd play for the hospital against the police. It was an annual game they had but they were gettin hammered every year by the police. An Davie said would myself and ma friend from Hightae, Glen Graham, who was a very good football player, would we play? An the police agreed tae us playin, so we played at Palmerston, an there'd be a crowd o, it was over 3000, it was for charity, Saturday afternoon. By the way, at the finish-up we won 7–6, but durin the game came the first goal. Davie was in goals, of course, and the ball went down the park, one of the boys passed the ball back, and of course there was no goalkeeper there and the ball was, that was them one up. Here was Davie round the back o the goals signing autographs for the females, durin the match (laughter). That's the kind o character he was. But he was a marvellous man.

*Yes, a man greatly missed.*

Exactly. But we won that day 7–6 against the police, an my father-in-law, which Ah didn't know then, obviously, was in goals for the police and he was six foot six an in these days you could heave the goalkeeper and of course with my build, it was no match for him but his feet were off the ground an Ah bundled him intae the net. Well, he was going to, what he was going to do tae me was nobody's business. An the next time Ah met him was when Margaret took me to her house but, fortunately for me, he didn't recognise me (laughter).

*Did you ever admit to that?*

No, but that didnae make any difference.

## Maitland Pollock

*So, you went to Lochmaben Primary and then Lockerbie?*

That's right.

*So, when did you leave?*

Ah left in 1968, when Ah played for Scotland Schoolboys. Ah had the chance to become a professional footballer, which Ah took, and Ah went to Nottingham Forest.

*So, how long were you with Nottingham Forrest?*

Ah was there five years.

*And then where did you go?*

Well, Ah stayed for the following year, because Ah signed for Walsall and then Burton Albion and Luton within the next year, but Ah stayed in Nottingham and then Ah moved to Luton after that.

One of the younger interviewees talked about footballing opportunities available to him in the town.

### Andre McCrae

> But, you know, we still have, we've got two football fields and they're free to just play in and they've both got football goals and the grass is nice and clean, it's not like all mushy or anything.

*What other things can you do?*

> There's parks and they're maintained quite well, you know, they're not just like, left to go and nobody really vandalises the stuff. And when someone does, they'll be seen because everybody knows everyone in Lochmaben, so they'll report it to the police, and they'll get in trouble, so they won't do it again. But there's a community centre and they have activities on in pretty much every day of the week and I just think they don't really have anything on, on a Sunday, but there's football on, on a Sunday, and a lot of weeks, as well, there's actual football matches at the big football pitch where Lochmaben play against other footballs teams.

Lochmaben Golf Club, has been in existence since 1926 with its course on the banks of Castle Loch. Originally a nine-hole course it was expanded to 18 holes in the 1990s. Paul Roxburgh and James McWhirter recalled the days when sheep grazed on the greens, a common practice on golf courses in the past. Hal McGhie, the club president for many years, spoke about the hard work and dedication of the members that has contributed to the expansion of the club. On returning to the area, after his career as a professional footballer, Maitland Pollock resumed his ties with the club and he explained what he has done to encourage young people to play, resulting in an increase in junior membership numbers.

### Paul Roxburgh

> Well, that's another story, how Lochmaben Golf [Club] was re-formed after the War. The greens were all fenced off because it was still used by Castle Hill Farm, they still had a lot o sheep on the golf course for many, many years after it was used, and aw the greens were fenced off to keep the sheep off them.

*They didn't have sand in the bunkers.*

> In the bunkers either, no.

### Isabel Wells and James McWhirter

*And the golf course would just be nine holes then?*

> JMcW: Nine holes an it was covered in sheep, matter o fact they virtually belonged to that ferm, Castle—

*Castle Hill.*

IW: Castle Hill, aye.
*We aye used to call it the Greigs, used to call that Greig's road.*
IW: Aye.

## Hal McGhie

*Another of your, Ah think, your achievements that you're quite proud of, is your connection to the Golf Club.*

Well, Ah've been the president of the Golf Club for as long as Ah can remember, just about.

*And what handicap did you have at your best?*

At ma best Ah was 14 which is—

*That's not bad.*

Not bad, but not good, and it's now up to 23 and Ah can't play to 23, I find it very difficult. But it's very enjoyable and it's nice to be associated with a successful club like Lochmaben. There's a lot of committee members put [in] a lot of hard work. In this past year, for example, the amount of people that have put hard work into creating a new green for the 15th hole, ye can see it now, it's starting to, the grass is starting to grow and it's looking green already. A huge amount of work that's been done. [At] Lochmaben Golf Club, the money's always spent on the course, and it's a good course. It may not have a very fancy clubhouse but it's a very good, picturesque and challenging golf course.

*When you look around, Lochmaben's been a very successful and very forward-looking club, really.*

Yes.

*They haven't sat back and expected people to come, they have attracted people.*

They've attracted people. Well, golf, you know, a few years ago there were waiting lists at the County, the Galloway, Southerness, now there really aren't any waiting lists, there's a very short waiting list for Southerness. When the economy started to bite they found that golf clubs are quite an expensive hobby and people [who] would be a member of two or three golf clubs, they've cut back to one, memberships dropped, and you have to have a, give a very attractive package to both get members and visitors and Lochmaben does that.

## Maitland Pollock

*And how many changes do you think you've seen in Lochmaben itself, I mean, from when you were a kid? Has it changed for the better or the worse?*

I'd better not say that (laughter). Some things are better. I look out here, where we're sitting just now, and this place has changed dramatically since I left in '68. The golf course has come such a long way in such a short time. And the membership, there's quite a nucleus of people who will the club to succeed, want the club to succeed, want it to be the best. Ah'm one o them Ah've got to say. Ah worked in this golf course when Ah was 13 years old, shovelling sheep manure off the greens wi the long-shank shovel and Ah got £1 a week for it. People wouldnae get out their beds for £1 nowadays. But, as Ah say, times have changed, everything else has changed. But Lochmaben as a whole, has grown quite a lot. We just need to look at Dumfries, when Ah left home there was, Ah think the population was 18,000, now it's 36,000.

*Yes, doubled. So back to the golf, then, you've become quite a* (laughs) *personality, let's say, in the golf world. What happened last year with your award?*

For the last twelve or so years Ah've coached youngsters and when Ah was captain, in 2006, of the club here, Ah noticed a huge dip in the membership in certain age groups, and Ah'd always gone around thinking, you know, people have got this wrong ... how shall I put it? They've got this ...

*Attitude, maybe?*

... feeling, the attitude that golf's an elitist sport. Yes, it's expensive at times, but it's not [elitist], anybody can play the game. There was a lack of juniors coming into the game. It does take a bit of time up, but Ah decided that Ah could help the club in some way to bring juniors on, because we didn't have a very big Junior Section. And Ah went out and got ma qualifications from the PGA [Professional Golf Association] and Ah went about the business. People got in touch with me to go into the schools, to coach, and Ah've done that for the last twelve years or so. And last year, Ah was nominated twice for the Scottish Golf Awards, Volunteer of the Year, because I don't get paid, I'm an amateur, and I prefer, at the moment, to keep ma amateur status.

*Yes.*

So, I was nominated, and I got the award, and the following week Ah got the Annandale and Eskdale Award[2] as well.

*Great.*

Which is great.

*It's a nice feeling.*

It's lovely to be recognised for something that Ah've done, in the right way. But Ah don't do it for awards, Ah do it for the club, Lochmaben Golf Club has become very, very special to me. It took over, golf took over from football in ma life when Ah finished playing and, although Ah work, Ah spend a great deal of time here. I'm the Membership Treasurer as well.

*It's a beautiful course.*

And I like to be involved, it's the setting that ... any of ma friends that come up, funnily enough Ah've got one guy that Ah played Scottish schools football with, and he's, through social media, got in touch wi me again, and he's been up and he can't believe how good this place is.

*Yes.*

And Ah think it's one of the success stories of Lochmaben and it's thriving compared with other clubs in the area that are struggling a bit.

*Yes, that's right. And how do the youngsters respond? Are you getting a number of them [attending] then?*

Ah've been fortunate that the mums and dads bring the children and they're very responsive to what Ah'm doing, they listen, they're very well behaved, Ah've only ever had to ask one child, in the hundreds o kids that Ah've coached, Ah've only asked one to sit out the session because of his behaviour. All credit to them.

*The school's got a good reputation, of course, as well.*

I think Lochmaben's always had a good reputation as far as schools and education goes. But to bring Lochmaben into the sort of national limelight was special to me.

*Yes, you should be very proud of that.*

The club have been very supportive of what Ah've tried to do. It goes down to ma wife as well, Brenda's always been there. Because you're sort of, you've got to take registers now and be disclosed and everything else.

*Oh yes, oh yes, absolutely.*

Which was not the case in our day, it was just 'go out and do it'. So Ah've got a lot of helpers, Brenda, and Davie Wright, Jimmy Lennox, so I get a bit of help now, which is great. It was hard work at the start but from the first year that I did it at the start of the season Ah got maybe eight, ten kids coming along every week and it took an hour, now it takes two and half, three hours, because we get between 20 and 30 kids every week, coming along.

*That's really good.*

And the Junior Section's starting to benefit from it which is great.

*And that'll have a knock-on effect for membership later, of course.*

Of course it has because, with being Membership Treasurer, Ah'm kinna party to all the details o the membership and it still frightens me that we have this: at the start, now, we've got quite a high volume and then in the middle, between 20 and 50, dips and that's the area that frightens me a little bit because the Seniors, shouldn't say the Seniors, but the full membership and the ageing membership is still there and it's still the highest so there's still a lot of work to do.

*Aye, it's maybe a lot of people are at work and then they don't have the time, they say that they don't have the time and then it's a …*

Then there's the money. This area's not the most affluent area in country.

*No, no, exactly, exactly.*

And the first thing that goes if— Let's just say a young lad wants to play golf, he wants to go out on a Saturday night with his pals but he hasn't got enough money.

*Yes.*

What does he choose?

*I know, I know, it's difficult, very difficult. And then you maybe find that some folk maybe go away to college and university as well.*

    That's the other thing, you lose a lot between 18 and 20 because they're at university or college and everything else.

*We need to keep them here.*

    It's difficult, yes, we've got a university in Dumfries now but it's not the same as going away to Heriot Watt or something like that.

Other activities to the community were bowling, snooker and badminton. There is a bowling club in the town and Hazel Sloan spoke about change in its membership demographic over time. We hear that the sport was open to all age groups. Indoor bowling is also popular and played in the local community centre. There was a snooker hall in the town and Paul Roxburgh recalled working there in the evenings, for pocket money, when he was a youngster.

## Hazel Sloan

*So, can you tell me a bit more about the bowling? I mean did you join the bowling [club] when you first came to the area?*

    Not quite, ma children were small but Ah've been a member at the bowling, I think, since 1972.

*1972. So what's, what was the situation with women bowlers at that time?*

    Well, men previous to that, we opened in 1890, Ah think it was.

*Oh, that's right.*

    The club was started and it was only men that was in it then and I'm not quite sure when ladies were invited but in 1972 the proportion was two-thirds men.

*Really.*

    One third women.

*And it's changed now, it must be the other way round, is it?*

    Nowadays we have, last year we had 41 lady members and 25 men.

*That's strange isn't it, it's very different. And that's the outdoor bowling.*

    Yes.

*What about indoor bowling?*

    Well, we have a local community centre where there is various activities but we do have a Tuesday morning and a Wednesday morning for short mat bowling and we just come and play, you don't need a membership fee, you just pay as you come and on an average each day there might be 20 people playing.

*That's good and that's various age groups as well.*

    Various age groups, definitely, yes, uh huh.

*Good, good.*

## Beth Corrie

*Your granny does bowling, do you not fancy doing some bowling?*

My brother did bowling, actually.

*Uh huh?*

He used to come along with Granny when he was in nursery and he used to love it. And then, but he was so disappointed when Granny doesn't do the outdoor one because he loves that.

*Uh huh, it's got a lovely pitch, a lovely green down there.*

Do they do the younger ones?

*I think they sometimes encourage some of the younger ones, yes, the ones—*

If they wanted to do that.

*It's always possible, there's bowls, I think, for younger, you know, small ones for younger people.*

That'd be good.

*And there's the tennis as well, and golf.*

I used to play tennis and golf actually. Russel's got my golf clubs now, handed them down.

## Paul Roxburgh

In the winter Ah used tae go to Joe Crolla's Snooker Hall, do you know where that is?

*No, Ah don't.*

No? What dae you call that wee vennel?

*Blacklocks Vennel?*

Blacklocks Vennel, aye, there's council houses built there now. Joe Crolla, who had the chip shop, had a snooker hall there and ma mother didnae approve o me going but anyway, Ah still went, an Ah used tae mark the scores up. There was a game called skittles, it was a gambling game, played on the snooker table and we yaist tae get 1s for half an hour's markin the tables up an did it for maybe two or three hours tae get 4s or 5s. An then we went an blew the lot on the skittles, the snooker tables maself, aye.

*An that was burnt down, was it, did you say?*

No, no it wisnae burnt down Tom.

*Was it demolished?*

It wis demolished to make [room for] council houses, that's another story (laughter).

*And that is, again, is separate from to the building next to it which had the …*

Oh aye, the recreation hall …

*Recreation Hall.*

… where they played the carpet bowling

*Did you ever go up there then?*

Occasionally, ma aunt yaist tae clean that, so she used to take me in, Ah was always curious about it. There were public toilets doon that wee road as well, next door to the snooker hall.

*Ah wonder if the facility was connected to the changing rooms that are there now, the water supply or the drainage, maybe.*

Aye, maybe Tom aye, there was an old chap cawd Jack Handby who had a shed down there and he used to sell kindlers.

Badminton was also a popular sport as recalled by Hal McGhie

## Hal McGhie

*You did work hard but you also had some recreation that you kept going.*

Well, badminton suited the hours we worked very well and Ah played badminton all winter. They were all, the churches had, a churches' badminton league and you could play badminton six nights a week, if you wanted to, without moving very far, so Ah played badminton. Ah played table tennis when Ah was in the Army a bit too, which Ah still do occasionally, I've a table tennis table in the basement that we still use occasionally, not as much as we used to.

*Well, they're looking for members for the Dumfries, the Lochmaben table tennis.*

Well, Ah'll go and try it (laughs).

*Anyway, age is no barrier.*

No.

*Ah mean that is interesting to hear about badminton when now there's not a lot of badminton played because there's been the rise in all these other sports.*

Yes. Ah think there's still quite a reasonable amount of badminton played but not an awful lot. Ah mean, we played it in Malaya, it was outdoor badminton, we played there.

*Of course, they're very good at it.*

Yes, and we used to play, in general you got a calm about six o'clock in the morning and you would play from six to seven and then come home, come back to the camp. We played [UNCLEAR] in Taiping in a league of sorts. So, badminton was, it was a good mixer, it's a good mixing game because both sexes play badminton, so you meet the opposite sex.

*Good social occasion.*

Good social life, yes.

Going to 'the pictures', a popular pastime enjoyed by several of the interviewees when they were young, is recalled in the following extracts. George McCall remembered films first being shown in a tent in a field and then, after the Second World War, a disused church building being converted to a cinema. He also spoke about a circus which came to town. Isabel Wells and James McWhirter remembered playing with their friends and pretending to be the heroes and heroines of the films they had seen on the big screen. James also recalled travelling to Lockerbie to attend the Saturday matinee screenings. Many of these films were of the popular 'Western' genre recalled by Ian Tweedie.

## George McCall

*There would have been some entertainment going on. What can you remember of that?*

Well, the entertainment was, there were jist ordinary sport, there wis football. The dancing of course, there were always dances going on every week, that was all really. We just sort of found our own entertainment, really. As a boy, Ah spent a lot of time in the wood, down at the Bogs down there, we used to build bridges and stuff like that, and we had great fun. The cinema started just after the War finished, a chap called Cummings, Mr Cummings, he was a real gentleman, but he hadnae the money to do it like, he tore the church to pieces to make it into a cinema an Ah don't think he could afford it.

*That was the one at the Barras?*

Aye, the one at the Barras.

*It got off tae a bad start?*

Well, the first film was *Lassie Come Home,* and it kept breaking down and it put people off, but at the finish-up Ah think he just completely gave up.

*When it was operating though, were there a large number of people went there to the cinema? They liked going?*

Oh yes, it was well supported for a wee while anyway, aye. It was quite good but Ah don't think he would make a lot of money out o it.

*And you were saying that the circus used to come occasionally?*

The circus used to come once a year, Pinder's Circus. They used tae have an animal parade.

*Through the High Street?*

Jist down at the High Street, Queen Street. There was a tap there wi a basin an we used to go in there and see the elephants drink the water and squirt it out. It was great, aye, and it was well supported as well. Ah think the animals finished the circuses, when they stopped using the animals.

*Yes, aye. An you also remember a ghost show that used to come?*

Aye, Biddle's ghost, Biddle's ghost, and Henry's pictures of course, I forgot about that.

*Aye, Henry's.*

Henry's pictures, aye, that was the first cinema, that was a cinema as well, but it was done in a tent as well. An it wis doon Jeannie's field, what they called Jeannie's field, opposite where the park is, the Mill Park, these are houses. It was just one big billboard at that time for, you know how they used to advertise soaps and everything, it was a billboard.

*Aye, keep everybody informed about things?*
> Everybody, aye.

## Isabel Wells and James McWhirter

*So, across the road, you played there, then?*
> JMcW: In the builder's yard.
>
> IW: In the builder's, aye, we used to make, well, the lassies made wee hooses oot o the builder's blocks, we made them into wee squares, you got chairs made and everything (laughter) using your imagination.
>
> JMcW: Used tae be a fight wi the lassies whae wis gonna be Esther Williams.
>
> IW: Esther Williams, aye, Esther Williams.
>
> JMcW: Or Jane, fae Roy Rogers, is the best (laughter).
>
> IW: That's right, aye.

*You're talking about films. Did you go to any films, did you go into Dumfries or Lochmaben?*
> JMcW: Oh yes, aye.

*You went to that one did you?*
> IW: Oh, aye.

*So, that was still going in the '50s an that, at the Barras?*
> IW: The Barras, aye, that would gaun on for quite a while, Jimmy, when we were young.
>
> JMcW: It did actually, Ah can mind gaun up there and watching the pictures a lot.

*Can you remember some of the films you saw?*
> JMcW: Maist o them wis cowboy films like Tim Holt and Hop-Along Cassidy, Roy Rogers (laughter).

*Oh Roy Rogers, and was it expensive to get in or—?*
> JMcW: Oh, [it] would be aboot sixpence Ah would think. An then when it shut down we went tae Lockerbie in the afternoon, [the] matinee.
>
> IW: The Rex on a Saturday, aye, get the bus. Ah think one and thrupence would get ye intae the pictures and get ye on the bus as well.
>
> JMcW: That's right, aye.

*Aye, so it was cheap entertainment.*
> IW: It wis, aye.
>
> J McW: The boys didnae get the bus, they walked hame an kept the money (laughter).

*That's quite a long walk. You wouldnae get kids doin that nowadays.*

## Ian Tweedie

> Aye, aye, and then there used tae be the picture house, of course, the picture house.

*That was at the Barras.*

Yes.

*You were at the Barras at the picture house quite often, were you?*

Aye, oh, many a time, aye.

*Do you remember any pictures there?*

Oh, it was the cowboys.

*Cowboys and Indians?*

Indians, aye, Roy Rogers and company.

*I was probably watching the same pictures where Ah was brought up too, cause cowboy pictures were very popular at that time weren't they?*

Yes, aye.

*Aye, they were.*

Because we used to sit right at the front.

*Yea, dodge the bullets eh, dodge the bullets, aye?*

Aye.

Dancing was another popular pastime. Isabel Wells and James McWhirter speak about some of the venues and dance bands that they enjoyed.

### Isabel Wells and James McWhirter

IW: … in thaim days, even when ye were a teenager, there wis lots of dances like at Johnstone and Hightae and that, an you walked, ken.

*Anything in Lochmaben? Balcastle would be around by that time was it?*

IW: Well, we never really, … my daughters went there but we didnae go there. They had dances in the Toon Hall.

JMcW: Oh aye, they did.

*So, the Town Hall was quite well used?*

IW: Oh aye, it was used quite a lot.

*And that's upstairs was it?*

JMcW: Aye, that's where aw the Christmas parties were for the weans and that.

IW: Aye, that's right.

*Oh, I've heard about these parties, Ah know there was one after the War ended, a big Christmas party, but was it a regular thing?*

JMcW: The dances maybe wid be aboot one a month or something.

IW: Something like that aye, but there would be a lot of folk there.

JMcW: Oh aye.

IW: It wisnae just two or three, there would be a lot o people.

*And was it a live band or—?*

JMcW: They played as if they were half-dead (laughter).

IW: Aye, some o them would be, sometimes ye got yin like the Wamphray band.

JMcW: The Wamphray band. The yin that auld Willie Edwards had, the

Run Rig or somethin.

IW: Oh, Ah cannae mind. But it was him an his twae brothers.

JMcW: An Davy, him an his twae brothers, …

IW: Aye, Davy Edwards an then there wis Jimmy that steyed in Moffat, he played in that.

JMcW: Cos Ah can mind o saying tae him, when Ah was gaun in the door, tae auld Wullie, Ah says: 'Dae ye no get issued wi ear plugs?'

He says: 'What dae ye want ear plugs for?'

'For that noise.' (Laughter).

*So, what kind of dances then, were they waltzes or was it Scottish dances?*

JMcW: St Bernard's Waltz, the Gay Gordons.

IW: That kinnae thing.

*They're Scottish dances.*

JMcW: That's right.

*Cos Ah remember learning that at school, you know, ye did that?*

IW: Aye, that's right, ye did.

JMcW: It used to be quite guid, you'd get aw the boys standin in this corner an all the lassies in that other corner (laughs).

*Exactly.*

IW: Aye they didnae, well they seem to mix mair noo.

This chapter ends with Hal McGhie and Wilma Twidale, who talked about their personal hobbies. First Hal explained his love of horse racing, an interest that he inherited from his father.

## Hal McGhie

*You were very modest when Ah asked you about your ability with horses, but you said that your interest in horses was confined to certain mundane tasks.*

Well, ma father didn't think Ah had the necessary skills. Apart from that Ah was too heavy, by the time Ah was 16 Ah was eleven stone so …

*No good for a jockey.*

… not very good for a jockey but Ah didn't have the skills anyway. Animals didn't take to me, although Ah did ride them out, one of them. He had a black mare, we called it Trixie, it was called West Croft, that Ah used to ride occasionally. We'd ride, go out walking, walk them for four or five miles or six miles and Ah could handle that one, Ah was very friendly with her. But Ah wisnae any good at tackling horses that had a bad temperament so Ah would groom them when they came back, clean out the boxes do whatever.

*You were doing the real work.*

Well, it wasn't the real work, it was menial work.

*You mentioned that your father had some success as a trainer, and you mentioned flapping races[3]. Could you maybe say a little more about that, please?*

Ah remember after the War there was gymkhanas which were held locally, there was one in Lochmaben, there were New Galloway, there was gymkhanas in Dumfries, everywhere, where he competed on horses. It was things like the saddling up race where you rode a horse bareback and picked up the saddle, put the saddle on and raced back.

*Ah, yes.*

There was the Musical Poles where there was a potato or something on a pole and when the music stopped you all dived in and grabbed whatever it was on the top of the pole. Apart from gallops, and ma father was very good at that, he was a good horseman, very good with animals. Apart from being a farrier he had a good eye and then he graduated to flapping. He had been involved, at Halleaths, when the Johnstone's at Halleaths had their own private stable. The last trainer I remember being there was a bloke, Davy, who went on to train in Yorkshire, at Malton. But he learned about racehorses at Halleaths and shoeing racehorses and about the ailments that racehorses had and he took to flapping. I mean his most famous horse in flapping was a horse called Annandale, it won the Tradesmen's Handicap, which was the principal race at the Hawick Common Riding, three years in succession. Ah think it was carrying about 13½ stone the last time it won, it was a big sprinter.

*That's interesting, Ah mean, again, Ah met Geordie Rome who was the factor at Halleaths.*

He wisnae, Ah don't think. Was he the factor?

*Oh, maybe not.*

He worked at Halleaths, yes, Ah remember the house he lived in.

*Ah remember him telling me, I was intrigued at the two long fields down from the stables …*

Yes.

*… Ah didn't appreciate that the horses were…*

There was a gallop there.

*Yea, a gallop area and sadly, Ah think, they have not kept these long fields as a sort of historical memento. Ah think they're all split up now.*

Well, Ah think agriculture's more important (laughter).

*Aye, you couldn't argue that they should keep a field for a historical reason, Ah suppose.*

That's an expensive hobby, keeping fields for historical reasons.

Hal talked about several of the racehorses he went on to own and had some success with.

Well, this is the experiences as an owner of racehorses, which goes back away to the 1960s. Ma father talked us into, the four boys, into buying a share in a horse. It should have put us off forever because the horse was a total disaster. But anyway, we got into others later on. Ah had, in 1982, Ah bought a half share in a horse called Able Albert, that finished up winning the Ayr Gold Cup and went to Holland to stand at stud. That was quite successful. Ah had, when Lennie Lungo came and opened at Hetland he talked me into buying a horse, Wattle Syke, that managed to win a seller but it was not very good and then after that Ah had Attadale, which was probably ma favourite horse of all time. He was a lovely horse with a good temperament, and he won a lot of regular races. He didnae win any very big races but he won a lot of races, both in the flat and principally over hurdles. He won six hurdles in a row one season and then two the next season and then Ah was out of them for a wee while. Well, we had, after Attadale, I had Noyan, who went on to win the Punchestown Heineken Gold Cup, at Punchestown. Now, at this particular stage, Ah've just got one horse called Ginger Jack, that's been doing reasonably well, he was second at York last week. Unfortunately, I couldn't go, because Ah was at a wedding. So, horse racing's been a bit mixed, some successes, quite a lot of failures, but not very financially successful, but Ah've had some very nice days' horse racing.

*But it's interesting that that is a continuation of what your father was interested in.*
Yes. He talked me into buying the first horse Ah had, Caxton Hall, on ma own, which won a race but it won a race Ah had a big gamble on, away back, Ah think that was in about 1978. And he had the horse called Asset that, when he died, Ah fell heir to, and it was a nice horse as well. So, he wanted me to get involved because he liked to have influence [over] what I'd be doing but Ah've maybe been a little more successful since he died. Ah still wish Ah had his knowledge of horses, particularly of the confirmation and what to look for in a horse. It's difficult, you either have an eye for that or you don't.

*Ah, so you can't teach that form.*
Ah think it's very difficult to teach it, it's like judging cattle, Ah think, judging horseflesh, there's different things to do but the top people like the Irish, Ah think's the ultimate person on how to make the money out of horse racing because he does it very successfully and he's done it for 30 years.

Hal also spoke about his keep fit regimes.

*Now, you don't look your age, if Ah may say so. How do you keep fit?*
Well, ma wife helps me to keep fit. Ah do a bit of walking, Ah play golf, Ah do a form of Canadian Air Force exercises once a week, sometimes twice a week, which keeps me reasonably flexible, just bending and stretching, more or less. Although I'm not very good at bending and stretching nowadays, Ah still manage to do it. Ah've a fairly healthy diet.

*You also mentioned that when you go to the likes of Majorca, you indulge in another activity.*

Well, it's mostly Portugal we go to, and we've bicycles in Portugal and we, once we get there, we're on the bike, I'm on the bike every day, play golf two or three times a week, walk quite a lot, eat a lot of fish and find it a very healthy atmosphere and I come back not needing a holiday, feeling refreshed.

Some hobbies are non-competitive and quite personal. Wilma Twidale explained how she spent her free time.

## Wilma Twidale

*… I know, time flies, doesn't it? But you do your art and singing and—*
Well, Ah mean, Ah never have a problem filling ma days, from the time Ah retired things jist seemed to start coming ma way that Ah wanted tae do. Ah go to ma art class now, Ah sing in the choir, Ah'm an elder of the church, an Ah have the Guild, I read for the blind.
*Oh, you do that as well, yes, very good.*
Once a fortnight, Ah do that. But I haven't been since the New Year because Ah haven't been well, hopefully Ah'm going this week. That's in Dumfries. And what else do Ah do? Ah love doing crosswords.
*And you've got a lovely collection of owls* (laughter).
Oh yes, ma owls just kind of, Ah don't know Ah jist thought, Ah'd been given one in a present an Ah was in the chemist's one day and Ah saw this one. It's a Royal Albert an Ah jist fancied it, an Ah bought it, an that was the start and now—
*How many have you got?*
Ah think they hatch out when Ah'm no looking (laughter), people keep buying me them.
*Well, that's the thing.*
An really, Ah'm running out of space.
*You must have about what, 200?*
Ah've got more than 200.
*Oh yes, anyway, yes.*
This is ma latest acquisition.
*Oh, my goodness.*
Ma granddaughter brought me that from Vietnam.
*Oh, lovely.*
And it's made of marble, feel the weight.
*Oh yes, it's heavy, yes, an it's lovely it's beautifully carved.*
An hasn't it got an oriental look?
*Yes, yes, the sheen of the marble as well, that's lovely.*
She gave me it for Christmas an she brought it from Vietnam.
*So, there's never a problem of what to get you for your present.*

Well, no, but Ah mean Ah'm really running out of space, very rapidly.

*You'll need to get some shelves.*

Very rapidly. You start a hobby and through there Ah've have got donkeys.

*Donkeys?*

It was donkeys, Ah started out to collect but they sort of seemed to go out of fashion.

*I think everybody likes owls.*

I think they do, Ah think they do.

# The War and Military Life

On 3 September 1939, Lochmaben's town crier announced the start of the Second World War. In the days and weeks that followed, while locals began to leave town to enlist in the armed forces, the town became a hub of military activity. Most of the interviewees were born in the 1920s, '30s and '40s and had childhood memories of the military presence in the area during the War.

The first five selected extracts give us an insight into the awareness of these children of the preparations for combat that were taking place in the area. They also recall lying in bed listening to German bombers passing overhead and, later when peace had been declared, being given and playing with toys which the prisoners of war in the local camps had made for them.

### George McCall

*George, you would you be in Lochmaben when war broke out, were ye?*

Ah was in Lochmaben when war broke out, yes, 1939, 3rd September 1939.

*And how was it announced in the parish?*

It was announced by the town crier, which was a Mr Trotter at that time. An he went round wi a bell and announced that war had broke out. Well, Ah wis young at the time, but Ah went and seen some of the locals away on the train, that was conscripted. Conscription just started in 1939, just more or less when war was declared.

*And how many men would go away from Lochmaben? Quite a few?*

Ah, when Ah went, there were a few but even at that time Ah would say there were about five: Bobby Bell, oh there were, a cannae remember, Tommy Mitchell, Peter Mitchell, Wilson's son got killed, some o them wis in the Army before the War, of course.

*Before the War, yes, right. And did they leave Lochmaben on the train, did they?*

They went on the train.

*To Lockerbie or something?*

Lochmaben.

*Aye, but to Lockerbie an then away.*

Aye. That was the start of the War.

*But it was tough times again, was it, during the War years? It would still be tough, aye.*

Yes, it was tough during the War because there was rationing, and stuff was very, very scarce, because the shipping was all upset and everything, in the war years.

*... you mentioned Halleaths, though?*

Halleaths Camp, well Ah can start off. That was the first that we saw o the War, how it was affecting us. Ah cannae jist remember how long it wis after war was declared, but we found that there were aboot 250 men frae the Royal Engineers came to Lochmaben to build the camp, and they were billeted in Lochmaben, in the houses, people took them in. They were, of course, fed in the church hall an the cookin was all done in the wee houses along tae the right of the church hall ... I don't know if you know the Aldersons, or no, decorators, Terence?

*Aye.*

His dad was one o the cooks an he married in Lochmaben.

*Oh, right, I see.*

After the camp was built, for some reason or another, they sent men fae every regiment in the British Army, Ah'm sure, there were. There were Welsh men with their fancy uniforms an aw the sort o replica gear on, the regiments, an they aw came tae the camp. An [of] course the next thing we heard that the camp wis, that they were gonna turn intae one regiment, which become the First Reconnaissance Corps.

*So, it was a post for British soldiers then, was it?*

It was a post for British soldiers, yes, aye. It wis a big camp, it wis a big camp. The square's still there yet, the parade square. We used to go down there, they used tae allow us to go down for entertainment, dos, parties, concerts, things like that. Dancing, and it was quite good. One of the local worthies, Smith, they called him, his nickname was the Aga Khan, he was a sergeant an he wis a drill instructor. He wis very sore on the men, really. In fact, a lot of them used tae say they wanted to kill him (laughter), that was the Aga Khan. But he was a Lochmaben man, actually, an for some reason he was posted. He had a family in Lochmaben, they had rough times.

*... apart from the camp, was there any other signs about the place of the War?*

Yes, Millhousebridge, that big mansion house that belonged [to the] Jardines, Ah cannae remember the name o it.

*Jardine Hall.*

Jardine Hall, aye, it was a hospital.

*It was a hospital?*

Yes. Now another thing that Ah wanted tae say wis that ..., next door tae where Ah stayed there was a British Legion hut and the S[A]S [Special Air Service] took it over. Now the S[A]S, ... trained here and up the Mill Road was the gas house. There was this big chimney and they used tae do a lot o work training and that, house to house fighting and that sort of thing, in the area, and that detachment that was trained in Lochmaben, they were first, on D-Day, to land on the beaches.

*Oh, is that right?*

An the Major that was in charge o them got killed just at the beginnin o the War. The field was a big camp area. It was mair or less, ye could say, it was the 4th Field Hygiene Section, it was the RAMC [Royal Army Medical Corps] and they supplied the laundries, the laundry for the hospital and aw the camps round about. There was Millbank where the 10th Battalion, the Black Watch, they were stationed there an they used to come with their band, they yaist tae come an play at Lockerbie, Lochmaben and round about. The aerodrome was operating, it was a big affair as well, the RAF over at Heathhall, Dumfries.

*At Heathhall, aye.*

It wis a big affair, an they had a military band as well, and they yaist tae come an play. Ah think that's what made my love for military bands.

## Paul Roxburgh

Anyone in Lochmaben who had spare bedrooms was asked to billet soldiers from the local camp at Halleaths. Sweeties were very, very scarce, even for a shopkeeper's son. We were lucky, we had two soldiers, Royal Engineers, billeted with us, they used tae bring me wine gums fae the NAAFI at Halleaths. That was their greatest asset as far as Ah was concerned. An toys, a lot o the toys that we were given were made by German prisoners o war. Beautiful aeroplanes, you know, wooden planes, handmade by the prisoners of war, an they were exceptional toys.

*They were prisoners of war that were … camped at Halleaths, were they?*

No, no, there were no prisoners o war at Halleaths. The big prisoner-o-war camp was at the Barony, … up Parkgate actually, no at the Barony itself. Ah think the ground would belong to the Barony, but [there was] a really big prisoner-o-war camp at Parkgate.

*So that's where the toys would come from, then?*

Parkgate, aye, mind, a lot o the prisoners were released ontae working on farms, immediately after the War, the ones that didnae want to go back home, and they might have made quite a few o them after they were released. The Army camp, of course, was a very exciting place for a young boy. An aw the activities associated wi it, particularly in the lochs where the soldiers built jetties an Bailey bridges. An the empty houses, the derelict houses in Princes Street, where they practised hand-to-hand fighting, thunder flashes flying, really, really great stuff for a young boy, an collectin empty bullet shells, but you know there werenae live bullets, they were jist dummies, but aw really worth collecting. An the soldiers used to have manoeuvres up in the hills at, what dae ye call it?

*Is that Beacon Hill?*

The Beacon, right along there, used to have night manoeuvres and used mortar flares wi wee parachutes on them. An these were really great, collectable items on some o ma walks up over the hills.

*That is interesting, I didn't appreciate so much had taken place in Lochmaben itself.*

Oh, aye.

*At that time Halleaths House would still be there, was it occupied by ...?*

It would be the officers; Ah believe the officers were billeted there. They used to have, an odd time, open days at the camp as well, where ye could have a walk round and that was a really exciting day, anything to do with the Army. There were Royal Engineers there mainly, but there were also soldiers belonging to the Reconnaissance Corps. Ah don't know exactly what they did, they were a sort [of] mysterious unit, they didn't partake in the manoeuvres, as far as I can remember, the same as the Royal Engineers did.

... Ah remember talking to Ernie Boyer as well. Do you remember Ernie?

*Yeah, I remember Ernie.*

An Ah knew Ernie had came tae Lochmaben during the War, an Ah never realised what he had done durin the War. Did you know?

*No, no Ah didn't.*

Ernie was in an Observation Unit at Skipmyre Farm, I'd no idea there was such a thing, for the Air Force. An he was attached tae the RAF at Chapelcross, Ah think, an it was constantly manned, an he spent his war days manning that Observation Unit.

*He was a very dapper gentleman.*

Oh, aye, great football player.

*And he latterly worked for McCall Wells.*

He did, aye, he was a foreman. Ah remember as a young boy in ma bedroom, and tae think of that, how the windaes used to frost up in the winter, an ye could write your name on the windows in the morning, beautiful frosted patterns. An lying in bed at night, [Ah] heard the German bombers going over tae Clydebank. We must hae been in the direct route, an they had a particularly loud noise, a distinctive noise, the German bombers. It was really quite exciting an in the distance, it must have been doon about Gretna, there were searchlights going, Ah never saw a German bomber.

*Of course, that might have been connected to the Mossbank munitions[1] there, having searchlights at Gretna.*

Aye.

*That would have been one of the places they might have been targeting.*

Aye, that's right.

*Did you have blackout at home?*

Yes, aye, an of course the vehicles had their headlights blacked out as well, God knows how they could see.

## Roy Thorburn

*You have several memories of life in Lochmaben during the War. Can you tell us about what went on at Townhead?*

Well, at the Townhead, there were derelict cottages there. They used to do exercises, Army exercises, combat training and so forth. There was bullets and hand grenades, and goodness knows what, left lying all over the place, there was no difficulty in going and collecting these.

*Were they live?*

They were live. We used to put the bullets in a wall and hit them with a nail, which was a very dangerous practice when you think about it now. As Ah said before to Tom, here, Ah had a hand grenade we found. We took this hand grenade out to the outskirts of Lochmaben which, again, was probably a bit foolish but we were about nine, ten, year old then, pulled the pin, threw it away and lay there for about six hours waiting for it tae explode, which it didn't do. I got into a bit of bother with my old man because it was dark by the time we got home and that's one of the vivid ones Ah remember.

*They also used the lochs for another activity, the Mill Loch and the Kirk Loch.*

Oh yes, during the War the Mill Loch …. They had a pontoon bridge across there from approximately the swimming pool and Vendace Drive, an Ah remember one occasion they lost a tank there. The water's very, very deep in that particular place and they also had a jetty at the Kirk Loch, which is still visible to this day.

… There was a lot of activity. The soldiers used to run past our front door. They used to do the circuit from round Halleaths to Lochmaben, back to Halleaths. The first soldiers would come through, maybe one or two and then about an hour and a half later you seen the ones, the tail-enders. You'd wonder where they had went to on a three mile [exercise], it was takin them a very, very long time. So that was the less fit soldiers, there. But anyway, I also remember an American, Ah must have been very young, a convoy coming up through Marjoriebanks, the soldiers in it, it was going very, very slowly and they were throwing chocolates and sweets out, so it was quite an experience actually, something you only seen once in a lifetime. But again, that would be probably about 1940, 1941.

## Ian Tweedie

*So, your dad was called up to the War you said.*

Yes.

*An he went off to fight.*

Uh huh.

*Do you know much about his war service? Where did he go?*

Oh, well he went, he was in the Gloucestershire Regiment an he come out at Dun—

*So, he must have been in Europe fighting.*

Yes.

*An then he [came] back, came out at Dunkirk?*

Dunkirk, uh huh, an then he got discharged.

*He got discharged after that? Had he been hurt or something?*

Ah don't know that.

*An then he came back to Lochmaben?*

Lochmaben, aye.

*And do you remember any difference when the War was on?*

The War?

*Ah mean anything about what life was like in Lochmaben during the War?*

Yes, Ah can. Do you want, they used tae, you know about Halleaths?

*Aye, Halleaths, the big house, aye.*

Aye, an … the soldiers used to come and go to the picture house and things like that. An then they used to walk them from Halleaths tae the train, in a big mass. Because one o the times, there wis a lot this day an they were aw walkin down the street towards the station an then aboot, och, a wee while later we were told that the boat that they went on had been sunk.

*An Ian, you said there was something that you remember about the Kirk Loch where they used to practice landings and things and building things, the Engineers.*

No, the, what do you call it, the Mill Loch?

*The Mill Loch was it? Right, ok.*

The Mill Loch, aye. … what was the name o the farm?

*Robson's farm was it?*

Yea, they used tae go up there an then they used tae come down the field and they'd get intae a boat and they'd to come just across the loch an come up the street at Lochmaben and they used to shoot their way up there, and there was smoke and everything.

*Ah've heard before about people finding bullets and things. Did you ever find any of them?*

Aye, we had the thunder flashes as well.

*You'd have a bit of fun with them, had you?*

Oh aye, oh aye, well there wis three o us were always together an we found two thunder flashes.

*Thunder flashes. And you'd jist tae throw them away did you?*

No, we used to drop them an whatever. … Jimmy and me used to … take it out of the, what do you call it?

*The casings.*

The casing aye, and get [it] intae a piece o paper and set it alight, but this other young man took it into the house an he had a bit of wire in the house at the front o the fire an [makes exploding noise] … what a row we got.

*I bet. I'm sure you did, aye.*

Oh, aye, aye. But they say that there was up Queen Street, an then up, what's the other street?

*Princes Street?*

… there was a house there, right, that's Princes Street. There was a house here an this is Queen Street an they used tae fight their way across there an at this, here, there was a wall an they used to throw smoke over an jump over, aye.

*Oh, right? Trying to show what it would be like in war conditions.*

Aye.

*Yes, so that must have been quite interesting.*

Aye, it was aye, aye.

*And there were quite a lot of soldiers around Lochmaben.*

Oh aye, we used to gaun tae the golf course when the guys were there wi their girlfriends in the town and we used to follow them.

*Aye, right okay, typical boys eh?*

## Hal McGhie

*What do you remember about Halleaths Camp during the War?*

Well, there were obviously a lot of soldiers, Ah think they were Engineers or in the Pioneer Corps, and Engineers there. They had soldiers billeted out in Lochmaben an the church hall, Ah think, was used as a sort of dining area or canteen of some sort and 6 Princes Street, which wasn't our neighbours by then, because we'd moved into 10 Princes Street, was, Ah think they had a soup kitchen, a kitchen in it, where they fed the soldiers. Ah remember them building the bridges or starting to build bridges out into the Kirk Loch and, of course, there were always various activities there. Ma father … became the captain in the Home Guard and they would have exercises when the Home Guard would take on the regular soldiers. A bit of a Captain Mainwaring, except ma father wisnae quite like Captain Mainwaring.

*So, could you maybe explain, [for] people who are quite young, what the Home Guard was? What was the role of the Home Guard?*

I think it was originally called the LDV, the Local Defence Force [Local Defence Volunteers], which we called it the LDV, the Look, Duck and Vanish (laughter). But it was supposed to be in place in case we were invaded, and we were supposed to repel the invaders. How effective it would have been, Ah think it was slightly more than, it would have been more effective than it was in Dad's Army, but how effective it would have been against a German Panzer Division, I doubt it very much.

*Did you see any combat training in the streets in Lochmaben then?*

No.

*Just when ye were talking about building into the Kirk Loch, one person Ah inter-*
*viewed remembers a sort of Bailey bridge across at the Mill Loch, you don't?*

Ah can never remember it for the Mill Loch.

*And they said that one of the tanks, or whatever, crossing, fell in the Mill Loch. Ah*
*don't know if this is a story or not, Ah don't know.*

Ah don't know, Ah can't remember it.

… Ah remember them working on the Kirk Loch because we would tend to
go, when we came home from school, we'd sometimes come home over the
golf course.

*The wee stumps in the Kirk Loch are supposed to be relics of that.*

They were relics, in fact they were definitely relics of them building the
bridges.

*I suppose they were preparing for the D-Day invasion.*

Well, Ah don't know whether it was, Ah don't think that was done here, but
they were preparing to build bridges, the Engineers, it was practicing. It was
a different system they used for the D-Day landing, Ah think.

The next five extracts are from Paul Roxburgh, Ian Tweedie, Hal McGhie, Tom
Allan and Roy Thorburn. After the Second World War these young men were all
called up for National Service in the decade following its ending. While inter-
rupting their working life, this nonetheless gave them an opportunity to travel the
world and to take part in significant events in the places that they were posted to.
While serving in the Army, Paul trained as a tactical sketcher, drawing maps,
and Ian, Hal and Tom were deployed to Malaysia. Roy, who joined the RAF, was
selected for the camp football team, travelling to RAF bases in Europe at weekends to play in competitions.

## Paul Roxburgh

Oh aye, when Ah was 18 Ah was served notice that Ah was required for His
Majesty's Service for two years, doing National Service, or conscription as
they called it. All young men were called on, at the age of 18, to do two years
in the Army, Navy or RAF, usually the Army, you were very, very lucky tae
be selected for the Navy. An generally it was the Army unless ye were physically unfit to do it or in one o their selected occupations [so] that you
werenae required to do it. Because Ah was running the shop at the time, Ah
applied for exemption and had tae go before a tribunal in Ayr and got a
year's deferment. But a year later they were back again an it was probably
futile, I'd hae been better gaun in the first place.

*So, you were called up for National Service, where did you go?*

… while Ah was workin in the shop, the van man left so we were left withoot
a van man an Ah would be jist turned 17 at the time. Ah had tae go onto the
van an, of course, Ah hadnae a driving licence so Ah had tae apply for a

driving licence and set off in the van. Ah applied for a driving test an took lessons an after two months luckily managed to pass my driving test at ma first go. Ah was stopped by the local police sergeant two days later an aw he said was, 'Thank God ye've passed yer driving test.' So, he was quite sympathetic to our plight. But, as Ah was saying, a year later Ah was called up for National Service. Ah've explained tae ye what National Service was, an Ah was required tae report to Aldershot, which was the ends of the earth, as far as Ah was concerned, an set off in November 1953, to Aldershot. Ah had basic training there for about eight weeks, which was square-bashing, as we called it, and [Ah was] taught discipline and went on further courses, finally qualified as a map maker, tactical sketcher was the proper name for it, and had managed to stay at Aldershot for six months, quite unwillingly, really, because Ah didnae like it there. It was termed as the home of the British Army. They hinted at me to go on at Aldershot an qualify as an instructor but there was no way Ah wanted tae spend two years in Aldershot, so Ah was posted tae Nottingham, which was quite a good posting. An it was handier to get home, as well, because Aldershot, if ye had a weekend off from the Friday night, in Aldershot, it was practically impossible to get tae Lochmaben an spend any time an get back to Aldershot for six o'clock on the Monday morning. However, Ah was posted to Nottingham, which was quite an interesting place, the headquarters for North East England. An it was a place cawd Bestwood Lodge, a mansion house beside a mining pit, a coal pit, an Ah quite enjoyed it there for over a year. Then ma mother took ill in the shop an required an urgent operation. Ah got a fortnight's compassionate leave tae get home an got in touch with the local rep for SSAFA (Soldiers, Sailors, Airmen and Families Association) which was a society to help servicemen with any problems of any kind. And Mrs Kerr from Templand Farm, Colonel Kerr's wife, came to see me, took notes, put ma case forward to the Army. An Ah got a compassionate discharge about three months before Ah was really due to come home. But it's amazing how these things were given consideration in the end so that was me back intae the family business which, as I said, Ah never really liked. Ah did apply for a job with Ordinance Survey because Ah would have liked to have been a map maker but Ah didnae have the educational standard to qualify for it so Ah was never considered and that was me stuck in the shop for quite some time.

*It's quite interesting you said that, because it wasn't an educational standard, really, they would be looking for, in a way, it's the facility to be able to draw well and make maps and so on.*

Aye, aye, but mind you, in an awful lot o jobs you were trained for in the Army, they werenae rated in civilian life, you know, they werenae treated as proper qualifications. Ah mean take an Army cook comin out an applying for a job as a chef, he would get very poor consideration, wouldn't he?

## Ian Tweedie

*So, you left school at 15?*

Aye, an then Ah went to the Army when Ah was 20.

*Where you called up to the Army, was this National Service?*

National Service, yes.

*So, you left Lochmaben then and went where?*

Ah went to, down south.

*Aye, to your basic training?*

Uh huh.

*An do you remember where that was?*

The Lincolnshire … Battalion of the Royal Lincolnshire, aye.

*And then you were posted abroad were you?*

Aye, well oo were actually, oo were actually geared up tae go tae the Suez Canal, remember when, it was only a five-day job? So, we didnae go, they put us on a boat, HT *Nevasa*, then we went tae Hong Kong but we sailed, before, you know how you had the canal was blocked, well we came, the boat come right down.

*Round by South Africa?*

Aye round the—

*Cape [of Good Hope].*

Cape [of Good Hope], aye. Ah can remember … when we got there, gettin off the boat, the first thing Ah heard was Matheson and Jardine[2] an that was the Jardines [from Lochmaben.]

*From Lochmaben?.*

Aye, aye an they used tae take opium, up through the country, [REDACTED].

*How long were you … in Malaya?*

… we were only there for a very, very short time an then they sent us tae Malaya. We did operations, jist like gaun intae the territories an goin to the different places an findin how much good food an whatever, because the Chinese were taking it, like.

*So, did you spend time in Singapore?*

Yes, aye.

*You were in Singapore and then you were up country as well?*

Aye, aye.

*… how long were you over there?*

Where? In Hong Kong?

*Aye.*

Ach only for a couple o months.

*An did you travelled by ship there and back?*

No, we flew from Hong Kong tae Singapore in an old Valetta. It was the first time I'd been in a plane an Ah'm sitting there an the wings, you know what Ah mean? Green, sittin there.

*Terrified* (laughter).

> Terrified, aye, an then because when we come intae near Singapore there's a lot oh, what dae you call it? We were gaun along an it just goes 'whoosh'.

*Ah remember going into Hong Kong airport, an Ah was frightened there because it just came down and 'whoosh'.*

> Aye, did ye?

*Aye, Ah was frightened there.*

> How lang were you in Hong Kong?

*Just a couple of days, really, just for a couple of days. … Yes, it's quite an experience going in there. And you spent your two years in National Service, then, away from Lochmaben?*

> Aye, oh, aye.

## Hal McGhie

*So, the next date Ah have in yer life is August 1950, when you were called up for National Service, could you tell us a little about what happened, where you got your training and so on?*

> Well, Ah was enlisted into the Royal Army Service Corps, in Aldershot, and we had eight-week basic training there, then we went to Farnborough for another two weeks, then we went to Colchester for some reason or other. And eventually we set sail from Liverpool, in January '51, and it took us 25 days, Ah think, to go out on HT *Pride*, [HMT, *Empire Pride*] to Singapore, where we were camped in tents for approximately, Ah think we were there about two weeks, and then I got sent up to Taiping in northern Malaya, where Ah spent the rest of ma National Service. But I enjoyed it very much, at least looking back I enjoyed it, Ah just remember the good things. Some people look back and remember the bad things, I like to look back and remember the good things.

*Was this during what they called the Malayan Emergency[3]?*

> The Malayan Emergency, yes.

*And who was fighting whom?*

> Well, when the Japanese invaded Malaya they went down through Malaya in about a week. And the British helped the Chinese communists, Ah think they were then, in the hills and they armed them and when the Japanese were defeated, as they did in Korea and Vietnam and everywhere else, there was a, the Communists tried to take over. And these people that we were fighting, if that's the right word to use, were guerrilla, it was guerrilla warfare, and they were in the hills. And Ah was in the Royal Army Service Corps attached to 48, an MT [Mechanical Transport] Company, attached to 48th Infantry Brigade, and we were giving back-up to them. We never actually went into the jungle but we would go in occasionally in the middle of the night and surround a village, along with a lot of other people, while

the real front troops went in and interrogated them to try see if they could find who was helping them because the guerrillas were obviously relying on local help quite a lot. Ah was in a Malayan Company. There was about 430 Malays which included Chinese and Indians and Ah think it was about 18 British other ranks gonna join. And when Ah left there was twelve and a very good friend o mine, who was a Chinese sergeant, just disappeared and we were told that he was a communist and somebody had told them about him because they had a, at Changi, in Singapore, they had a place which maybe we shouldn't know about, where they got a hold of these so-called terrorists and tortured them till they gave information. The British weren't any better than anybody else. They had the first concentration camps, in the Boer War.

... We were in a support role for the Malayan troops. We worked very much with them and when you go back now and say you were there in the Emergency you're very much appreciated, there are not many of us left Ah suppose now.

*Aye, you obviously made friends there because you have regularly gone back to see them.*

Aye, Ah've lots o friends there but Ah've never seen any o them [when] going back. Ah just go back to the area and when Ah've gone to the camp Ah've been shown round the camp, [but Ah've never seen] friends Ah can remember [from] during the emergency.

*How did you find the climate compared to here?*

Well, there was no frost (laughter). There was plenty rain but it was warm rain and Ah still go back, Ah'm going back in three weeks, four weeks, Ah go back on the 19th November, Ah go back for three weeks.

*The humidity didn't trouble you then did it?*

Well, we got prickly heat, but you just live with it, don't you?

*You get used to it.*

You get used to it, aye.

*And of course, you were young.*

Ah've been back a few times and for some reason or other it doesn't seem to upset me as much as the cold, damp winters do nowadays.

*You found that, obviously, you benefited from your National Service and you must have grown up quite quickly in these conditions.*

It was much better than ... ma father was quite a strong, strong man in the sense that he was strong-willed. You did what you were told, you didn't need to be told twice, you were just told once an you did it (laughter). It was when he said 'Jump' you just said 'How high?' (Laughter). And it was quite unusual to be away from that influence and it helped me to grow up, I'm quite sure. Because Ah could stand on ma own two feet and save, I was always quite a good saver in these days. Ah brought a lot of money and presents home from the Army. … at the finish-up, Ah never got any promotion, but Ah was passed all ma exams. And so Ah was a five-star private and was getting £5 odds a week and ma keep, which was a lot more than Ah was getting at home (laughter).

*Ah've heard that before, Ah think* (laughter), *it's not a good idea to work for your family probably.*

No, in the long-term if you work hard it can succeed.

*So, you came home, and you didn't hang about in August 1952, when you came home.*

No, Ah got off the bus at a quarter past seven and by half past seven Ah was delivering milk (laughter).

*Ah just wonder what many of your listeners are thinking about that.*

There was no going away carrying—, no going away party and no coming back party. You stopped work when ye had tae stop work and when ye come back ye were straight into it.

## Tom Allan

Of course, two or three years efter that, the Queen asked me tae join her company.

*The Army.*

So, Ah went tae the Army. Ah went when Ah was 18 because Ah didnae want ti go another three years and then go. Ah wanted tae get it over with, get it past and—

*So, you were away from Lochmaben for how many years?*

Well, Ah was away for 18 month because Ah went, as Ah say, Ah did ma training at Berwick-on-Tweed, went tae Ireland, a place called Ballykinler. Sailed fae Belfast on a troop ship, the *Devonshire*, an went tae Malaya where we did internal security. There was a wee bit o trouble in Singapore itself so we wis stationed at Selarang, which is next to Changi Jail, Selarang Garrison. Did internal security there and then Ah went up tae the FTC, the Federation Training Centre [and] did oor trainin for jungle warfare. An then Ah went back doon country intae Johor an then we were distributed tae compounds, you know.

*Different places?*

Aye. Every company, C Company or whatever it wis, went different places. But Ah'd had a problem, medical problem, wi ma neck, an eventually Ah landed in hospital in Singapore, the BMH [British Military Hospital]. To try an recuperate me they sent me to the Cameron Highlands which is in the north, mair or less up at, Ah forget the name of the place, but Ah come back doon tae Singapore an had a medical there and they said: 'This man is not fit for any further duties in this theatre of the War'.

… So, Ah wis dispatched home bi ambulance plane and Ah landed at Lyneham into Aldershot Hospital, had an operation there.

THE WAR AND MILITARY LIFE

*Ah right Tom, so that finished your visit to Malaysia, let's call it.*
That's right.
*And you came back to Lyneham, did you?*

Ah come back tae Lyneham, wis in hospital in Aldershot and, of course, out and in the hospitals fae there on tae Ah wis demobbed in the March '57. Of course, efter earnin 15s a week, of course you allowed yer mother 10s, 15s a week, ye had tae get a job, you hadnae saved very much.

## Roy Thorburn

*So, the next date in your life really is 1957, when you were called up for National Service.*

Ah went to the RAF then, Ah'd be probably about what, 21½, 21, somewhere about there.

*You were allowed to defer.*

You got deferred for, to get your time out. Of course, when Ah was, Ah had started late, obviously Ah was going to be finishing late. Ah was a bit older than the ones that Ah was in with which, 21½, 22, well Ah wisnae that old. Anyway, Ah done quite well there, Ah got into the RAF Command football team. We used to fly to Germany, Belgium, alternate weekends, an of course Ah met Margaret, ma future wife, and Ah used tae hitchhike home to Lochmaben and Ah used tae score my name off the football team, which was a bit foolish because you got away on a Thursday and you didn't have to return, you didn't return till the Sunday and ye got Monday off so you were only working really three days a week, better than a minister.

*Now, you mentioned that one of these weekends you didn't make it.*

No, the train actually froze up, the diesel froze up on the train when Ah wis going back to Swinderby one weekend.

*That's near Lincoln.*

Near Lincoln, aye, and of course Ah was 2½ hours late with ma pass which expired at eight o'clock in the morning. Of course, Ah got arrested immediately an thrown in behind bars, Ah thought Ah was a criminal, really. Then Ah was put before the Commanding Officer, an there was about 6000 men in that camp at the time, an Ah was put in front of this Commanding Officer an he asked me what Ah meant by coming in late. An Ah told him, an he says: 'Is that the best story you can come up with, Thorburn?'
And Ah says: 'Well, Ah've been taught to tell the truth all ma days, sir. That's exactly what Ah'm tellin now so Ah can't vary it.'
So, he says: 'Ah gather you don't like the RAF', an I said, 'No sir'.
'Why?'
'Well, as ma father just started in business he was relying on me. Ah'm here an Ah wouldn't mind if there was a purpose but Ah don't see the purpose.'
Immediately he said, 'Sit down', an he told the two police officers to go and

give me ma hat back. At that he asked me if Ah would be interested in doing work in his house which, five minutes later, Ah was sitting in his limousine going up to his house to do work, an half an hour prior to that Ah'd been in chains (laughter).

*Quite a change.*

Quite a change. So, Ah worked at his house for two or three days and his wife called me Roy an he called me Thorburn, of course. An every time he came into the house Ah used tae stand tae attention but he relieved me of that. Anyway, one day Ah was sittin having coffee wi him and he asked me if I'd like a home posting, a compassionate posting. Ah said Ah would, so Ah got sent to Leuchars. He put me to Leuchars the next day. He had a good friend, the Commanding Officer at Leuchars, an he become a good friend of mine. So, my experience in the RAF was quite good.

*Excellent. And so, of course Leuchars was in Fife and it was also close to St Andrews, where you developed another of your passions.*

Aye, that's right. We got concessions on the golf course at St Andrews, the RAF did, between half past four and five [o'clock] it was 1s 6d [pence] a round for the golf, a penny a hole. Well, you couldnae beat that, when ye think nowadays, Ah dunno, it's probably about a £150, if ye can get a game.

*Yes, that's right and, in 1958, you and Margaret got married and she moved to Leuchars.*

Aye, … we got married when Ah was halfway through ma service. Margaret moved to Leuchars and we bought a small caravan. We borrowed £120 to buy this caravan and we went to Leuchars and, of course, the inevitable happened and Margaret was expecting and she came and stayed down here with her parents until my RAF time terminated.

In this final military recollection James McWhirter, who started his working life as a bricklayer before joining the Army as a regular soldier, shared his military experiences.

### Isabel Wells and James McWhirter

JMcW: But then as the year went on Ah found [bricklaying] wasnae for me so Ah joined the Army an Ah joined the Argyll and Southern Highlanders. … An Ah was there for twelve years.

*And did you go abroad?*

JMcW: Yes, Ah was abroad quite a lot. We started off in Inverness, Fort George, for four weeks and then it shut down an then oo had tae go tae Aberdeen. And we were in Aberdeen until oor training was finished in '64. And we got caught up in the typhoid, in Aberdeen.

*Oh, Ah remember that, yes. Goodness.*

JMcW: We got caught up in the typhoid in Aberdeen, cos Ah wis supposed to get taen out tae Singapore an it was cancelled until the July. When Ah was in Singapore, you did six months in Singapore and six months up the jungle, that's when the Indonesians were infiltrating Borneo.

*Oh, right, ok.*

JMcW: So, we went in there tae dae that, an then after, when oo were finished in Singapore we came to Plymouth, wi Mad Mitch and we went across to Aden.

*Aden, oh yeah.*

JMcW: Aye, Aden. Cyprus, Ah was in Cyprus for a year, wi the United Nations an then we were stationed, the Argyll's got disbanded, but before that we were in Berlin.

*Berlin.*

JMcW: Ah guarded Mr Hess.[4]

*Really?*

IW: Really, did you Jimmy? Gosh.

*Was he not the only prisoner or something?*

JMcW: He was the only prisoner in there, an every country taen a shot [of guarding him].

*Of course.*

JMcW: British, French, American an Russian. It was the only time the Russians were … allowed intae oor bit.

*IW: Oh, right.*

JMcW: [The Russians] used tae take aw the papers an music away fae him when they came.

*So, did you see him?*

JMcW: Oh, aye, aye. There was 32 people in there, 16 at a time, you had towers.

IW: Oh, right.

*Guarding one man?*

JMcW: Guarding one man.

IW: And he would be getting on for bein an auld man.

JMcW: He wis an auld man then. An the Argylls got disbanded an Ah went tae the Gordon Highlanders an that's where Ah wis, a year in Limassol, with the United Nations. And then they got reformed and Ah did aboot three or four tours o Ireland. We were stationed at a place called Kirknewton, jist outside Edinburgh.

*Oh yes, Ah know where that is.*

IW: Is that where them barracks still are, aye?

JMcW: Pardon?

IW: The barracks at Edinburgh, is that where they still are?

JMcW: No, the big barracks in Edinburgh's cawd Redford.

*Redford.*

JMcW: This was an ex-American place where the Americans used tae go.

IW: Oh, right, aye.

JMcW: It was mair or less just ammunition huts, ken, where we were. Where did we go after that? Germany again, Osnabruck. Well the kid's gaun tae be going to school and Anna, ma wife, didn't want to come with me to Germany, so Ah went across there for aboot six months but Ah couldnae settle so Ah came out. An then I went to Gates Power Transmission, it was Uniroyal at that time, an Ah spent 25 years there.

*'Join the army and see the world' that's what they say.*

IW: Aye, that's what they say.

JMcW: Got the General Service Medal for, they've got bars on them, got one for Singapore, four for Borneo, one for Aden, one for Ireland, what's ma other yin, for [UNCLEAR], one for Ah got another yun for [ UNCLEAR].

*So, it must have been quite difficult to settle back in Lochmaben after being, you know, touring and being—*

JMcW: Oh it wis, aye, especially working in a factory, cos Ah went tae Uniroyal, Ah wanted tae be a security officer but there were two o us in for it and he said Ah was too young for it. But he says, 'Ah'll offer ye another job', so he taen to this new place they'd built, Power Transmission. How Ah lasted 25 years, Ah don't know.

# Notes

Chapter 1
1   Scottish Natural Heritage, now NatureScot.

Chapter 2
1   Currently known as Dumfries and Galloway Royal Infirmary, the hospital was for a time based at Nithbank before relocating to Bankhead Road. Since 2018 the hospital has been located at Cargenbridge, just off the A75.

Chapter 3
1   Belle Vue Stadium, Manchester was a venue for greyhound racing.

Chapter 5
1   Lochmaben GP Dr Jack Wilson wrote extensively on his experience as a general practitioner as well as the history of Lochmaben and district.
2   Devil's Porridge was the colloquialism for cordite used by those involved in its manufacture.
3   Regulation 50 of the Defence (General) Regulations, 1939 which requisitioned the removal of metal railings ostensibly for munition manufacture. In fact, most of the metal so gathered was unsuitable for use in the manufacture of munitions.

Chapter 6
1   The GP14 is a general purpose sailing dinghy which is 14 feet in length.
2   Dumfries and Galloway Coaching Awards, 2016.
3   Flapping races are horse race meetings on the flat held from April to September, mainly in the Scottish Borders, but also in Annan.

Chapter 7
1   Mossbank Munitions was part of HM Factory, Gretna where cordite was manufactured.
2   Refers to Jardine Matheson, the large trading company based in Hong Kong which continues in business.
3   The Malayan Emergency, also known as the Anti–British National Liberation War, was a guerrilla war fought in British Malaya between communist pro-independence fighters of the Malayan National Liberation Army and the military forces of the British Empire and Commonwealth.
4   Rudolph Hess, Vice-Reichs Führer, imprisoned in Spandau Prison, Berlin.

# Glossary

| | |
|---|---|
| beds | Also known as peevers or hopscotch. A children's game which involves hoping from squares marked out in a bed using a stone, or peever. |
| 'Big Sna' | 'Big Snow' of 1947 in which much of Europe suffered an extreme harsh winter with prolonged, heavy snowfalls through January–March. |
| guddling | Capturing fish by hand only by tickling the fish as it swims over sunken hand(s) and lifting swiftly out of the water. |
| Nissen huts | Buildings prefabricated with concrete and corrugated steel, often used as temporary billeting for military personnel. |
| parish money | Monies distributed by parochial boards as poor relief. |
| quoits | A traditional game which involves the throwing of metal, rope or rubber rings over a set distance, usually to land over or near a spike (sometimes called a hob, mott or pin). The are several variations of the game. |
| tawse | Leather belt/strap used for corporal punishment in schools. Its use was outlawed in 1987. |

# Bibliography

Carroll, D. *Old Lockerbie and Lochmaben* (Catrine: Stenlake Publishing, 2001).

Gow, I. C. *Lochmaben Primary School: "a Guid Wee Schule": a History of a Typical Scottish Rural Primary School from the 1890s to the Present Day* (Dumfries: Solway Offset the Printers, 2005).

Gow, I. C. *World War Two: Annandale Connections* (Dumfries: Creedon Publications, 2009).

Gow, I. C. *Nithsdale at War* (Catrine: Stenlake Publishing, 2011).

http:\\www.lochmaben.org.uk

Lochmaben Town Council. *Royal burgh of Lochmaben official guide*, (Lochmaben, 1968).

Williams, M. *History of Lochmaben Hospital* (Dumfries: Dumfries and Galloway Community Health NHS Trust, 1996).

Wilson, J. B. *The royal burgh of Lochmaben: Its history, its castles and its churches*, (Lockerbie, 1974).

Wilson, J. B. *Further glimpses into Lochmaben's history* (Dumfries, 2008).

# Index